Systemized Thinking Models for Entrepreneurs

Effective, proven methods to model successful entrepreneurs and upgrade your Personal Operating System using Stoicism, Emotional Intelligence and NLP techniques

Joel E. Winston

© Copyright 2019 - All rights reserved.

The content contained within this book may not be reproduced, duplicated or transmitted without direct written permission from the author or the publisher.

Under no circumstances will any blame or legal responsibility be held against the publisher, or author, for any damages, reparation, or monetary loss due to the information contained within this book. Either directly or indirectly.

Legal Notice:

This book is copyright protected. This book is only for personal use. You cannot amend, distribute, sell, use, quote or paraphrase any part, or the content within this book, without the consent of the author or publisher.

Disclaimer Notice:

Please note the information contained within this document is for educational and entertainment purposes only. All effort has been executed to present accurate, up to date, and reliable, complete information. No warranties of any kind are declared or implied. Readers acknowledge that the author is not engaging in the rendering of legal, financial, medical or professional advice. The content within this book has been derived from various sources. Please consult a licensed professional before attempting any techniques outlined in this book.

By reading this document, the reader agrees that under no circumstances is the author responsible for any losses, direct or indirect, which are incurred as a result of the use of information contained within this document, including, but not limited to, — errors, omissions, or inaccuracies.

Hello fellow Entrepreneur,

As a successful entrepreneur you´re no stranger to long work days. But you also want and need to level up a lot of your leadership skills.

Skills you need to use on a weekly basis:

Self-awareness, having a clear vision and goal so you don´t get distracted

Decision making based on sound logic instead of on your emotions

Smoother communication, both 1-to-1 as in groups

Negotiation skills, to get better and more profitable deals

This all will lead to better personal results and higher profits in your business.

So, don´t wait longer to receive not 1, but 4 PDF´s by typing the link or scanning the QR code below:

http://systemizedthinkingmodels.businessleadershipplatform.com/

As a successful AND productive entrepreneur, you :

Download the PDF´s

Print the PDF´s

Put or stick them in a visible place, like your bathroom mirror or the monitor at your work.

Start reading the book

Let´s 10X your business ....

Enjoy,

Joel

Table of Contents

EMOTIONAL INTELLIGENCE FOR ENTREPRENEURS — 9

- Introduction — 11
- Part 1: Understanding the Foundation — 17
- Chapter 1: Human Emotions — 17
- Chapter 2: The EQ Models — 45
- Chapter 3: Introspection — 59
- Chapter 4: Extrospection — 81
- Part 2: The 30-Day Emotional Intelligence Booster Program — 107

NLP FOR ENTREPRENEURS — 141

- Introduction — 143
- Chapter 1: NLP EXPLAINED — 153
- Chapter 2: ENTREPRENEURIAL MISSION/MOTIVATION — 169
- The Swish technique — 174
- Chapter 3: CONFIDENCE — 197
- Chapter 4: SELF-APPRECIATION AND SELF-ESTEEM — 229
- Chapter 5: PRODUCTIVITY AND TIME MANAGEMENT — 255
- Chapter 6: COMMUNICATION — 263
- Chapter 7: NEGOTIATION AND SALES — 279
- Conclusion — 285

STOICISM FOR ENTREPRENEURS — 289

- Introduction — 291
- Chapter 1: Stoicism and Journaling: Plan, Reflect and Achieve Success — 315
- Chapter 2: "Stoic, Prepare for the Worst!" Negative Visualization and the Secret to Overcoming Obstacles, Adversity and Failures — 337
- Chapter 3: Get to Work, Stoic. How to use Stoicism to Increase Motivation, Cultivate Discipline, and Enhance Productivity — 355

CHAPTER 4: THE STOIC IN THE WORLD: HOW TO STOICISM CAN IMPROVE SELF-CONFIDENCE, COMMUNICATION WITH OTHERS AND MAKE YOU A BETTER NEGOTIATOR — 365

CHAPTER 5: PRACTICAL EXAMPLES OF HOW INTERCONNECTEDNESS CAN HELP YOU RELATE TO EMPLOYEES, PARTNERS, CLIENTS AND IMPROVE YOUR WELL BEING — 379

CHAPTER 6: CONCLUSION: WHAT THE STOICS CAN TEACH US ABOUT OBTAINING AND MAINTAINING SUCCESS IN BUSINESS — 405

FURTHER READING — **413**

REFERENCES — **419**

RESOURCES — **421**

Emotional Intelligence for Entrepreneurs

How to Use the Secrets of Emotional Intelligence to Achieve Better Sales, Increase EQ, Improve Leadership, and Skyrocket the Profits of Your Business

Introduction

Starting a business is an exciting adventure. Once you first thought of the idea, you probably felt a thrill at the exciting things to come. Maybe you already tried a business and it didn't succeed like you wanted it to. Perhaps you picked it back up or started a new one with a fresh vision.

Maybe you do not have a business yet at all. Perhaps you are thriving, or maybe you need help to lift your business off the ground. No matter where you are in your entrepreneurialism, there is always more information to be learned that can really help drive your business to success. One of the best ways to ensure your business is running smoothly is to attune your emotional intelligence abilities and understand how we react and interact based on our levels of EQ.

This book is for ambitious entrepreneurs who want growth and to get better results with less effort. Sometimes it can be so draining to desperately try to make sales. Perhaps you have done some things you wish you didn't have to do, or maybe you pushed yourself past your limit on occasion, all in the name to make a sale. Maybe you see exactly what needs to be done, but you have trouble interacting with your employees. Whatever the problem might be, there's a good chance that an improvement of your emotional intelligence can help grow your business.

You can do this by understanding how to handle your team better as well. Though you are the backbone of your company and the ideas and visions that drive your business started with you, at this point, you have to realize the importance of your team as well. If we aren't conscious of how we can better lift our team up and work with them rather than against them, then our business will never succeed.

Aside from just working with our team, we also have to be aware of how we can better work with prospective clients and investors. We need the support of more than just ourselves and the people that are working for us. We need the inspiration from those that are a part of closing the sales after all!

One great book that helped inspire some of my greatest ideas around entrepreneurialism and emotional intelligence comes from Daniel Goleman's famous book, Emotional Intelligence. This book is enlightening for how emotions in our life can really drive our actions. Your emotions are part of you that can either help drive you forward or they can hinder your ability to properly operate throughout this life.

The first two chapters are going to focus on the ideas of his like these and all the other great psychological findings needed for the basic understanding of who we are, as well as the psychology needed to understand in others. The third and fourth chapters will be all about how you can start to apply these ideas and findings in your life, including important emotional intelligence models that outline approach and response.

You will find that you can better handle other demanding clients, sub-contractors, business partners, and shareholders when you increase your EQ levels. Most of the time, the way that we respond starts first with the basic emotion we feel. When we might sense attitude or animosity from someone else, it can either cause us to get defensive or perhaps our apprehension shows to the other prospect. This can be a turn-off or at least, start a power struggle in which we are destined to lose. Your emotions do not have to be a power-play and a struggle between competitors anymore. There are plenty of healthy ways that problems can be worked through, no matter how challenging they might feel initially.

Your working relationships will improve. You will find it easier to get what you want from others, while also having the emotional ability to stand up and say what you think is fair in any given setting. You will know how to ask for what you want and receive it in a way that is beneficial not just for you, but for the business overall.

Generally, this book is going to help you be more effective and productive by analyzing people. You will better understand how body language and facial movement can give you insight into what other people might be thinking, the way that their minds might be working.

You will learn how to use social skills in the work setting. The better your social skills are, the easier to becomes to actually drive sales. The easier it is to make sales, the faster the money comes in! This is not just good for you, but for your team. More profit means higher pay for your workers and better amenities for the business. Your clients will become more satisfied with this higher quality of work, only driving sales further.

We are going to discuss using the right emotions at the right time. There are times when you might need to really show your emotions and others where you have to remain as professional as possible.

This can lead to better deals with partners, clients, subcontractors, and shareholders while reducing stress. People will trust you more and at the end of the day, relationship management is most important. When your stress levels are lower, it will show and it can help people be more trusting of you and the things you might be asking.

The main focus is going to be self-awareness, self-regulation, social awareness, social skills, and assertiveness to become more productive, become a better entrepreneur, and to get more done with less energy and time.

Success is less determined by IQ and is more determined by EQ. The importance is self-awareness and social-awareness. Statistics show that the influence of IQ as well as EQ, in careers and working relationships is incredibly important for you and your employee's success.

To understand emotional intelligence, you should understand that there are some notable research and publications on the subject that are worthy of mentioning. We will dive further into this at the beginning of the book as well.

The first part of this book is an explanation of what EQ is. The better you can understand this, the easier it will be for you to constantly improve on it. The second part, we are going to give you practical steps to help improve your levels. We set it up in a thirty-day challenge so within a month's time, you will already be able to see the ways that you can improve your company all on your own.

Part 1: Understanding the Foundation

Chapter 1: Human Emotions

Everyone has emotions, feelings, ideas, thoughts, and opinions. We all have a range of emotions that help to define who we are. Emotions come more naturally to us than most other aspects of our life. We do not always need to be taught how to feel certain things. When you stub your toe, you feel hurt. When you slip and fall, you can feel embarrassed, when you lose something or someone, you feel grief. There are many emotions that come very naturally to us. In the same breath, we certainly learn how to feel other emotions. You might feel guilty, but would you still feel that same guilt had someone not told you that you should? You might feel ashamed, but is that just because someone told you that you needed to feel this way?

Emotions are what separate us from each other and they separate us from animals as well. We all react differently to various stimuli, so we can't always be sure that one moment would have the same emotional reaction for everyone. Your emotions can be learned but they can also be inherent to your personality.

Many emotional responses are the same. When you see someone trip and fall, everyone might become concerned. You might hear a loud "Oh!" when others see someone trip and really smack their face or knees into the concrete. After that initial "oh!" you might see a branch in the kinds of emotional reactions.

Some people might laugh, thinking that the fall was no big deal. Others might stop and ask if everything is OK, becoming concerned that even though the person who fell says they are fine, there might be something else wrong. And then there are those people that would just keep walking if they saw someone fall and go on with their day as if they hadn't seen anything at all.

Your facial expressions can be the first sign of your emotions. Have you ever been studying something hard just to find that your face was sore from being scrunched up? Maybe you are excited and watching something amusing, your face in a gentle smile in anticipation. Perhaps someone is giving you a ton of attention and love, and you can't help but smile hugely. Maybe someone is making you mad, telling you a story that's a blatant lie, your face is confused and annoyed.

Our emotions can cause us greater feelings that extend beyond that initial reaction. Maybe you hear that a friend is newly engaged, your mood might end up being more excited for the rest of the day. Perhaps you woke up and read something in the news that angered you right away and the rest of your day is met with an inability to concentrate and general concern over the world. These simple reactions can be stretched out, all based on our emotional intelligence.

Our emotions can destroy us. A small hint of jealousy could turn into endless stalking to the point that you could violate someone's privacy. Perhaps a tiny fear over losing a job means constant stress and anxiety for the next three months as one tries to perform their job to the best of their abilities. Anger over something that happened in the past can stew into hatred that blinds us and controls the decisions we try and make.

They can inspire us to do something. Maybe you are sick of being broke, feeling the intense emotional turmoil, stress, and anxiety of your finances. This could inspire you to go back to school to get a higher degree and a better paying job. Perhaps you are feeling angry about the injustices for a certain group of people, so you spend your time devoted to fighting for their rights. Emotion has inspired some of the greatest people in the world to live out their dreams, in turn, inspiring more to try and achieve theirs.

They can also keep us held back out of fear. How many times have you stayed home from an event because you were scared? How many times did you stay quiet when you should have spoken up? The more that we start to understand what our emotions actually are, the easier it will be to find methods to manage them.

Basic Human Emotions

At the root of all your emotions are your basic emotions. Whatever it is that you might be feeling can be traced back to just a select few kinds of emotions. Whether there are two, four, six, or twenty-seven is all up for debate. There's no manual for what it means to be human, so most scientists are just theorizing what the basic makeup of human emotions might be. We might never fully understand what they mean exactly, but we can determine what it means to feel them.

These emotions can seem like they hold the majority of the power over who we are. Your emotions have probably taken the driver's wheel on more occasions than you'd like to admit. Maybe you threw something when it wasn't working. Perhaps you texted an ex-girl- or boy-friend you didn't want to talk to. Maybe you slapped a friend, skipped an event, broke a glass, threw up, cried, spit, and did whatever other unpleasant, unattractive thing it was that left you with yet another emotion – guilt, shame, regret.

If there is one thing that we do hold reign over in our lives, we can be certain that it is our emotional reactions. You will not always be able to control the way you initially feel. If someone makes a joke about your appearance, maybe you feel hurt. After a moment of reflection, you realize it was just a distasteful joke made out of poor judgment, but that initial gut reaction of hurt is not something that's always within our control.

What you do have; however, is control over your reaction. When that person said something mean to you – you could have reacted by saying something mean back. Or you could have reacted with a laugh. That hurt was still there, but it is the emotional reaction that differs.

In order to really become an emotional expert, one must first ensure that they fully grasp what emotions are. You have to learn to separate the emotion from the reaction. Some people will say, "I couldn't help it! I was mad!" but that's no excuse. You are not at fault for how intensely you even feel an emotion, but it is still your responsibility as a human in a certain society to get a grip on the things that you feel.

When you have the ability to hold reign over these emotions, it will help you to become a more influential person. No longer will you be ruled by them. Others will see your willpower and admire the strength you have over the things that you feel.

Think of your basic emotions like colors. Yellow, red, blue, white, and black. These are the most basic building blocks of the color wheel. You can't have anything else without these fundamental pieces. Green, orange, purple... these colors are just combinations of the others. We will discuss the combined colors in a later section but for now, let's look deep at what these basic emotions are.

There are six common basic emotions referred to by a psychologist named Paul Eckman. These were happiness, sadness, anger, disgust, fear, and surprise. Since then, much other research has been done and many will narrow them down to four basic emotions, with as many as 27 others to be picked up from facial recognition. For the sake of this book, we'll refer to four and from there, expand into the advanced combination of emotions (Cherry, 2019).

Happiness

The first emotion, the one that we all really strive for the most at the end of the day, is happiness. This is one of the best feelings in the world. When you have everything you need, you are happy. When you get what you want, you are happy. When you have an unexpected positive surprise, you are happy. When the opposite of any of these things happen, guess what? You're not happy.

When you are happy, you are feeling whole. There is not anything else that is required to make you feel more fulfilled. You are satisfied and living in the moment. You might understand there is not perfection present, but that doesn't stop you from being happy in the moment. You are distracted when you are happy. Maybe you are laughing at a funny joke or a TV show. Perhaps you are dancing with friends at a party. You are in that moment, happy with who you are and what's around you.

Happiness is usually shown through smiles. Though some people might laugh when they are feeling manic or delusional, laughter most of the time indicates someone is having fun. Happy smiles indicate that the other person is satisfied. It is a little assurance that you didn't do anything wrong. Once you start to dive deeper into what kind of smile is being flashed – that's when you might start to discover that there is a deeper meaning to this smile.

When we are happy, we are relaxed. We lack fear, and any fear we do have might be positive excitement. We might be scared, but our excitement for the good that is to come outweighs any other negative things we might be feeling.

Happiness is something we measure as well. We might look at the people and the things around us and use this as a scale for whether or not our lives carry joy. Perhaps you are happy based on the things that you have; the number of cars, houses, and bags you own. Perhaps you are happy because you have so many amazing people in your life, a positive support system. It doesn't take a lot to be happy but when happiness is not present, it can take a lot out of you.

Sadness

Sadness is the emotion that we try to avoid the most. Really, if you think about it, these two emotions can be the most basic. When you are experiencing good emotions, you'll automatically be happy; and when you are not, you might be in a state of sorrow. We shouldn't look at our emotions this stripped down; however, as they are so much more complex than that. However, it does help to make the comparisons between different states of emotion, as it will help you better see the way that these emotions can influence behavior and overall mood.

When we are feeling sad, it is hard to get anything done. We are distracted by the thing that happened. We might be going over and over in our heads everything that we wish we would have done differently. Even if you are sad about not having any money now, you might think back to two years ago when you purchased a $300 pair of shoes you only wore once. When you are sad, you are thinking about how other people are happy. It might make you even more sad to imagine the amount of happiness that you are not experiencing.

We are usually focused on finding a solution to make us feel better in order to bring ourselves out of the sadness. When you are sad, you might be thinking of what is needed in your life to make you feel better. However, we can sometimes be too consumed with our sadness to even have the strength to do anything about it.

We often forget what it is like to be happy at all when we're sad. We wonder if we are going to stay that way forever. We might be happy all day, but then that one moment of sadness sours every other good thing that we felt.

It can be easy to inflate sadness over happiness because we imagine that sad is not a place that we are supposed to be. We think that happiness is normal, that this is how things should always be. In reality, we should find an easy balance in the middle – a place of content. This is not how life will always be, but we have to learn to embrace this one basic emotion or else our entire lives will just be a fight against it.

Sometimes, we are even feeling sad on the inside but will try desperately to show that we are really living life in a happy way. Since feeling sad can be so challenging, we assume that it is something bad, something we need to hide. We pretend we're not sad, but so does everyone else, making it even harder to talk about the real things that we're feeling.

Fear and Surprise

Both fear and surprise can sometimes go hand in hand. You might fear that your spouse is cheating on you, and still be surprised when you walk into the bedroom to see them with another lover. Perhaps you are fearful that you are going to get kicked out of your apartment, but you are still surprised to see the letter of eviction taped to your door.

Fear is usually a feeling to an unexpected circumstance and surprise is that reaction. When we are feeling both fear and surprise, we can sometimes react in the same way. The initial reaction doesn't always mean that we are showing our real feelings. As we go throughout life, we create certain expectations as a means of survival.

You expect that tomorrow you'll wake up again to your alarm, and then get ready for work, go to work, come home, and repeat. You have these expectations so that you are prepared to do what you have to do. When those expectations are not met, it can cause an emotion in us – fear or surprise. Fear is also something that we might experience beforehand. This is where surprise becomes the opposite to fear. When you are anxiously anticipating a big speech, maybe a surgery, or the arrival of a new baby, you might be fearful. You will be scared of everything that can go wrong.

For some, surprise could still elicit this reaction, especially if they consistently have negative perspectives and frequent pessimistic attitudes. Have you ever seen one of those makeover shows where the person is completely unhappy with the makeover? They knew it was happening, yet they were still reacting with negative shock, likely because they just do not as easily adjust to change as some others might.

Fear can quickly transform into surprise, and vice versa. For example, a mother might show fear in her surprised reaction at her 21-year-old daughter announcing her engagement to a man she dislikes. She might show that she's angry because the surprise didn't give her time to emotionally react. In time, she accepts her daughter's decision, changing her emotional reaction. Another mother might meet this daughter with intense surprise and an overall happy feeling. However, she might find out the wedding is only happening because the daughter is pregnant and the groom doesn't have a job either. Her surprise suddenly turns to fear as she has time to emotionally adjust to the situation. It's important to understand how fear and surprise, two things seemingly so different, can also be incredibly similar.

Fear doesn't have to be bad all the time either. We are fearful of spiders, but we might seek out watching spider movies because they thrill us. We can fear heights, but the surprise drop of a roller coaster is something that we still seek out. It is an adrenaline rush, an unexpected sensation, and a shockingly good feeling when it is felt in a controlled environment.

When we are startled, we are surprised, and we can also be fearful. It's really the situation that would depend on if it is something good or bad, whether your scare made you laugh or cry.

Anger and Disgust

Anger is another emotion that can be defined as one of the most basic we have, along with feelings of disgust. Anger seems to come just as naturally as fear, happiness, and sadness. Toddlers can show their anger when something is taken away from them. They might also show their anger through hitting, kicking, and screaming. As we become teenagers, we can start to feel that anger directed inwards. We can quickly become self-loathing when we might have anger we do not know how to express. Rather than hating others it can become easier, and eventually more comfortable, to hate ourselves.

Anger comes when we are feeling as though something is not fair. We grow angry when things do not go our way. We might get angry at someone that gets more than us. Maybe we get angry when someone else gets their way and our opinions are forgotten.

Anger can be a result of us feeling threatened like something might be taken away. If you are afraid that someone is trying to take your position at work, perhaps you grow angry because you think that another person is taking the job from you. Anger can also be linked to sadness or fear if you really connect it as well. You might be sad that someone hurt your little brother, so you are angry with their bully. It can be a secondary emotion to one that is felt more basically. It is still an emotion that will help to drive others in a different direction.

When we're angry, then we can often show other signs and symptoms of disgust. We might feel like a person is using repulsive behavior. They might be acting in a way that we never would, and we end up thinking they are terrible people for choosing to do the things they do.

We might not see the use of something. We might be disgusted at the idea of someone using a leash on their child because we do not understand why anyone would want to do that. We might grow disgusted at those who spew hate and bullying online because we do not understand why they feel the need to be so detestable.

We can be disgusted when we do not understand. Those people that do spew the hate and partake in cyberbullying might be disgusted at their victims because they do not understand the challenges that others face. When only one side of a story is understood, it can be easy to grow disgusted as we do not fully grasp what it means to be on the other side.

You are simply disgusted at things that are bad for you. Have you ever seen a cat walk up to a bug on the ground, sniff it, and walk away? They could have eaten it, but they were able to see it wasn't good for them and walked away. We have similar reactions to other stimuli. We might see that it is not for us, so we go to the extreme and think that it is disgusting, based around our opinion.

Advanced Combination Emotions

Your combination emotions are what results as a mixture of the basic emotions. In reference to the color comparison in the last section, think of your combination emotions as the more complex colors like green, purple, and orange. These only exist because of a combination of other emotions. Then you add in some white or black, and those emotions can start to get more positive or negative as well.

Perhaps you have a pretty green color and you splash some more yellow in to make it lime. You could also splash some blue into that to bring it back to a neutral green. Then throw in some black and you start to get a forest green.

Can you see how one emotion can greatly affect a combination of two other emotions that have already been blended? This is where our personalities start to form. We can pick up different traits based on consistent emotions that we've felt in the past.

All of these complex emotions can really boil down to the basic ones, but if we want to really understand how to feel and pick up on what others are feeling, getting to know the entire color wheel will be rather helpful. The more aware you are of the mixing of emotions and what effects can end up happening, the easier it will be to try and get what you want beforehand. Think back to the colors.

If an artist has no idea that blue and red make purple, they are just going to keep blending colors until they get something. What will end up happening is that they just mix every color together and get some sort of brown color! A talented artist will know how to blend and correct colors. A person with a high level of emotional intelligence will be aware of how emotions can be affected by things so minuscule.

Some emotions will be because of the same stimuli but based on an emotional reaction. For example, you might have a video released of you singing. You could either be proud or ashamed.

One feels good and one feels bad. If you are of a certain ethnicity, maybe you get offended by racist jokes while another person likes to make them. These are all based on our emotional connection to that stimuli. If your friend makes a rude comment to you, you might brush it off. If a stranger on the street shouted the same thing from their car, you'd want to run up and attack them!

A combination of the love for your friend and the understanding of the joke helped to alleviate the situation. For the person shouting from their car, the shock of that statement along with the hurt from the comment caused you to emotionally react and want to chase them down.

These combined emotions are assessed on their level of intensity felt by the individual as well. Maybe you and your friend are watching your favorite team play baseball. Your team loses brutally and you are both mad. You sit in silence for a bit, but you decide to shrug it off and open another beer. Your friend, on the other hand, gets up and throws their beer across the room, stepping outside to chain smoke while they calm down. You were both angry, but your friend felt that anger more intensely – potentially based on their past or simply based on their emotional intelligence - and reacted to it in a much stronger way.

While there is a basic underlying emotion to all that we feel, these kinds of more complex combined emotions will help us better articulate the things that we're actually feeling. When you can break apart these complex emotions, it becomes easier to also ensure that you can analyze the reaction typically associated (Donaldson, 2019).

Easy Emotions

Easy emotions are ways to refer to those that come easier to us. These are feelings of happiness, love, joy, excitement, and positive surprise. Easy emotions are the ones that you feel when you are doing your favorite activity.

When you can get cozy on the couch and turn on your favorite show, belly full of some delicious takeout and not a care in the world, you do not have to think twice about how you feel. You might be ultra-appreciative and think, "how lucky am I?". But often, if this is a nightly routine as well, you will simply feel that emotion without having to put any effort into it.

When it comes to surprise, you might feel speechless, astonished, stimulated, amazed. Perhaps a friend surprised you with a birthday party and you are filled with joy. Not only is this a good feeling because you feel loved, but it is pleasing because it came naturally. You didn't have to think about getting surprised.

For joy, you might be feeling optimistic and hopeful. Perhaps a feeling of euphoria comes over you. Maybe you are satisfied, grateful, or proud. Maybe you just finished your semester with a report card that shows straight A's.

Finding out about a promotion could also be great news. It took a lot of negative emotions to get there but in that time when you are ultra-appreciative, you aren't thinking twice. You are usually basking in that easy emotion.

When it comes to love, you are feeling compassion, desire, and affection. Love can be incredibly complicated, do not get me wrong. It can make you feel all twisted up inside. But the good parts come easy. When you can just sit and chat with someone you really love, sharing jokes and having a good time, that's easy.

Love certainly is not romantic either; it is not just about feeling good during intimate moments. Love is when you have children and see their happy faces at the things you have provided. Love is holding your warm cat as you both snuggle up in bed at night. Love is seeing your mom after not visiting home for over a month. These things just happen. You might work hard to get them, but as you are feeling that emotion, it is simply something that you ride out.

Love is peaceful, it is romantic and sentimental. All of these words are ways to describe the combined emotions of the things that are good.

Challenging Emotions

Challenging emotions are the ones that put us in bad moods. We do not want to refer to them as negative emotions because then that means that they are bad. We do not want to look at these as bad things because they come just as naturally to you like the easy ones. However, they are more challenging as we have them.

They are the emotions that we have to push through, confront, and sit in misery with as we deal with them. These challenging emotions are the ones that leave us thinking, "why me?" or ones that make us wish we were anywhere else. Challenging emotions can cause thoughts that we have to confront.

We might ask ourselves, "why am I thinking this way?". The challenging emotions are ones like regret, making us question if we are bad people. We might wonder if we have made too many mistakes, should we have done something different, or if there is any hope for us at all.

Sometimes, these challenging emotions are so hard to deal with that we will push them out of our heads. We can block out things we do not want to think about, thoughts we do not want to believe, all because they are just too hard to deal with.

If you are fearful, you might be insecure, dreading something, or in a panic. Perhaps every terrible scenario is playing out in your head before you have to attend an event. Maybe you are thinking about how the plane might crash before your vacation, or you might lose your luggage as you make it to the airport.

On a date, you might be thinking of all the terrible things that you are saying, wondering if you are making a fool of yourself. These emotions can pop into your head and some people are good at pushing them out. Others will latch onto these emotions like they are the truth, allowing them to control the direction of their actions.

Anger can build into rage, jealousy, and resentment. Perhaps a friend is living a life filled with everything you ever wanted and this makes you incredibly angry. That jealousy can soon turn into resentment toward that friend when that emotion is not dealt with.

Sometimes we will not even be aware of this kind of jealousy we feel. We might simply hate a person, only to realize later, once we're separated from that situation, that all along we were just jealous of someone that we hated so much.

You might be annoyed, frustrated, and agitated. Perhaps someone is just really getting on your nerves and driving you nuts. These aren't easy feelings to deal with. We question why they have to be the way they are or maybe question why we are so easily agitated.

Perhaps you are mortified, hostile, and exasperated. These are all just different words to describe a wide range of complex emotions that form as a result of varying combinations of basic feelings.

Then there are the sad feelings. You might be in agony, feeling hurt, and suffering. Perhaps you feel neglected or carry shame and sorrow. Maybe you are regretful, guilty, and remorseful. All of these kinds of thoughts can turn into rather intense feelings that stew and fester in our lives.

They can lead to intrusive thoughts that never seem to go away. We can obsess over the past, replaying things in our head over and over. Though it might seem like we will find an answer in the embarrassing memories we relive, they only cause us more agony.

Perhaps you are holding onto isolated feelings, you have no power, or are overwhelmed with grief. Simply feeling lonely can be a horrible feeling. Everything that we discussed in this section is not easy to deal with. Some people will internalize these feelings, hating themselves and becoming depressed or closed off.

Others might use these emotions to lash out at others, usually pushing people away. The best way to ensure these challenging emotions do not destroy our lives is to learn why we have them in the first place and how we can use them to actually enhance our lives.

Why We Have Emotions

There is a biological purpose as to why we have emotions. Think about every purpose your body's functions serve. Your heart pumps blood everywhere to keep all your limbs alive. Your stomach processes what you eat, doing its best to get as many vitamins and nutrients as possible from each food source. Then your brain tells you what's right and what's wrong in the hopes that you'll make the best decision. What about our emotions, however? What purpose do these serve?

They are responses to different threats that we might be presented with. When you are angry at your spouse for keeping secrets from you, you feel threatened that something bad might happen. You are fearful over the end of your relationship and up until that point, part of your survival was dependent on your relationship.

The biological purpose of emotions has been to keep us alive. You are afraid of certain things and this can protect you. You are afraid of falling off a cliff so you might stay a little further back from the edge, your brain knowing the threat that this can have. When we're afraid of the dark, that can be something that dates back to more primal times when a predator might have been lurking in the dark bushes.

Emotions weren't only created so that we're scared all the time. They also came about through years of evolution because we need to be able to identify different opportunities. When a bowl of food looks especially tasty, we eat it because who knows if that will be the last time that we get to eat for a while. When we are given the chance to meet somebody new, we might feel positive emotions from this, knowing that they could end up being someone that changes our lives.

Emotions used to help us survive. When there was a threat, your body would go into either a "fight" or "flight" mode. You would sense that there was danger and thereafter, your body would ready itself for the best possible resolution to this attack. Think of it like an animal. If you ran up to your cat and started screaming and swatting at it, he is going to either scratch you back or sprint and hide under the bed. If you saw a bear in the wild and you were acting all loud and crazy, that bear might run and hide as well or they might completely destroy you (Stosny, 2019).

The fight mode gets your muscles tensed so that you know how to fight back. Your arms clench, your heart starts beating faster, and you ready yourself to start swinging fists should you have to. Your eyes widen and your attention focuses. This sort of adrenaline rush can make you feel somewhat "pumped up." Your body's trying to get ready to fight, so you have this sudden burst of energy. For some people, this can result in the idea that they need to push the fight further and get it going. In one way, it is them validating their own response, maybe trying to look for reasons that this fight is the best. Others might also do this as a way to have the upper hand.

Think of an especially inebriated buff college frat boy at a bar who wants to start a fight with someone that's pretty much a carbon copy of him. He might say something like, "come on bro, do you want to hit me?" egging him on and trying to get him to start the fight first. These are all just survival tactics when you really start to break things down.

The flight mode gets you ready to sprint as fast as you can. You might start to feel more anxious, as if you have to leave. Perhaps you have trouble breathing, feeling as though you need to get up and out of the room. You might shake your leg, feel your heartbeat, and look for the quickest exit. These kinds of responses, both the fight and flight, do not just happen physically.

Nowadays, we do not need to worry about a bear gobbling us up as we sit and relax, but we do need to be cautious of other factors for survival. You might be someone that never punched anyone in your life and never will. When you are presented with a threat, you might still respond in fight mode, however. Let's say a friend starts to question your honesty, maybe calling you out on a lie they think you made. You might get defensive, feeling as though they are questioning your credibility. Rather than hearing them out to really get to the bottom of all the rumors, you could start questioning their credibility, taking their character in defense.

We can "flee" mentally as well. When someone is yelling or screaming at you, you might be the type of person to just shut down and start to disassociate from the situation. This happens often in abused children. They do not have the option to fight back because they aren't strong enough, but they can't flee because their parents are the only caregivers they know. It can be easy to just shut down and try to tune out what is going on as our body's way of fleeing the scene of the attack.

When you feel such negative emotions, it can be challenging to be able to look inwards about what the root issue is and why you might be feeling a certain emotion so intensely. Now that you understand the evolutionary purpose of these emotions, let's look at why you are still having them today and how you might be able to interpret them in a way that benefits your life.

Motivation

Our motivation might sometimes also be referred to as our arousal. When something elicits a feeling of curiosity or gets us excited, that can lead to more feelings of exploration. One motivation for our emotional reactions is to simply explore them deeper and see what the root of them could be. We might like to test our limits, see what thrills us, and understand why we get so mad at some of the things that we do.

As the mammals that we are, we are wired to explore as a way to get the supplies we need. If you let a cat outside, they are going to start sniffing around, maybe eating bugs or looking for rats along the way. This curiosity is natural and part of their survival. This can be a reason that we might start to feel emotional connections to certain stimuli. Some things might give us interest, so we are motivated to discover even more.

Our motivation is a reaction to an emotion that therein helps us respond to the feelings that we might be having. All emotions can motivate us, even the more challenging ones. As we start to get more into discussing your control over your emotional intelligence now, start to think about how each feeling you have can be one that drives you.

Not every emotion will be a motivator. Some days you just might be in a bad mood and need to sleep and eat and relax. Other days, you might find that you are perfectly comfortable with just sitting with your happiness, basking in the glory of ignorant bliss.

Interpretation

Of course, we can't only talk about our own emotions when referring to different human thoughts and feelings. We have to be aware of how others play into our emotional roles. Whether they are influencing how we feel or we are playing a role of persuasion in their lives, it is important to see how human emotions can all mingle together.

The major part of emotional intelligence is understanding how others are feeling. When we start to come to terms with the emotions that others have and really recognize what it is they might be feeling, that is when real persuasion can start to happen.

We need to recognize how perception can entirely change someone's ability to emotionally react.

How you perceive someone's emotion can be different from others as well. Maybe you leave a party and say, "didn't she seem mad?" and someone else says, "what are you talking about?". You can pick up on, and equally misunderstand, something that another person has the opposite perspective on.

Others might perceive your emotion completely different from what you are trying to express as well. Maybe you are really in a good mood, but just feeling exhausted. Others might see a lack of excitement as a sign you are in a bad mood, constantly asking you "what's wrong?".

To see emotions in others requires you to have a strong understanding of what they look like in yourself first.

As you start to become an emotional master, both of your own and other's feelings, it becomes so much easier to understand emotional awareness. When we fully improve our perception of emotion, we will start to better use it to drive logic and influence decision making.

Emotion versus Logic and Decision Making

Many decisions are based on emotions over logic and we aren't always aware of this connection. Now we are really going to start to get into why all this matters to you as an entrepreneur. Of course, we first had to go into detail over what emotions were and what it can mean to feel certain things. Throughout the rest of the book, we are going to put an emphasis on why it is crucial you maintain a high level of emotional intelligence.

We might start to get fearful, so we rush something that we know should take time and patience. We might get angry, so we cut connections that would be better off improved. If we use emotions, we react too quickly, not giving ourselves any time to see what would be the most beneficial in the situation overall.

We also need to ensure that we are able to use emotion in our sales in order to drive decision-making in the people that we want to influence. Emotions can be very strong and they can be what helps us to finally win over clients and convince investors that we are worth their money.

You'll first need to start to be fully aware of the emotions that have been driving your decisions. How has happiness, fear, anger, and sadness played into your decision-making process?

Emotions shouldn't be totally removed from our ability to choose whether something is good or bad, but it shouldn't take the front wheel and drive that decision overall.

Let's start to look at the models of emotional intelligence so we can better pick up the ability to figure out how to improve our own (Levine, 2019).

Chapter 2: The EQ Models

In this chapter, we are going to discuss the different emotional intelligence models. You know you better than anyone else, or you should at least. Though talking to other people can really help you get to know yourself more. For the most part, you have a true sense of self around your identity that's stronger than what other people think.

When it comes to understanding your emotional intelligence, it can be hard to measure. What's important is understanding the difference between what you think you would do in any given situation and what you would actually do.

Now that we know everything there is to know about emotions (if only...), we can move onto what emotional intelligence is. Emotional intelligence is similar to your intelligence quotient

Your emotional intelligence is the ability for you to manage your own emotions, while also recognizing and understanding the emotional state of those around you.

Emotional intelligence is objective. You are able to see the good qualities that you have to offer the world, while also being conscious of the things it wouldn't hurt to work on. Simply being self-aware does not always equate to self-loathing. There is such a thing as being too aware. This might get to the point where you become scared or paranoid, maybe thinking everyone hates you, always ruminating over the things you said. Most people aren't even going to be aware of these smaller things about yourself that you might pick up on.

Someone emotionally intelligent understands there is important influence that you need to be aware of on one level, while still being able to see that you are a beneficial and influential person in other ways.

Someone emotionally intelligent understands that they are in charge of their emotional reactions – not necessarily their emotions. You might not be able to help it if you get mad that your sport's team lost, but you are 100% in charge of whether or not you choose to punch a wall.

If your emotional intelligence is high, then that means you have a high ability of influence by using your emotions. This means that you can understand how critical thinking can affect your exact emotions.

One quick method to improve intelligence is The Six Seconds model. You should notice three things, all in just a couple seconds. Know yourself and what you do, choose to do what you need to do, and decide to do this for a reason. It can be vague but, essentially, it is a great way to determine where you are at in your emotional intelligence ability. When someone makes you mad, you might know that they offended you, choose to insult them and do this because you want to make yourself feel better. That would demonstrate a low level of emotional intelligence.

Each of these models gives us insight into what emotional intelligence is and what level you might "score" at in each of these categories.

Ability

This model was developed by two different people, Perter Salovey of Yale University, as well as John Mayer, who attended the University of New Hampshire.

This first model is a newer version of a way to define what a person's emotional intelligence level is. You can decide where you might be based on coming up with your own scores.

Is what we're describing behavior that sounds like you or do you think you could honestly work on it a bit? When thinking of these kinds of scenarios, ask yourself if you think that other people would answer for you. It can be helpful to consider another's view on you in an objective way.

Many of us can be emotionally intelligent without even trying. It's not always something that you have to practice and can just be a part of who you are. However, the ability model helps to point out areas of weaknesses that you might want to work on (Salovey, Brackett & Mayer, 2007).

Ability to Perceive Emotions

The first part of the model is inclusive of how nonverbal signals are understood and processed by an individual. Those with social disabilities, such as social anxiety or Asperger's, might struggle with picking up on what others are trying to say not through their verbal language.

If someone is in a rush, we might see them tapping their foot, anxiously wanting to leave. If someone is sad, they might not be making eye contact, frowning, and unfocused. There are plenty of little cues that let us know how the other person might be feeling without them having to say anything.

Any facial expression or body movement; whether it is in a picture, in their voice, through their words, or whatever else, can be an indication of a person's emotion. Can you pick up on the things about a person that might signal what emotion they are feeling? Can you tell when someone might be feeling uncomfortable? Do you understand what it means when someone is wanting to leave?

This doesn't just go for how you recognize emotions in others either, it is also important to note how you might be able to recognize different emotions in yourself. Let's say that you are in one of those moods where everything annoys you. Maybe your assistant asks a question and you get a little snappy, a friend texts you about dinner and you are quick to write it off. Even the cat might get on your nerves to the point you feel like exploding.

Are you able to recognize that it is not all of these people that are annoying, that instead, you are just in a grumpy mood? Though the initial emotion might be annoyance, how well can you say to yourself, "OK, I just need to destress a bit before I snap on anyone else.". It can be easy to blame everyone else for our bad mood, but those with a skilled ability to understand all emotional perception will have a higher EQ.

Emotional Reasoning

How well can one use emotions to cognitively investigate? How well can emotional activity spark intellectual exploration? Do you notice one of your behaviors and have the ability to link it back to something in the past? Are you able to take a terrible mood and turn it into a moment where you learn something deep about yourself?

When you have a desired outcome, there is a way that you can use both your emotion and the emotion of another person in order to guide you both in the direction of the things that you want. Are you able to catch someone in a good mood and use that in order to inspire them? Perhaps you and someone else are both in a distant or even lazy-feeling mood and you take that opportunity to just have a chill day.

Are you considerate of others' emotions while making decisions? Most of the time we do what is best for us while making sure no one else gets hurt. Do you allow yourself to make some sacrifices so that you can get to a decision that's best for the both of you?

Are you appropriate with the expression and discussion of emotions? Can you bring up things that make you upset in the right setting? It's never easy to talk about our feelings, but someone with a higher EQ knows that it is vital to have moments of discussion and reflection in personal relationships.

Understanding Emotions

Can you recognize the emotion that someone is displaying? It can be easy to think that someone is mad but sometimes that is just our insecurities getting the best of us. We might think everyone hates us or is judging us, when we're really fine and just feeling extra sensitive to scrutiny.

Once you recognize these emotions, how well are you able to interpret them to find the most realistic situation? Is someone mad because no one came to their party or is someone mad because they are really feeling lonely and angry at their friends? Can you push past the surface level idea and really see the root of why someone is upset?

Do you get why people are mad, even in situations that wouldn't make you angry? It's easy to write someone off and say, "I do not get why they are mad," but understanding why someone is mad doesn't mean that you have to agree with the reaction. You can still see their hurt without feeling the offense yourself.

Are you understanding of the complexity that one emotion could hold? Once you start to see how deep feelings can really go, it becomes easier to start to understand why someone might be displaying that certain thought or feeling.

Do you have the ability to look past just the words someone is saying and really get what feelings they want to express?

Management of Emotions

Are you able to regulate your own emotions? When you stub your toe, this is a good sign of how well you have your emotions under control. Can you walk it off and feel fine or do you have to scream a loud curse word? When someone cuts you off in traffic, can you wave and smile or do you feel the need to lay on your horn and tail them? No one is wrong for having the initial upset feeling, but there are many different ways that emotion can be taken, and it is not always good.

How well can you articulate a response and keep it appropriate to the situation? Even though you might have the urge to say something rude, are you able to just keep your cool and shrug the comment off or do you have to say something equally snarky right back?

Do you have trouble responding immediately to an emotion you have? Do you make impulsive decisions? Maybe the server came up and said your food is going to be out ten minutes later than they said. Can you simply say, "ok, that's fine, thanks!" or do you throw a fit that gets the attention of the entire restaurant?

Do you often apologize for your behavior after it has happened? There are many people that will snap, yell, fight, and argue but ten minutes later apologize. Even though it is good to recognize it and say you are sorry, it is not good to consistently snap like this, simply hoping every time that others will just so easily forgive.

Does stress cause it to be more challenging to focus? Do you have trouble liking someone when they have upset you? How well do other people's emotions affect you as well? All four of these sections are ways that you can start to measure your emotional intelligence. They represent different branches of emotions and how they are utilized. In order to be emotionally intelligent, you have to have all four working in harmony, not some that are great and others that aren't. The more you work on these, the better and stronger they will all become individually as well.

Mixed

This model is one that we will likely be referring to the most because it is so detailed yet inclusive of the basic ideas understood in the other sections. It was created by Daniel Goleman, whom we referred to in the introduction (Goleman, 1995).

Self-Awareness

This is inclusive of one's confidence. Do you have the ability to recognize that you are a valuable person who matters in the world? We can easily see how we affect the world, but it is important to be conscious of all the ways you have been able to positively affect those around you.

Do you recognize the strengths that you have? These will be the things that you do well, what others admire in you, the things others ask you to do often, and simply, the things that you love to do the most. Even if you are not necessarily a good singer but still love singing, this is still a trait that many will admire!

Can you identify what weaknesses you might run into? Do you need to work on communicating? Maybe you have to increase your level of self-discipline? Whatever it might be, someone with high EQ levels understands what they need to focus on strengthening.

They will also have the ability to recognize their own feelings. Can you tell what makes you upset, identify your triggers, and work through your inner turmoil on your own? Those with a low EQ will not be self-aware. They will not understand why they are in a bad mood; they might treat others with disregard and they will often be self-loathing and overly judgmental.

Self-Regulation

Do you have the ability to display self-control? When we're kids, teens, and even young adults it is easy to look at the authority figures to tell us what to do. You have to wake up and go to school, do your homework by a certain deadline, and do your best to follow the rules the rest of the time. Now that we're adults, we're the ones in charge! Are you able to come up with your own schedule and actually stick to the things you say you are going to do?

Are you trustworthy? Do you struggle to keep secrets, or find yourself enjoying the discussions of others? We all like our occasional gossip or the juicy news on the street, but consistently discussing another person and breaking them down when they are not even there is not healthy. You might like to share the secret that your co-worker's spouse got arrested for public indecency, but if you and your mom constantly talk about your sister and all the problems she has and never discuss this with her in person, this can show a low level of emotional intelligence.

How well can you adapt to any given situation? Do you have the ability to take control over yourself and cool down when you have to suddenly switch plans? When things didn't go your way, are you able to make sure that this doesn't cause you discomfort, or to grow really angry?

Motivation

Motivation is one's ability to use their emotions for a beneficial drive. Can these feelings you have become something that actually powers you into a beneficial action? Maybe you are feeling angry. You could drink a beer, and then another, and then another, and then another until you are so numb you do not feel any pain. Or, you could go on a run and release your anger, come home and enjoy a reasonable amount of beer while you joke and hang out with close friends. It's not like you aren't allowed to have fun, in terms of enjoying alcohol, but it is about how your motivation to do certain things might be driven by positive or negative emotions.

Not only are you motivated, but are you committed? We all have great ideas all the time, but how many of those ideas turn into half-planned ventures? By being an entrepreneur, you are already doing a great job of turning your goal into actionable steps; what's important going forward is the level of dedication you have to this.

Do you take initiative when you know that it is needed? Sometimes we know what's best to do, but we might be too afraid to start. When you know what needs to be done and you have the ability to take the lead, then this will be a good sign of your emotional intelligence.

How optimistic are you about what it is that seems motivational? Optimism can sometimes be blinding and we always need to pay special attention to the things that could go wrong. However, if we're motivated, then we're optimistic and we need to ensure we have the right balance of both.

Empathy

Empathy is your ability to not just understand, but to feel the emotions of those around you. We will get into this a little later in the book, but for now, empathy refers to one's ability to feel what it is that others might be also feeling. Can you relate to that pain? Can you understand what it feels like to go through what it is that they are experiencing?

This is important to have because you need to also be politically aware of the world, at least your society, and the diversity required in your team.

Social Skills

Finally, social skills, leadership, communication abilities, and conflict resolution are incredibly important in measuring your emotional intelligence in this model. Again, we're going to dive deeper into the important social skills that are needed, especially as an entrepreneur. Be conscious of how you are able to interact within this world, as it can show what your level of emotional intelligence might be.

How can you take all four of these things we just discussed and apply them in a way that helps others?

Trait

Konstantin Vasily Petrides defined this model by referring to it as a constellation. He believed that our emotional self-created perceptions are based on emotion and these would become the drivers of our personality (Srivastava, 2013).

Now that you have a better idea of what your emotional intelligence level might be, let's take a look at how this can directly affect your personality.

It's important to remember that just because you have a high level of emotional intelligence doesn't mean that everyone else will always see that. Since you perceive others in ways differently than someone else might, others will perceive you different as well. While you might be an emotionally intelligent person with a really high score, that doesn't mean that others will always see you as empathetic because they have their own personal perceptions.

In the next chapter, we will start to breakdown more about how you are going to be able to influence others based on improving the skills and emotions we talked about throughout this chapter.

This model forms more around the idea that your EQ is based on personality traits, not necessarily your ability. So rather than asking, how well can you do this, it is whether or not you can do that if it is part of your personality.

The trait model is one based in your own self-perception of how you can emotionally manage. Some reject this model on the basis of self-assessment.

How well can you understand your own emotions? Do you also have the ability to be aware of how others might be perceiving some of your emotions?

With this trait model, you have to really look at your personality in the past and your history of choices you have made, rather than the "what-ifs" of what you might do now.

One has to have an understanding of their personality framework in order to better recognize their ability to judge their emotional intelligence level in the first place.

Chapter 3: Introspection

In this chapter, we are going to focus more on the EQ levels as much as possible. By this point, you should already understand of someone with both a high and a lower EQ level might look like. We went over the levels of a high emotionally intelligent person in the last chapter – someone that can recognize emotions in themselves and others and use those for good. Those who have lower emotional intelligence will be reactionary and dismissive of the feelings and thoughts of people around them.

This chapter, we are going to be discussing the way that you can recognize emotions within yourself. This is going to be directed in a business and sales way now as well. Rather than talking about personal relationships you have with friends and family; we are going to keep your attention on what matters the most as an entrepreneur. You can still apply these kinds of ideas to your personal life but in the context that we're discussing, it is all about making business relationships and focusing on sales regulation.

The point of all of this will be to help you understand the importance of sales negotiation. That is why you are applying this to your own business, after all. You want to learn how to be an emotionally intelligent person to ensure that you are focused on business when it matters – never your emotional feelings that could derail a sale. That sounds cold and calculated, so it is also vital to remember how our emotions can still play an imperative role in our lives. You shouldn't react emotionally right away, but you should still let your feelings and passion help to drive success overall. The key is using your emotions for something beneficial, not in a way that could make things worse.

There will also be an emphasis on relationship management. Where does relationship management start? With yourself, of course. The next chapter will be more focused on emotional intelligence with others but right now, we are going to emphasize building your emotional intelligence within yourself first.

Self-Awareness and Self-Esteem

You are likely already more self-aware now than you were at the beginning of the reading. What you need to work on now is how you can be more self-aware in your business. You are the boss; you are in charge. You're the manager of managers, the head guy, the number one that everyone will go to at the end of the day. There are already expectations of you in place before you even get a chance to meet some of your employees and clients. It is up to you to now focus on getting into the right mindset to operate as an emotionally intelligent individual.

Always look for ways that you can give to others first. Be aware of how you wouldn't be successful if it weren't for the people that are working just as hard under you. Give without expecting anything in return. Give and forget that you did, so that you will not be waiting around for others to give back to you. Don't give to a point where you are sacrificing yourself and do not give often to someone that you do not think would do the same for you if they could. Not everyone is going to give back to you but remember, when you might feel guilty about not giving enough, would they do the same for you?

While being self-aware, always look for ways that you can improve. What do you feel you need to do to help your team? How can you also help them in return? You might try to figure thisature of this chit chatting with the boss about what their problem is. Look for ways that you can give people a voice without them being afraid to share. Do surveys, and anonymous ones will help people be open even more.

While being critical is an important aspect of being self-aware, you must also ensure that you are doing your best to have a high level of self-esteem. You have to believe in yourself first if you ever expect anyone else to believe in you as well. Having high self-esteem doesn't mean thinking that you are better than everyone else. It means that you know your own worth and it doesn't always matter if everyone else feels the same way.

Always put yourself in your employee's position. Yes, you need to focus on yourself, but how can you really improve your business if you do not know what it is like to be the middleman? Don't expect things from your employees if you wouldn't be able to do the same, at least in their situation. If you are the owner of a construction business but do not know how to operate a certain piece of machinery, that's understandable. However, if you had their same training, would you feel comfortable doing what you are asking of your employees?

Be aware of how much work you are putting in as well. Depending on the position, you should be working just as often as your employees. A great manager will also do the same things that they are asking of their employees. They do not want to feel as though they are working forty + hours a week when you are only available for one hour a week. You can't do it all, especially the larger your business is, but you can still make an effort to show to others that you are willing to work just as hard as them.

Confidence and Assertiveness

Part of being self-aware is also going to involve having confidence. There's a difference in being assured and being someone that is too cocky. Don't be afraid to say what's on your mind, but phrase it in a way that others will respond well to. Let's say you run a small clothing store. You walk in one day and notice that one of your employees is leaning up against the counter on their phone and there are a few out-of-place clothing items on a messy rack.

Your first instinct is going to be, "doesn't anyone do any work around here?"; however, this will just instill fear in the employee. Instead, you might still be wondering what the reason for the messy store is, but you'll want to phrase it in a way that can turn into a productive conversation.

That will give you a little insight into what was going on and give you the chance to express concerns over their work ethic. You might say something like, "it looks like it was a busy day, were you able to get a lot done?" They might proceed to tell you the tasks they did and you could ask something afterward like, "have you been able to get to the clothing racks yet? I noticed one is a little messed up over there." This helps the employee give an explanation.

They might say something about how they just got a chance to catch their breath after a rush or that they needed to take a quick break in between cleaning up. This is understandable and you could remind them of your appreciation for their work. This employee could have been lying to you, but they will still be more likely to respect you and want to improve their own work because they respect your authority.

They might also say something about how they didn't notice and reveal that it wasn't that busy of a day at all. You'll then be able to use this moment to tell them that when the store is slow, they need to pay more attention to keeping the racks tidy. This is going to be based in your own words but as you can see, their revealing of the lack of work that day shows they aren't doing the tasks they are supposed to be performing. It gives you a chance to educate them so that they do better next time, while still in a respectful and authoritative way.

Confidence means that you believe in yourself. You accept that you are not perfect, but you know that you have the ability to do what needs to be done with the supplies already at your disposal. Too much confidence can make you seem frightening and that will not give your employees any respect over you. When you are around, they'll do their best. But when they have free reign, they'll probably slack off because they will not really care about the business. They might believe that you do not respect them, so they will not show that back to you.

The same goes for when you are working with clients and contractors. You'll want to show them that you are open to discussion and approachable. You will not be able to give them everything they want, even if they are especially demanding. Confidence doesn't mean rudely telling them no. you simply have to find a way that the both of you can benefit and communicate the reality in an effectively authoritative manner. We'll get more into working with others in the next chapter.

Part of lacking confidence is having the difficulty to say "no." This is a vital word that we need to include in our vocabulary, if we ever plan on getting the things that we want. Sometimes, we can get afraid to tell people "no," because we grow fearful that they will not need us anymore. If anyone is only around you because they need you and like how frequently you say "yes," then they are not someone that you should focus your energy on.

This is where we fall into being assertive. An emotionally intelligent person is aware of what they want and knows how to get it. They aren't blinded by power, but they are able to see a situation that will benefit them while also aiding others in the process. When you are only focused on your goals, you lose sight of what is right, what is fair.

When you are only focused on everyone else, then you forget about yourself and you can quickly become exhausted, losing some of your identity on the way. Focus on finding the balance between pleasing others while ensuring you are still taking care of yourself.

At the same time, you also want to assess when their wants are things that aren't going to harm anyone else. For example, you are going to want to pick and choose some battles. Accept that not everything that you want is going to be realistic. Ensure that you aren't hurting anyone else along the way.

When you are confident, more people will believe in you. When you aren't afraid to stand up for what you want, it shows that you are trustworthy as well.

Remember that there is a huge difference between just being a boss and being someone that manages others. Don't just tell people what to do; work with them to make sure they understand what they need to do. Don't just say "yes" to everyone that makes requests through your business. Explain to them the process and give them flexibility, maybe a few options to choose what they feel most comfortable with. When you open these doors of communication, then it can help you build relationships. Don't think of yourself as just a business owner. You are a facilitator between people that want your service or product and others that want to help you in return for something valuable as well, whether it is money from income or simply experience through internships. It's not just a business transaction, even if that's what your business boils down to. There is a valuable exchange between all parties and your confidence and assurance are required to see this.

You want to be assertive, but never aggressive. You might be able to gain power with anger and being more aggressive, but you will never gain respect. Your employees having respect for you is going to be more important than anything else.

How to Make Requests as a Socially Intelligent Person

A socially intelligent person knows how to make requests. It can be scary to ask for things at times but once you learn how to do it, it can come so easily. First, remember that you are entitled to ask for things from others. There are some entrepreneurs that will even be afraid to ask their own employees for help! That's what others are there for! As long as you communicate in an effective way and be open and honest with others, you are never wrong for making a request.

Those with a high EQ level ensure that what they are asking of others is first and foremost, reasonable. Never ask someone of something you wouldn't be willing to do for them, again, if they were in the same position. Let's say you need a personal loan from a friend for around $10,000 and since they net over $1,000,000 a year in their business, it is really not that much money.

As a struggling entrepreneur, it is a lot for you. Of course, if they asked you for that money, you would have to say no because you do not have it. However, if you were in his position, would you be able to say "yes," to what it is that you are requesting? If you say "no," then it is probably something you shouldn't ask.

When making requests, keep it as simple as possible. The more reasons that you give for someone to listen to you and help you out, the more ideas you are giving them for reasons not to help you out.

If you need that loan and you start to say, "well I need it because it is just money to get me started, and I ran out of my funds already, and I need to buy a bunch of things, but I'll get it back to you soon," and ramble on with more and more excuses, then you are basically listing out all the reasons the other person would say "no."

They'll see that you need money to get started, which means there's a chance that you will not finish. Then they'll hear that you ran out of funds, which means that you might not be good with money, and so on. Each of these reasons why you need the money can be twisted into a reason that they should not give you the money.

When making requests, frame it in a way that will benefit them, and never lie. This doesn't mean you have to give the juicy details. Simply state your request, tell them you understand if they must decline and from there, you can communicate. They might ask "why" anyway, but this gives you time to prepare a proper response that will not scare them away from the request.

Ask yourself if you would feel comfortable with the request. If you think it is absurd, then you probably are asking a little too much. Never bank your requests on luck.

Find a way that the other person's needs will be met by your request. Start by telling them how you'll be helping them before you even get into how you'll be helped.

Never lie. Sometimes you might want to exaggerate one part to make another look less atrocious. However, lying is one way to instantly make everyone else around you untrustworthy of your actions.

Never show emotion when you do not get what you want. Maybe a client says "no," or someone else refuses to invest. It might be a denial that really changes the course of how you thought things were going to go. Perhaps you were really banking on their saying, "yes," so you get emotional and upset. Don't show this with anger. It's OK to be disappointed, but you do not want to take it out on them for turning you down.

Don't burn bridges. Some people say that it is fine to burn bridges because then that means you will not be tempted to look back. Sure, there's a reason that you left in the first place. However, if you continue to burn bridges, you might find that you eventually become isolated on your own island!

Don't put pressure on anyone, even if it is a really pressing matter. They might say yes, but you do not want to be in a position where they later withdrawal, realizing that your request was too much for them. Let's say that you asked your business partner for a loan and once they approved, that gave you the chance to make another small investment for your business based on a lead from a different colleague.

However, when you asked your partner, you really put the pressure on them. They said no at first and it took a lot of convincing to get them to cave. While you might have won, he might end up pulling out. Then you have already invested the money, putting you in an even more challenging position than if you would have just dealt with him saying "no" in the first place.

Asking Others for Help

When it comes to asking for help, always do so in a way that you will be able to pay the other person back. This is not for the exact monetary amount but look for a way that you can help them too. Never just ask for help and then abandon the other person. This will only make things worse for you down the line.

Let those who are helping to guide you as well. Don't just ask for one aspect. Don't pretend like you "know it all," when they are responding. If they start to offer you advice, take it. Maybe you ask for some help promoting your business through a friend. They agree, but they also make some suggestions to your branding that you do not totally agree with. Rather than turning them down right away, maybe you take part of their advice and twist in a way that works to your advantage.

They clearly know what they are doing or else you wouldn't be asking them for help. Listen to them and they will appreciate that you are willing to grow. They will then be more willing to help you out if you need it again in the future, rather than if you would have ignored them and blew off their suggestions.

Tell them the reason that you are asking for help in the first place. Maybe they'll be able to come up with a better solution for the issue at hand. If you ask for $1,000 in investments from someone but they do not feel comfortable giving you that money, perhaps you can throw in additional labor or a higher percentage of return if they do go through with the investment.

They might counter with a better offer that saves both of you money, while you still get the outcome you were hoping for when making the initial request for the investment.

Let the other person know that you specifically chose them to help you out. Use phrases like:

"I asked you because I knew I could trust you."

"I do not feel comfortable asking anyone else."

Of course, only say these things if it is the truth, but it really is a good way to be more personable and show just how much you appreciate what they decided to do for you. These phrases make the other person feel important and they will be more willing to help because you have added compassion. Again, this is part of the process of building a relationship, not just working the motions of a transaction.

Remember that when you ask for help, you can never be too grateful. Send a "thank you" card, have them over for a nice steak dinner, buy them tickets to a fun show, or do whatever other small gesture you can. If they gave you a $100,000 loan, even taking them out to dinner once could be enough to show how much you really appreciate what they did for you.

Make sure that your timing is right. Don't wait until they are stressed. It can be tempting to ask when you know you will not have to face them. Maybe you leave a voicemail when you know they are not home, so you do not have to talk in person. Don't do this! People will be so much more likely to respond when you take time out of your day to ask for help.

Don't bombard with gifts first. It will make people think that they are being bribed or that you only care to do nice things because you need something from them. It might seem like a good idea to take them out to dinner, get a little wine in them and ask when they are in good spirits. It could work, but it could also make them feel like they are being set up. Instead, ask them up front or at least preface the dinner by saying, "I want to take you out because I have something really important I need to ask." The more honest you are, the more likely they'll be willing to help out. Most people will say "yes" in times that they are able to fully help, so it will not always be a matter of whether or not they can do it; it can sometimes be up to whether or not they feel like they want to do it based on if they should be helping you out.

Self-Regulation and Self-Control

It's important that we are aware of the impulsive behaviors we might exhibit in the workspace. If you are feeling anxious, maybe business is dying, your employees lack motivation, and clients are pulling out left and right, you might start to panic.

It can be easy to want to do something drastic; maybe fire someone, rearrange the office, change the logo, take out a loan for marketing, or do something else that you think will help you out of the rut.

Practice self-control and remember that most good things will take time. You will not just snap out of that rut. Have meetings, talk with employees, get candid with clients, and find ways to improve over time rather than demanding the situation gets fixed right away.

Part of having self-control is practicing patience. Just as mothers and fathers are models for their children, so are you for your employees!

When it comes to your personal life, you need to consistently regulate how this might transition into your work life. Are you always on vacation? Do you bring designer purses into work? Your employees will see this! Do not flaunt your wealth in front of them. They will start to resent you because they can't go on vacation as often or they have to wear used clothes because they will not have as much money for nicer designer pieces.

Regulate how much of that personal life you share with others as well. It can be tempting to talk to your employees because they will always be willing to listen, but they are not people to always spill all the drama to. Being personal is important, but there are some things that shouldn't be involved in a boss-employee relationship.

You must have self-control as well. Make sure that you are staying until the time that you were scheduled. If you are leaving every day an hour before time is up just because you can, then you are letting others know that you do not care about the business. If you do have to leave early, make sure you express why and keep your phone on you to check emails an hour after others are scheduled just to show that you are willing to still work.

Discipline yourself to stay on track with your goals as well. Don't be tempted to "sell out" for more money if it means that you are going against the original ideas of the business. There might be times when you have to make sacrifices for the company, but do not do it in a way that jeopardizes the future. Plan ahead and even though something might seem like a quick fix, ask if it is just a Band-Aid or the long-term solution to ensure you do not fall back into a place such as that again.

Dealing with Stress Created by Yourself

A lot of the stress we feel comes from things that we have created within ourselves. When we do not control our anxious thoughts, they can turn into paranoid delusions rather quickly. We have to constantly check and see if the things that we are worried about are valid or if we are taking things way out of proportion.

You need to make sure that you are setting a time period away from work. You should have at least a quarter to a half a day every week that you go radio silent. Maybe it is Sunday from 8 am to 2 pm, or Friday nights after 6 you refuse to check your email. No matter how bad you might want to look, just give yourself some peace and quiet away from the job. Ideally, you'll dedicate a little more time, especially if your business is not even open every day. For a store that's open over 12 hours a day Monday-Sunday, it is hard to not always be there. Someone's always calling off or there's an especially angry customer. However, the business will survive for a few hours without you.

As entrepreneurs, it is hard to not constantly be stressed out. For many of our employees, they can simply clock out and go home! That's not so easy for us to do. Instead, we carry the weight of work with us wherever we go because it is our life! Don't let your business be the boss of you, however.

Allow other people to do some tasks. If you have to hire a temporary position or even a part-time one just to alleviate stress, do it! You might lose out on some income because you have to pay for the work, but it is better than paying the hospital bills after a stress-induced heart attack!

Don't let past failures trigger you into a panic. Treat each new venture as its own. Perhaps signs of decreasing business have started and ones similar to a last failed business adventure. Take this time to look at what you did wrong and how you can make this business different. Remember that not every dip in income means that the business is failing. Sometimes there will just be slow periods. Keep in mind that usually, when it rains, it pours.

Recognize when the stress first starts. Identify your triggers. Maybe it is the constant phone calls, the one client that always seems to need something, or an employee who is not living up to their part. Try and work through these stresses, find ways to avoid them, or come up with a solution to alleviate the stress that they bring on.

Always combat your stressful thoughts. When you have a negative one, come back at it with a positive one. An emotionally intelligent entrepreneur is going to know how to turn negative thoughts into ones that will provide them with use.

Positive and Negative Emotions in Yourself

There are ways that you can manage the negative emotions. You should never block out these kinds of negative emotions. The moment that you start to do this is when you start to build up and hold onto emotions that will only cause you more stress!

When it comes to your negative emotions, imagine that you are a mentor to someone else starting their own business. How would you help them to combat those ideas?

Let that negative emotion tell you something about both yourself and your business. What is it that you are afraid of losing?

How can you take that instance and, at the very least, learn from this negative emotion?

We make mistakes that turn into lessons. You might invest too much money at once and you learn that you need to start small once that investment fails. How can you take that negative feeling and learn from it before any mistakes are even made?

We will also want to put an emphasis on leveraging the positive emotions. Your mind is clearly one of greatness, that's how you have been able to become an entrepreneur. Every thought you have can be useful, it is simply up to you to find that overall purpose.

Always look for a change when everything else fails! Remember all that excitement at the beginning of your business adventure? How can you turn that around now and use it for something positive?

When you are angry, how can that passion be directed towards improving some aspect of your business?

Remember that you are always going to be anxious and fearful of the future. You just have to now focus on putting that energy to good use and using it as a passion-driver, not something that destroys you and your company.

Self-Motivation

The key to motivation is knowing what needs to be done. What is it that you want to do? What is the goal of your business? You are not just an entrepreneur; you are a leader. You are someone established who is in charge of directing many people's lives.

If it is just to make money – be honest with yourself! We would all probably just sit around and relax, lay in the sun and eat if we could. But we have to make that money! Now that you have gotten that part out of the way, how else can this business add value? You might be able to make a ton of cash, but how can you make others' lives better? How can you make yourself feel more fulfilled?

Money is not the only thing that should drive you, either. You need to find a way that this method of making money is good for you and for others. An emotionally intelligent entrepreneur can take that passion and let it be the driver, the conductor, the pilot.

A successful entrepreneur knows exactly what needs to be done and they believe themselves. They see a goal and, even if it seems big, they have the confidence to know that they are the ones that can do it.

Motivation is necessary because no one else is going to tell you what to do. You have to start to take charge of your own life and the things that are the most important. Other people will be happy for you. Those that love you will encourage you. No one else but you is going to be able to take charge and really guide your life. You are the one that has to decide where things go from here.

You have to be confident and compassionate for yourself if you want to find true motivation. Though it can be hard to not be self-deprecating and critical, you will still want to stay focused on encouraging yourself, especially when going through times of others doubting you.

Motivation is going to be developed around goals. Come up with personal goals, goals for your team, goals for the next month, six months, year, five years, ten years, and so on.

Your goals need to be realistic. What goals would you give to an employee? If you wouldn't expect someone else to be able to achieve a certain goal within a timeframe, you can't always expect yourself to do it either.

Make sure to have a looming goal that you want to reach. What is it that you want to do with your life? You can't just want to be rich! You should want to do something great. Do you want to help people? Do you want to be remembered? Do you want to improve the earth?

What is it that you would be comfortable doing, knowing it was your greatest accomplishment before this great life ends? This should be your main goal and the one which helps to drive all the smaller goals along the way. Once you have determined what your biggest dream really is, it will be much easier to figure out the small steps you need to get there. If you wanted to move a mountain, you wouldn't do it by pushing the whole thing. You would want to start by moving one stone at a time.

Chapter 4: Extrospection

Extrospection is a way that you not only get to know other people, but you learn more about yourself in the process of learning from other people. If you stayed in your apartment all day every day, never leaving or interacting with others, eventually, you would start to become more anti-social, just by default. You might become more focused on yourself, only seeing the world through your perspective. When we get outside and consistently interact with others, it becomes a lot easier to start to learn more about ourselves and who we are.

As you continue to interact with others, you will start to see your ability to understand their needs better, also helping you figure out your own wants and desires. When you can really connect with someone and get to know who they are deep down, it starts to become easier to see what they are trying to say without only listening to their words.

As much as you might be able to control your own emotions and figure things out on your own, you will still always want to put an emphasis on ensuring that you are open and listening to others. Some people have a bad habit of sitting there and thinking about what they are going to say in response while another person is talking. They will not listen to anything the other has said and rather rehearse the conversation over and over again in order to make sure that they "win" the conversation. When you really listen to the other person and open yourself up to hear what they have to say, then you will start to explore some amazing things about both yourself and that other person.

Recognizing Emotions in Others

Once you have recognized your own emotions within yourself, it is time to start recognizing them in other people. Part of really getting to know how someone else feels involves being empathetic to their needs. You'll need to understand their background and how that might have affected them as well. You will not get to know everything about your colleagues and employees when it comes to their personal life. It will still be helpful to try and have an idea of who they were before they became a part of your entrepreneurial adventure.

It is important that you learn to recognize emotions in other people for your own social well-being. You will get a better sense of when certain things are appropriate and when you should really just leave things as they are and not try to alter the situation. When someone is bad at reading social cues, it can show that they might have a lowered emotional intelligence.

When you can tell someone is mad, frustrated, or annoyed; you can accurately treat that situation. You might be able to help them calm down. Perhaps distracting them from that temporary emotion is all they will need to better focus on something else and work through their feelings.

When you can see that they are happy, you can encourage that behavior and aide them in growing stronger. You'll know what their happy mood is and assisting other people in being happy will really help your business. You will be able to see if they are feeling good and you will not have much work to do! If they are seemingly blue, you can brainstorm a plan to help them feel a little better.

You will be able to point out their weaknesses and the good things they do as well. This will make it easier to guide or praise. You can see what might trigger someone to not perform their best. Maybe you put one employee on cold calls and the other works on invoicing. However, that one working all the files is actually a more personable speaker, so you can switch and adapt positions based on their strengths and weaknesses.

Understanding others' emotions will help you to regulate your own as well. You will see how bad moods can affect other people, so it will be simpler for you to snap back into a good mood. You'll start to recognize what qualities you like and dislike in other notable leaders and you can either be inspired or avoid these kinds of traits.

What you have to also be aware of is how you can talk to others about their emotions. Telling someone "you seem mad," is not going to stop them from being mad. While you might be able to notice someone else's weaknesses and be aware of areas they need to work on, it is important to refrain from trying to tell them how they need to change. Let people come to some terms on their own. This is more important in your personal life, but your employees might become bothered if you are consistently giving negative feedback. When it does come time to be critical and assist with things that need to be fixed, offer up one great thing they do just as often as you would make comment on something that needs improvement.

One thing you will want to look for is the words that they are saying. Maybe they say they are "not satisfied," or that they are overly "stressed." Being stressed doesn't mean they are unhappy, but it could if they say it in a worried tone. Still, even when people say they are joking, there is going to be a morsel of truth in their words that you can understand to help you better decide which situations might need to be fixed and which are fine as they are.

Aside from their verbal language, let's take a look at how someone's body can tell us a ton about what emotional state they might be in.

Facial Expressions and Body Language

If you have the environment with your team to do so, you should try playing games to get everyone warmed up. This can help them to be more focused and active. A great game is one that many might call charades.

Split your team in two and have each team member pretend to act out a word or phrase that the other team came up with. It can be funny and a way to loosen others up, which is especially important when many people are meeting each other for the first time. It can also be helpful in teaching your team how they can understand each other based only on their body language.

Aside from using these games to help you warm your team up, they can give you insight into how they might hold their emotions. Is someone that seems reserved really emotive when in the right context? Does the person who seems to display emotions actually have trouble trying to fake them? You can get a lot of information form a person when you see what they are like in group and game settings, especially when forced out of their comfort zone.

When reading someone's body language, start from the top of their head to the tip of their toes. There are little signals in every part of our bodies that can help let the other person know the things we might be thinking.

Look into their eyes. Are they closed? Wide? Looking somewhere else? Unfocused? How a person is holding their eyes will reveal a ton of information about the things they might be holding back. Squinted eyes might mean that they are focused, trying to really pay attention. Eyes that do not seem to be focused at all might be a sign that they are not listening to you.

Pay close attention to their brow as well. A scrunched brow might mean they are focused but pointed downwards could indicate that they are mad. Brows that are wide on their forehead could mean they are shocked, or maybe even feeling a bit anxious.

Move down to their mouth/nose area. Tight and curled lips might mean they are holding something back. An open mouth might mean that they are focused. Tight lips could mean that they are angry about something.

Blinking frequently and scattered eyesight might indicate they are nervous. They might be looking around rapidly, not able to stay concentrated on what you are saying.

If someone has trouble making eye contact with you, they could be lying, but they could also just be a really anxious person that is a little threatened by your authority. You have to really look at the context of what is being discussed if you are going to start to judge whether or not someone might be lying to you.

If they seem unfocused, they might also just be confused or maybe a little nervous about keeping up with what you are saying. Part of being emotionally intelligent will be recognizing all the ways that others could be perceiving what you are saying. When you notice all the ways your words can be interpreted, then it will be easier to assume how others might actually be reacting to your words.

Their hand over their mouth could point to the fact that they are trying to hold something back. Maybe they are struggling with taking new information in and trying to keep themselves from making any comments. They might not want you to see how they are reacting as well while they process different information.

Now, look at their arms. If they are holding them clenched and tight, they might be closed off. Crossed arms can mean that they are protecting themselves, maybe wanting to stay on the down low. Don't look too into this when you are having a casual conversation, as it sometimes just becomes a comfortable way for a person to hold their arms. At the same time, they might have done this position frequently because they are closed off, therefore it became their regular stance.

Hands on hips is just a comfortable position some sit in, but it could also have an underlying meaning. It can mean that you have authority over the room or at least are trying to take that power. You might be dominant, trying to make yourself look bigger and more easily assertive.

Notice all of this in yourself. When you really want to open up to someone, drop your arms and face yourself towards them. Keep your posture open so that they are going to be more willing to share with you as well. The more open you seem, the easier it will be for others to open up to you.

Keep your hands in sight when you want others to trust you. If you have your hands in your pocket or behind your back it can make you seem sneaky. When you are talking about big ideas, make sure that you make use of your arm movement. Make big gestures and hype up what you are talking about using articulated arm movement. Practice talking in front of the mirror so you can get an idea of how you look when giving speeches.

Make eye contact but not to the point that you are intensely staring them down. If you stare too hard into someone's eyes, it can make them feel as though you are simply intentionally trying to make them think that you are listening to them.

Empathy Versus Sympathy

Pity is just when you simply know that someone is suffering. We can recognize when another animal is hurting and they can sometimes see when we are as well. Have you ever been around a mother and child when the mom started crying? When the baby sees the mother crying, they might start to as well. This is sometimes pity and sometimes fear that there is a greater issue at hand causing the person to be upset.

Sympathy is when you can feel sorry for someone, when you can hurt for them. We feel sympathy when people are sick or when they lose a loved one. We understand that the things they are going through are challenging and we are happy that we aren't the ones experiencing those trying times.

Empathy is when you really feel what it is like to go through what they did. Empathy is something that is hard to feel unless you have gone through a similar experience as the person that you are feeling empathetic towards. As people, we might understand what it is like to lose someone we love. It can be very heartbreaking to watch someone pass and grief can consume who we are.

Only when you are a parent; however, can you really understand what it would be like to lose a child. Only when you have lost your mother can you really know what it is like to lose a parent. Though we can relate to the people who are losing loved ones, we can really only be empathetic when we have a very deep understanding of the specific thing they are going through.

Compassion is when we will try our best to alleviate their symptoms of suffering. When you see someone hurting and you feel it is your duty to stop that pain, you are showing compassion. When you are taking care of their needs because you recognize their hurt, that is being compassionate. Most people will want to show compassion towards others, but it is less common than you'd assume. How many people do you think pass car accidents, thinking, "I hope they are OK." That's mostly empathy. Compassion is pulling over on the side of the road to really check if they are all right. You have compassion mostly for those that you care deeply for. If you saw a random car on the side of the street, you'd likely keep driving. If you noticed that car was the exact same one that your mother has, you might pull over because you are worried about her safety.

We always have to have empathy as a bare minimum for engaging with employees. We will likely have compassion but will not always have to tools necessary to alleviate that. We might want to help someone but not really have any idea how. This shows that we might still be lower on the empathy scale. If you really know what someone is suffering through, then you understand what they need to heal because you are doing what you would need in that situation to feel better. Sometimes, that simply means giving another person their space to process and heal.

There are some situations that you will not be empathetic about, but we need to do our best to try and get there. What might not sound like a big deal to you could be to your employee, so do not always base things just on your perspective. Have you ever done something scary with others and there was one person who was extra terrified? Maybe you went on a roller coaster and one friend had to get off because they were having a panic attack. Some people might call others dramatic, but that's just because they are lacking empathy. You might not be afraid of the roller coaster, but you have to understand what it might be like to be afraid of something like that and then to have to live through that fearful moment.

You need to have empathy so that you can understand how to improve the relationship overall. When you can show humility, compassion, and understanding [; that person is going to trust you so much more. They will have a way higher chance of listening to you and really believing in your mission. No one wants to invest in a robot! You will want to share that kind of humble understanding to get others to open up to you as well.

Empathy shows that you really care about that person. You are validating their experience and showing that you too are human. Again, you might not agree with why they might be feeling pain or anxiety. You might not have the same reaction to the situation. By letting that other person know you hear them, it can be all they need to feel compassion from you. This allows you to be more influential. No one wants to trust a robot!

Important Social Skills for Interacting

You need to have a high level of emotional awareness so that your social skills will improve. Social skills are a practice. Some people might be good at them right away but for those who aren't, more emphasis needs to be placed on working to tune these right. As an entrepreneur, social skills are crucial. You can hire many people but, at the end of the day, your employees and clients will still want to hear from you. Other contractors might be able to talk to your managers that you have hired, but there will always be cases in which your input is required over all else.

Knowing whether or not you can really trust someone is very important in any business. You have to have the social skills needed to let others know that you do care about them and that they will be willing to trust you.

You have to read beyond what people tell you so that you can best determine if they are accurate candidates. Look past just the words that they are saying and see what important information you can pick up on that is hidden behind their words. Only when you do this will you be able to accurately pick out those who are most valuable to your company.

Having a high level of social perception is a skill that can enable you to really figure out what the root cause of one of your employee's performances might be. When you notice how they interact, you can start to get a sense of what they are and aren't very comfortable with. They will show more through how they interact with their coworkers and customers than they will when you are together.

You can see things you might not notice about them when you are active in watching them work. When you have meetings one on one, they will, of course, be on their best behavior. It's important to start to actually get on the floor, or in the office, or wherever your business is and work with them so that you can understand the true nature of who they are.

Once you might have identified the issues that they seem to be having and the root of what their weaknesses might be, strong social skills will be necessary so you can start to discuss a plan of improvement with them. Some people will start to get defensive if you do not approach these kinds of conversations in the right way, so you should be prepared with patient and understanding language that will help them better accept your criticism.

"Reading the room," is an important skill, especially as an entrepreneur. Sometimes, people are simply tired and you have to let them go home and start fresh the next day.

You also have to ensure that you are able to have a high level of impression management. This means that you can elicit positive emotions from your employees. They should only be inspired by you, not fearful of you. When you can motivate your team and work closely with them, it will be easier to bring out those positive moods, which means that everyone else will be much more likely to work efficiently.

Don't be afraid to flatter others. When you can throw out a compliment, people will be much more likely to respond back to you in a positive way. Don't do it in an obvious schmoozer way either; however. If you compliment a bald guy on his hair, he's going to know that you are just trying to butter him up. Look for unique flatteries that you can throw out as well. Maybe you compliment their intelligence, their ability to talk to other people, or their own personal social skills.

Hide your distaste for those around you and always be willing to give them a second chance. Even if you have met someone a couple of times and they seemed rude, you should give people a chance to warm up. You always have to be professional, of course, but never stop giving people a chance. It's always better to "kill them with kindness" instead of working off their rudeness. It'll just create an ugly cycle.

Sometimes, you might simply have to agree with others, even if it means biting your tongue. Of course, if you are making a deal, you do not want to just simply agree. However, if someone makes a comment about politics or something else that is simply opinion based, it is easier to just laugh and nod. What you say in your head you do not have to share! It's best to just try and avoid making someone upset in a business setting by trying to be combative about something that you both are entitled to your opinions on.

Persuasion is an important social skill you will want to focus on. How can you recognize someone else's viewpoint and then change it so it is more in line with what will benefit you? Persuasion is not about convincing or tricking anyone into doing something that you want them to. It's about helping them to see the perspective needed to align with yours.

Others will see their side of the story, so you have to ensure they can see your side of the story most easily. Help them realize the way that both of you can benefit when you come together and form your own perspectives and outcomes in favor of both of you.

As an entrepreneur, you need to start working on your ability to adapt to certain situations. You are a leader! You need to guide and lead the room, take it to the appropriate situation. Don't just wait for others.

Most importantly, build your communication skills so you can effectively express your ideas and visions. Keep up with your vocabulary so you know how to better form and write emails. Keep up with the news so that you have conversation starters. Explore travel options around the world and keep up with geography so you can discuss different destinations of your clients that might be frequent travelers.

Handling Requests from Others

You will be getting constant requests from Business Partners, Clients, Shareholders, and Subcontractors. It is important that you understand how to best handle these requests. Some of them will be easy, and others might be asking too much of you. Most will be within your job description, but others might also seem like ludicrous requests.

Of course, if you are able to do so, then do it, first and foremost. Even if it takes just a little effort on your part, small favors can go a long way. Your job as an entrepreneur, especially in the beginning, is going to be to win people over. If you have to do a little extra, then do so! Just ensure that you are properly paying your employees and compensating them for the extra work. If they get the impression that you are using their labor to promote your business without getting an extra piece of the income, then they'll lose trust in you.

When it comes to things that you can't handle, there are a few things you can do. If you feel comfortable doing so, politely decline. If not, then it is time to brainstorm an option for how to alleviate the situation. What can you tell them that's not going to upset them and still keep them on as an important customer?

Be upfront and honest about it if you can. Let's say a client asks for a custom product that's just way out of your means for completion. Perhaps it costs too much or maybe it is simply a product you do not feel comfortable making. Let them know this and then you could offer up the option to create something else.

Come up with a solution and do not give them a "yes" or "no" option. When proposing two alternatives, think of other options. Let's say someone asks for a meeting on Wednesday. That's the only day you can't do. Rather than saying, "I'm sorry, I can't do Wednesday," say something like, "Unfortunately Wednesday is not available for me, but Thursday and Friday are great."

This lets them know that a meeting, in general, is still an option, just not on their date. Remember that sometimes scheduling things can be like a ping pong match trying to find the best time for both of you. If this is occurring with an employee, it is best to reevaluate their availability and dedication to the role.

When you struggle to schedule even an interview, it is a sign they are not going to be easy to schedule for work. As far as clients go, it might be better to tell them which dates you are not available versus the ones that you are. This shows that you are more flexible and others can trust you are willing to work with them on schedules.

Let's say they ask you for something that's just way too much work to do.

Let them know this by saying, "Unfortunately I am unable to do that at the moment, but I have no problem doing this for you. If that doesn't work for you then I am also comfortable doing this."

Ask them if there is a way that you could simply help out with that need in an alternative way. As long as you are showing others that you are open to working with them, it will be a lot easier to build a solid foundation for your relationship.

At the end of the day, you simply want to ensure that they know you are not refusing because you do not want to, just that you can't.

How to Respond to Other People's Emotions

Once you have an understanding of how to read the emotions of other people, now it is time for you to start to practice responding. The best way to respond is with a moment of silence. Never cut the person off. If they are asking a question, respond quicker. When they are explaining themselves, always give them a chance to keep going.

What you can always do to work through an emotion is to ask people questions. Wait to give advice. When you are trying to make a deal, this is when you will want to be the quietest and patient. When you aren't sure that you understand, keep asking questions. Even if you do have a good idea what they are saying, continue to ask questions to get them to reevaluate what they are saying as well. When you break apart their proposals, it gives you a chance to use influential language where needed.

People love talking about themselves and often, they just need to vent. They simply want to be heard and feel like someone cares about their feelings. When using emotional intelligence with both your employees and prospective business partners, ensure that you are giving them the grounds to talk. Never interrupt, even if you feel like what you have to say is incredibly important.

Always accept the emotion that they have. Never shame someone for being angry or upset. If you are discussing more personal things and there is a more heated moment, you will also want to make sure that people are getting their opportunity to talk.

Don't take things so personally either. If someone is frustrated with you, that doesn't mean they are questioning your character. Maybe you are telling your employees that you are unable to meet their demands and you have to turn a question they asked down. If they grow upset with you, you can't take it personally. If you do, then it can make you seem less trustworthy and they will not be as willing to open up to you down the line.

Be accommodating, no matter how ridiculous it might seem. When someone has an emotional need they really need to be met, be understanding and work with them rather than against them. If you give any indication that you are not supportive, it can quickly shut people off. They will then be more resistant in an attempt to validate their own feelings. Focus instead on finding a mutual agreement that works for everyone. When dealing with emotions, it is all about compromise.

Refrain from pointing fingers, even if they are in the wrong. Always state facts and never accuse. Even if your accusations are right, people can still be offended that you questioned their character. Be open and honest and give the other person a chance to tell their side of the story first and provide a legitimate explanation.

How to Handle Requests When You Don't Have Time

There's seemingly never enough time for anything. When you are trying to build a successful business, you are going to be busy. It's like a newborn baby! You'd be foolish to think you could have a child without multiple sleepless nights in a row. You're going to be working well over forty hours a week in at least the first year of your business. You'd be lucky if work slows down after that! You will have to get used to turning some people's requests down when time just will not allow it.

Time is very valuable, so we can't let it slip away from us. When we let someone know we can't give them our time, we might fear they'll think we do not value them or their own time. As an emotionally intelligent entrepreneur, what's most important is that you ensure the other person that their time is still incredibly important to you, even employees.

Start by telling them that you have other commitments. Let them know it is not about who's more important, rather, what's crucial for you is that you stick to your word. You simply told someone else you could accommodate them first.

Remind them that you want time so that you can give them the best quality possible. This is especially important to remind others when you have to ask for an extension on some product or service you are providing them.

Ask them if they would be satisfied with less of your time. Not in those words, of course. If they want an hour-long dinner as a meeting, ask instead if you could meet for a quick drink. Try and simply reduce the time, not completely ignore it.

Remind them consistently you have not forgotten about them. Check in on them when you have a free moment and do your best to keep in contact even when there aren't any active business relationships. Remind them of new products and get them excited for upcoming changes.

Explaining the Realistic Aspects of a Deadline

Some people can have some rather unrealistic explanations. People will get exciting ideas in their head and sometimes just run with that. Never make someone feel silly for having an unrealistic expectation. Simply do your best to describe why it might not be entirely possible.

First, do not be afraid to break it down for them. Be realistic. Step by step, go through the process of what they are asking and show them how things could take longer. Remind them that you respect your employees and that you have to work with them as well.

Just like you would in the last section, consistently remind your team that you are only taking the time to ensure the best quality possible. You aren't taking longer because you are lazy. You want to make it faster in the long run by ensuring there will not be any issues with quality. If you have to go back and do it again, then that'll just elongate the process.

Again, reiterate that you also have other commitments and that you are a person who sticks to their word. Remind those that are impatient that you also need to have time for things to run past when you would expect them to. In any kind of project setting, you might find that you will have issues with people running over when they say.

Give yourself a little wiggle room so you can consistently be early as well. It's better to have something early than have to apologize for having it late frequently.

How to Motivate Your Team

Motivating your team is going to be one of the most important aspects of your job! You are like the mascot of the company. If you are uninspired, you can be certain everyone else will as well!

The best way is with rewards in monetary forms. Offer incentives for when they sell more or provide higher quality work. Give bonuses to the hardest workers. When those who excel are rewarded, it makes everyone else want to work that much harder.

That's not always in the budget, so look for other free incentives. Perhaps they have access to equipment whenever they want, as long as they sign a waiver. Let them go home early without reducing their salary, as well. Just giving them one day off could go a long way over a six-month period.

As an emotionally intelligent entrepreneur, you want to be sensitive to how people will feel personally connected to your company. Your employees will want to feel special. They want to have a purpose in your company just as you have the motives that drive the business. Without passion in your team, your business will not be as successful as it could be.

Give them a chance to grow themselves. Perhaps you do not have managerial positions, but you could offer other training that can help them further careers outside their position with you.

Have regular meetings where their voices can be heard. Don't let these meetings become useless, however! Take your team out to lunch. Make sure meetings are during business hours because if you have to take time from them, they will not be as happy.

Don't reprimand them in a way that makes them afraid. Be human when they mess up. Have discussions so that they aren't afraid to come to you when they might need help. Always be open and willing to discuss how you can work together.

Positive and Negative Emotions in Other People

Once you have recognized these emotions and started to learn how you can sway them, now it is time to see how you can best turn those negative emotions into tools and use the positive ones as inspiration.

When your team is unhappy, it is not the end of the world. It is actually an improvement you can make for the future. When they are positive, reward this! Have an employee of the month program.

Give positive feedback on their attitudes and always remind them that they are appreciated.

How to Handle Stress Created Outside Yourself

A lot of stress is created within ourselves, but there is certainly plenty of stress that others can create around us as well. Have someone specifically for communicative purposes if this is something that consistently stresses you out.

Have all goals for your team together so that everything stays organized. Regularly ensure that everyone knows what they need to do. Have consistent moments of de-stressing as a group. Put an emphasis on making a fun and calm environment, so that even in moments of stress, people are still going to be happy to work there.

Maintaining Good Relationships

It is crucial that you start to practice how to maintain good relationships. What you will need the most is patience. Respect the way in which everyone is different and that we all operate in strange ways that others might not understand.

Always offer your ear to listen to others. The better listener you are, the more you can win over those who know you.

Be appreciative, grateful, and thankful.

Always check back in with others. At the end of the day, you need to ensure that they are feeling as though you care about them and they will, in turn, show that they care about you.

Part 2: The 30-Day Emotional Intelligence Booster Program

The focus of these exercises is all about improving **relationships**. As an entrepreneur, it is crucial that you build relationships, as these will be the foundations of the building of your company. If everyone you interact with is one and done, then your business will not be able to fully thrive. Those you work with are people that you'll want to be coming back on a regular basis.

We will also pay special attention to the importance of **trust**. When you have trust, it will be easier to make sales and have people invest in your ideas.

Negotiations are key to forming good business connections. These emotional intelligence activities will help ensure that you are better prepared for meetings, discussions, and other business deals.

You will have to learn how to understand, listen, recognize, and use emotions in the right way. When you can grow these skills, it will become easier to evaluate unplanned events. You can better adjust when situations do not go as you thought they would and help to avoid any mistakes.

These thirty days provide a practical step-by-step guide to raise your EQ as an entrepreneur. This is a personally curated plan to work on your personal goals. Find something to work on that is most important to you. Pick one overall goal that you will hope to achieve at the end of this.

Perhaps you want to see an increase in employee productivity. Maybe you want to make a big deal with potential prospects or see a jump in customer satisfaction. Whatever it is, remember that goal as you start to create smaller goals throughout each day of the upcoming month.

Your Daily Exercise

At the end of the day, take ten minutes to do an evaluation in a personal diary. Handwritten is better, but electronic is fine as well. Writing things down will help you to remember them better. Everything we discuss should be written down in notes, so having a dedicated journal to build your EQ is going to be very helpful.

Each day, we will have a different prompt, challenge, or thought process that you will want to experience. This will happen at the end of the day as a means to help you reflect. It will only take a few moments, but you should certainly spend longer reflecting if you have the time. You will also be required to think of one emotion when you wake up, as a way to sort of get you started with the day thinking about your emotional intelligence right off the bat. Here are the steps for what you should do daily:

Step One: Right in the morning, I want to pick an emotion to recognize within yourself. I also want you to pick out what your goal at the beginning of the day will be. There is no reading required. Simply pick out one emotion that you are feeling, or maybe had felt the night before if you are still kind of groggy, and what your goal for the day is.

Step Two: At night is when you will do the reading and it will only be around ten minutes. At the end of the day, you will want to pick out that same emotion, but who else you might have seen it in. How did you recognize that person was exhibiting the emotion that you identified in the morning?

Step Three: Follow the instructions below depending on what day it is.

This is all about building relationships, so you should never just think about yourself. Look at your own thoughts and the way that you operate, but always be considerate of other people's perceptions of you as well. This is a building exercise to get you to be a more emotionally intelligent entrepreneur.

Day 1

This morning, when you woke up, you should have started the daily activity of picking out one emotion that you felt. Perhaps you were feeling hopeful, angry, exhausted, annoyed, or scared. Whichever it was, that's perfectly fine! Once you finished your nightly activity of picking out the other person's emotion, it is time to do the next thing!

We will not remind you of the morning and night activities the rest of the days, so it is important that you remember throughout the month to go back and revisit these steps. Let's talk about your emotions now and how you recognize them. Perhaps you were having trouble finding the feelings within yourself. When you struggle to describe how you feel, pretend as though you are a child and you have to point to one of the frowny faces on the emotion chart. For each basic emotion that you felt, identify three more that could relate to that. Here's an example of what a journal entry would look like for today:

"I am feeling angry, annoyed, and tired. I am feeling frustrated with what's happening, scared that the things I need to do will not get finished, and I'm sick of others not doing what they are supposed to do. I am feeling irritable like every little thing is driving me crazy. I am confused as to why it is taking people so long to finish projects. I have a short fuse because of my anger and irritability, which is likely the cause of my annoyance. I am exhausted because I feel like I am doing too much and others aren't. I feel as though I'm overworked and underappreciated. All of these emotions are basically making me feel like this as well."

Can you see how as you start to explore those three basic emotions – anger, annoyance, and tiredness – it can help you really dig deeper to the root of the issue? From there, you can decide how to better prevent these emotions from happening the next day. Is there a clear root to this issue that you can overcome? This is something that you should be checking in on every day, but those just getting started with their emotionally intelligent journey will certainly have to practice this method of finding feelings within themselves.

Day 2

Welcome back to day two! Congratulations for not only making it through the book but for coming back again! Though yesterday might have been simple for some, it can be incredibly challenging to figure out what your own emotions might be. Now, we are going to talk more about what it actually feels like when you are angry, sad, happy, or whatever other emotion that you might be working through. Take a look at how you're feeling today.

Do you have the same emotions that you did the night before? You can use these emotions, or you can pick out three very new ones that you felt today. Now, your goal is to recognize how these emotions feel as you are having them. What do you feel in your body? Start from the top down when doing a body scan of feelings. You can simply pick one emotion to do this with today but if you have the time, certainly do more. Here's an example of what your journal might look like:

"Today I was feeling pretty happy. It isn't often that I'm feeling this happy, so I want to take special note of everything that I felt so I know how to get back in this mindset again if I want to in the future.

Starting with my head, being happy felt good. I felt a little buzz, one that kept me going even when I ran into a few annoying things that day. It helped my head out too because I didn't have those constant challenging thoughts that normally run through my mind.

As far as the rest of my body goes, I felt good all over. At one point, my neck did hurt a little, but I was able to stretch it out and ignore it for the rest of the day. If I had been in a bad mood, I might have let this minor annoyance ruin the rest of my day. I enjoyed feeling this great and hope that I can feel like this all the time."

Recording your emotional feelings can be helpful because you can look at the bad ones when you're in a good mood and discover a potential truth that helps you better get through them. Alternatively, you can also look at the good ones on a bad day and try to use these feelings to reverse and redirect your mood!

Day 3

Day three and what a journey it has likely been so far! The thing about becoming emotionally intelligent is that once you do, it's hard to go back to your old ways. Even on days when you're feeling entirely terrible, you might be able to quickly pull yourself out of it because of your emotional skills. Now that you know what your emotions are and how you can try to even elicit good feelings when you're having a bad day, let's dig a little deeper.

It's time to look at the trigger of your emotions. It's important to know the difference between the cause and the trigger. You are the one that causes your emotional reaction and outside sources simply stimulate them. When you're angry, someone else might have bothered you, but you are in control of if that anger carries with you throughout the day or if you're simply able to work through it.

Pick out one emotion you had today or use one from the previous days if you didn't feel anything particularly intense today. There are three questions you need to answer to better understand the difference between feeling and interaction. When you have determined this, it will help enlighten you as to how you can better avoid reacting the same way the next time.

What triggered the emotion you felt?

Did you react to this emotion in an appropriate way?

Was this a positive emotion that helped solve the situation?

Was this a negative emotion that made the situation worse?

Here's an example of what this journal entry might look like:

"Today I was feeling extremely grumpy. I wasn't necessarily angry at anyone specifically; I just had a bad attitude and negative perspective.

This emotion ended up being triggered by the fact that I was mostly tired, had a headache, and didn't really get a good meal all day. I was just feeling pessimistic in general, mostly because I didn't feel good physically.

I didn't react to this appropriately. I should have been aware of my bad mood and tried to resolve it instead of spreading to others. This was not a positive emotion, but it could have been had I instead focused on making myself feel better. It was a negative emotion and it made the situation worse by putting those around me in somewhat of a bad mood as well.

As you can see, the emotion was triggered by these small factors that led to an even bigger mood. When you look at the root of the emotion, it becomes so much easier to figure out how you can better resolve it. If I hadn't dug deeper and question myself, then this could have turned into another bad mood the next day, only to get worse and worse if I never look deep and try to make myself feel better!"

Day 4

Today we are going to focus on breaking down one of the most challenging emotions one can have – anger. Look back on the past three days. How often was anger on your list of emotions?

Did you mention being angry frequently throughout this time period? That's perfectly OK if so! It's time to really confront that.

Perhaps you didn't really seem angry at all before starting this but as you dug to the really deep trigger of emotion, you discovered that anger was really the root cause. We think of anger as some big muscle head with green eyes and red veins popping, yelling and punching. Anger can be rather dormant as well, hiding behind soft voices and constant nodding. Today, let's talk about anger! Answer these questions to start to break down what anger really is:

What does it look like when you are angry?

What makes you feel better when you're angry?

What is something that consistently triggers your anger?

What's the worst thing anger has ever caused you to do?

How has anger helped you or if it never has, how can it help you in the future?

When answering these questions, it can be really helpful to actually write them down before answering, as it will reiterate the message behind the question as well. Here's an example of what this journal entry should look like:

"When I'm angry, I get really quiet. I rarely express myself and instead try to take some alone time. What happens because of this is that I direct that anger inwards. I become madder at myself for allowing that emotional reaction than I do to properly express anger at others who triggered it.

When I'm angry, it makes me feel better to talk it out. I like writing down my feelings and taking moments to reflect to really understand what caused my anger.

My anger is triggered when I feel stressed. If I am feeling overwhelmed, annoyed, and detached from having any fun, then I can get really angry. The worst thing anger has ever caused me to do is throw my phone at the wall when I received an email I didn't like.

The best thing anger caused me to do was open up to my business partner about how I felt they weren't doing their part. I told them that I was angry they weren't carrying their weight and he actually responded by saying he felt the same.

We realized that we just weren't working together and needed to focus on playing on each other's strengths more. It helped me to improve my relationship. When I threw my phone, it broke. This helps me realize that my anger is better used when it can build a relationship rather than break an expensive electronic."

Day 5

You are becoming quite the emotional expert by now and you've likely been more aware of how your moods and thoughts can really interact with your day. Let's focus more now on how these emotions will help you thrive in an entrepreneurial way.

Let's take a look back at the Ability model that we discussed when first going over EQ models of intelligence. Take each four of these aspects for measuring emotional intelligence and identify one way in which that skill will help in your specific business. When you do this, you will realize the importance of focusing on building your emotions. The four were:

<u>The ability to perceive emotions.</u> This quadrant focuses on how well one can pick up on the way that others are feeling. This is also important when looking interpersonally to label your own emotions.

<u>Emotional Reasoning is next.</u> This is how you are able to use your emotions for a functional purpose.

<u>The next is understanding emotions.</u> How well are you able to really see the root of the emotion.

<u>The next is the management of emotions.</u> Can you control how you might react to any given stimuli?

Now, identify a way that each of these can help your specific business. Include your vision so that you better understand why it's important for you, not just entrepreneurs in general.

Here is an example of what a journal entry might look like:

"The ability to perceive emotions is going to help me at my coffee shop. When I can tell if my employees are happy or unhappy, I can better determine if the position they are in is the right one for them.

Emotional reasoning is important because when I'm feeling like others might not be performing to the best of their ability, I can communicate this effectively in a way that keeps everyone focused and working.

Understanding emotions is important because when an employee comes to me with a problem, I will be able to see the root of what they're saying as well as, the deeper issue that they might not even be aware of themselves.

Managing emotions is important for myself because I want my employees to respect me and be happy. It's important for me to know how to alleviate certain moods because it will help me be a better manager and leader to the rest."

Day 6

Welcome to day six! You have almost completed a week, and that is something to be immeasurably proud of. It is never easy to have to look inside yourself to see what's really going on.

When we're completely unaware of our emotions, it can cause us to end up being really destructive with them. Let's revisit another model for this activity. Refer back to the mixed model. Today, use each of those sections of the Mixed Model to identify how unregulated emotions within that category might lead to negative outcomes or how unrecognized emotions could cause a bigger issue. These are the five categories:

Self-Awareness: What's an emotion that if you are not aware of, could cause issues in your business? How could being not-self-aware cause a problem?

Self-Regulation: If you fail to regulate yourself, what damage could this cause your company?

Motivation: Why is motivation necessary for your company? Who is it that needs motivated?

Empathy: What good will empathy do in your company?

Social Skills: What could potentially happen if you do not have a high level of social skills in your business?

Now, answer these questions, and really understand why each of these measurements for EQ are important in order to keep your emotional intelligence in check. Here's what a journal entry for this day might look like:

"When I'm not aware of my anger, it can put me in a really bad mood. This could bleed into the moods of my employees at my writing company, so I need to ensure everyone is in a good mood so that we have a high quality of content consistently coming out. If I do not regulate my feelings and actively try to seek out the things that feel good, then I won't be able to recognize these feelings and use them in productive and healthy ways. I need to motivate myself to do better, but I also need to motivate my team, so they consistently come out with high-quality content that drives sales even further. I need empathy so that I can be understanding to their needs. If I show them empathy, then they'll show me respect and this is what a good working environment is all about. Most important are my social skills so that I can better talk about issues and communicate the things that I am wanting from my employees."

Day 7

Wow! It's the end of the first week and things are probably looking great for you! It can feel really great to fully identify all the things that we need to work on and how we might have been struggling in the past. You are likely feeling enlightened and inspired. Perhaps your confidence level has boosted or you've already noticed a way that you and a friend or colleague are working on your relationship.

For this day, we are going to work on identifying how our emotional intelligence has now become a personality trait. When you really open up the door of your emotions and start facing them for what they are, then you will be able to start to better recognize all the ways that they have changed your life for the better.

In the trait model, it explores the idea that you are an emotionally intelligent person and that those personality traits can either be hidden or flourished. It's not about learning a new skill like you might if you want to skateboard or play the violin.

It's a skill that already exists inside of you and you can form your personality to align with this.

Let emotional intelligence be a part of you, not the skill that you do. For this activity, rate each thing in two different ways. The first one, rate what you would say about yourself and the second, rate for what you would think others would answer for you. To keep score, 1 means completely agree and 5 means completely disagree.

1. When you are presented with a very attractive offer, you go for it right away.
2. When someone has a problem with you and starts to pick a fight, you get defensive and start to argue right back.
3. When you feel like you need to say what's on your mind, it's easier for you to bite your tongue than to try and speak up.
4. It is hard for you to really relate to other people. You have trouble seeing their pain and even think some people might be acting dramatically.
5. When you are stressed, it's hard for you to control those feelings.

If you want, you can even ask someone else to rate these for you. Then, add up your score out of 25 possible points and add it together with your score for how you think others would perceive you.

For example, you might think that you completely disagree with all of these things, but a friend would say that you are somewhere in the middle. Your score was 25 and theirs for you was 15. Add those together and then times by two. This will be your percentage out of 100. This would give me 80 percent, which isn't bad but I would need to work on how others perceive me and the way that I might express some of my emotions

Anything above 75 percent is good, but you should really be working towards getting all fives, where you completely disagree with the statements above. This is the last time that we'll be going over examples for journal entries or what the outcome of these readings might look like.

Now, it is time to move onto week two, where the daily discussions will be more focused on reflecting and writing rather than reading! The entries will be shorter, which means you'll need to spend more time writing. Ensure that you're not forgetting to do your daily morning and night exercises of identifying one emotion either. This will be very important in your continued practice of increased emotional intelligence.

Day 8

For today's activity, you will want to identify one emotion that you've had in the past. This emotion should come from the past week and it should be one that we would refer to as more challenging. Maybe you think of it in a negative light, but this activity is going to be all about how you can turn that negative emotion into the positive one. If for some amazing reason you had no negative emotions at all whatsoever last week, then look to a different time in your past where you experienced a negative emotion.

This emotion is one that felt bad to have – anger, grief, jealousy, rage, and so on. Here is what you will want to write about in your journal. Answer these questions and elaborate for more than ten minutes if you have the time. If not, giving yourself a minimum of five minutes to reflect will do as well:

What was the challenging emotion and the trigger/events leading up to it?

How did it negatively affect you, increase your emotions, or even affect others around you?

If you had a time machine and could go back to this moment, how could you have used that negative emotion for something good?

Day 9

A lot of times, it can be easier to simply repress our emotions than trying to have to work through them. This is never going to do you any good, however! Going forward, what you'll want to focus on is finding a balance between expression and repression, while doing your best to not worry about and freak out to your emotions.

For today's activity, it's important that you find three methods in which you can fully express yourself. To do this, start by looking at a way that you can express yourself when you're angry at yourself. Perhaps writing helps, going for a jog, or zoning out and playing a game. This isn't about pushing those feelings down but letting yourself be angry and work through them.

Your second method should be one that you can use with others. How can you properly express to someone that you are feeling bad? Maybe there is a word that you can use to let someone else know that you're feeling triggered or perhaps you have a specified room you go to when you're upset to use as a signal for others when you're angry. This second method is all about alleviating anger in relationships.

The third method is one that you should use to instantly alleviate your feelings. Perhaps it is a breathing technique, such as counting down from ten. Maybe it's a song that you can play that will instantly make you feel better. The third one should be focused on something that gives instant relief.

To recap, these are the things you need to come up with:

1. A way to relieve negative emotions within yourself.
2. A way to express negative emotions to others in a healthy way.
3. A way to instantly relieve negative emotions.

Day 10

This week, we are going to put an emphasis on making sure that you know how to take some time before reacting. It can be hard to not just say the first thing that comes to your mind. When you do this; however, you're putting yourself at risk for saying something that you don't mean. Our reactions can really cause bigger issues if we're not careful.

To practice this, I want you to think of a time that someone said something rude to you or a moment when you were really upset. What's a comment that someone else shared that really stuck with you? If you have trouble thinking of this, try and imagine what an insecurity you have might be and a comment someone might make based on that.

From there, I want you to come up with three responses. Your first one is instant, right away. Right it down without even thinking about it. Then, I want you to really think about an appropriate response. Once that is done, then tomorrow, come back and think of your third response. You don't have to write it down, but it will help you to look back on these responses and think of something more articulated and different from the first response. This activity will help you to start to see how reacting impulsively isn't always the best option.

Day 11

Tonight, make sure that you peek back at yesterday's journal to see your responses. Once you have done that, along with your other daily activities, we're going to focus now on how to recognize the emotions and feelings of other people.

Look back in your journal and go through and refresh yourself on the one emotion that you've been noticing in others every day in the past. For all of those people whose emotions you recognized, I want you to point out one strength and one weakness they have.

Once you have done this, then you should look back and reflect on those emotions and see if there is anything that might connect their emotion to their strengths/weaknesses. Is there something they could improve on? If these are your employees and you've noticed a pattern in their mood and their performance, then can you come up with a solution to resolve any negative feelings? This activity will help you start to see the correlation between emotion and behavior in other people.

Day 12

Today's activity might be something a little more challenging. I want you to think of someone that you aren't particularly a fan of. It could be someone you see on a regular basis – perhaps a client that's very difficult or even your spouse's sibling! If you struggle to think of someone you don't like, maybe you even consider a celebrity or notable figure that you just aren't very interested in. Whoever this is, I want you to really put yourself in their shoes. I don't want you to just think of this as them now – look back throughout their entire lives.

If you start to realize that there's a lot that you don't know about them, where they came from, how they were raised, or the experiences they went through, then perhaps there's something about them that you just don't really know. Maybe this is enough to have you reconsider why you don't like them in the first place! The point of this activity is to help you see why someone else might feel the way they do. You don't have to entirely agree with their behavior, but walking farther than just a mile through someone's life can be enough to help you see connections you might not have noticed the first time around.

Day 13

Remember that person we had you thinking about yesterday? You can do this activity with the same person in mind, but if you want to avoid thinking about them or just expand to someone else, that's fine for this part too. What you will want to do today is look at that person's triggers. What is it that might set someone off? What about a person could put them in a bad mood? Maybe the person you chose to focus on is someone that you dislike because they're so rude to you.

Look at the root of this – what happened in their life to make them feel that way?

When you can start to understand this, it will become much easier for you to "deal" with them or at least not be so upset when they're mad at you. When we dislike others, we think of them as how they're treating us. Remember that they have their own perspectives as well and each thing will give you insight into why they might act a certain way. This activity will help you see how even though you don't agree with their behavior, you can still be empathetic towards their actions.

Day 14

Welcome back! You've almost made it half-way through the readings! For today, we are going to focus again on understanding someone else. Rather than looking at someone you dislike, we're going to focus on someone that has hurt you in the past. Whether it was from your high school days or someone that really hurt you last week, pick out someone that has caused you emotional pain. Forgiving can be hard, but something you have to do not for them, but for you.

Now, let's look at the same things we have the past three days, but for them. Answer these questions in your journal.

What emotions and feelings do you think they had around the time they caused the hurt?

Why do you think they were OK with inflicting pain on someone else?

Where did their emotions come from? What was their trigger?

Why did they act, say things, or speak in the way they did that hurt you?

When you start to really break down someone else's actions, it becomes so much easier to see that they weren't always hurting you because of something wrong with you. As an emotionally intelligent person, you're going to need to focus on how hurt people can often end up hurting other people.

Day 15

There are plenty of useful and healthy ways that you are going to be able to use your emotions in different negotiations. The key is that you have control over these emotions. If you don't then that can hinder your ability to actually make a deal. Right now, I want you to identify three basic emotions that you often feel when making negotiations.

Then, you will want to identify one way that you can turn these emotions into something different. For example, anxiety can turn into passion if directed in a healthy way. Anger can be motivation. Make a list of these three emotions and turn them into something positive.

Then, I want you to look at the way that this will be able to help you better make negotiations. Identify the ways that the negative emotions are going to help you get people to trust you more and how you can close deals when you turn the good into bad. If you have time, try your best to find more than one emotion to change.

Day 16

You've officially made it halfway through this book and that's something that we all need to take a moment and be proud of. It's never easy to look deep inside who you are and start to pick apart the things that you might or might not like about yourself. You've done that so far!

The next step, after you recognize and understand what your emotions are, is to look where the feelings come from. Naturally, as you begin to question your motives, you've likely already thought of this. Now; however, it's time to really look at the root cause of your emotions.

For this activity, you are going to write a brief biography of who you are, using bullet points.

Start with the very moment you were born and work up to where you are now. Split these bullet points into two categories. One category is going to be good and one category bad. For memories that you don't like, things that are a little more tragic, maybe a death, an accident, a sickness, or something else that wasn't pleasant to live through, put that in one section. Then the good things, maybe a move, a new job, a baby, and other happy things, put that in one category. If you don't have time to go through everything, this will bleed into tomorrow's entry as well!

Day 17

For today's entry, let's ensure that you've finished your biography first. It shouldn't be too extensive; you're really just categorizing events. Now, look at those negative times and see if there are things from them that you haven't recovered from. Do you hold onto trauma from an accident? Are there still hurt feelings from a break-up? When you see that there are leftover feelings, you well better realize that you have emotions that still play into who you are today. For today's journal entry, write about what things from your past still affect the way you feel on a consistent basis.

Day 18

A huge part of maintaining healthy relationships is reacting to the way others speak and listening to them with a higher skill level. We often don't listen to others very well, or when we do listen, we might react in a way that makes them afraid to talk to us.

One way to practice your listening skills and increase the way you react is to watch more speeches online. For this activity, find a speech of someone on YouTube in a topic of interest. One pertaining to entrepreneurial skills you need to increase would probably be the best choice! Now, instead of listening to it at regular speed, increase it by two and see if you can really pick up on what they're saying.

Then, watch it through a second time at regular length, ensuring that you pay attention to every word they say. Take notes on what you learned immediately after. Each time you notice yourself losing interest and not focusing, make sure to redirect attention immediately. The purpose of this activity is to help you understand the difference between listening to the words someone is saying and the meaning of what they said overall.

Day 19

This activity is one that we're taking you outside of your journal to do! If you have already opened up to someone about this challenge, then that is great and you should choose them as they'll be understanding of this activity. If not, find someone that you feel really close with. Ask them how they are doing and really get them to open up.

Ask questions to keep them going and always repeat back what they said if you want to reiterate one of their points. This activity is to help you better listen. The challenge will be to not mention anything about yourself and to only have the attention on the other person. Think of it like you're interviewing a best friend! They'll have fun sharing their story and they'll appreciate the set of ears you have to listen!

Day 20

You are someone that's becoming quite the emotional genius! You know how to recognize your own emotions, pick up on others, and show empathy to allow others to feel more connected to you. How is your stress level, however?

For today's journal entry, you are going to want to identify the top five things that have been stressing you out. Once you have identified these, come up with a plan to reduce the stress. Is it something you can cut out, or cut down time spent on it? Is it something that you have to do a stress-relieving activity afterward? Tonight, focus on identifying your stressors and coming up with ways to alleviate them.

Day 21

Now that you're nice and relaxed, no longer as stressed, let's focus on something that might be keeping you still high-strung – complaining. As you're becoming more emotionally intelligent, it can be difficult to deal with others who are constantly complaining. Whether it's a customer, an employee, or even your business partner, we might notice others suffering by their own hands as we're becoming more self-aware.

Refrain from preaching to others about emotional intelligence. What you have to do is show that you are hearing the other person's suffering and you are willing to come up with a plan to help them with their complaint. For tonight's journal entry, think of the top three complaints you hear. Then, craft two responses to each that you can use next time someone comes to you with a complaint.

Day 22

The key to productivity is having an environment that not only enables that but encourages it. If you want your employees to give you the results you want, then you have to ensure that your working environment is one that they are comfortable in. For this activity, you are going to come up with a plan for creating a work environment. The keys will be:

Comfortability

Communication

Calming environment

Are your employees comfortable? Do they have a nice restroom to use, snacks available, a fridge to keep their food? You'll want your employees to feel at home. Next, consider your communication policies. Can they come to you whenever they want to talk? Do you have an anonymous way to report any serious issues? Finally, consider the overall aesthetic of your office or work environment. Consider having art, using some plants, or changing up the lighting to make it a place that people really feel inspired to work.

Day 23

For this activity, we are going to focus solely on giving the correct guidance. If you want to be the type of leader that people look up to and want to really work for, then you have to know how to provide them with quality advice and beneficial direction for both you and them.

For this journal entry, write about a small issue that you have in your life, but not one that you can't figure out how to fix. Maybe a friend is mad at you, you have a bill overdue, you have high blood pressure, or you need to buy a new appliance.

In your journal, also write a way to solve this problem. Write the solution to yourself. Let yourself be the guider. When you do this, you enable yourself to see how your advice might sound to others. Do you give advice that is just based on the easiest and most obvious solution or do you give guidance based on what works for the individual in their specific scenario?

Day 24

Throughout this thirty-day journey, you have likely grown immensely in your abilities as an emotionally intelligent being. Though this is true, there's a good chance that you've still had some moments where you let your emotions get the best of you. For your journal entry, look back on the past couple of weeks and pick out a moment that you were angry. Then, you will want to identify how that anger helped you. How were you able to push through it and use it for good?

After that, ask yourself these questions. When is it OK to get angry? What does your healthy anger look like? What is the way to get angry in a civilized and productive way? When you can pick these out, it becomes much easier to see the benefits of anger. Compare your anger reactions now, to how they might have looked when you first started this thirty-day challenge.

Day 25

The most important part of this all was to help you build on your relationships! For this journal entry, you are going to want to identify the most important kinds of relationships you have. What matters to you the most? Pick out the most important business relationships, your employee relationships, your clients, and everyone else pertaining to your relationship.

Pick out what you have to offer them and what they have to offer you. Decide if this is a fair amount being provided between the both of you. Is this something that needs to grow? Are you doing your part? Do you feel as though they are providing their part as well? When you pick this out, it becomes easier to see the strengths and weaknesses in your most valuable relationships.

Day 26

In order to maintain those strong relationships, you'll need to put an emphasis on the most important interactions between you and these other people. Preparing for important meetings, discussions, and negotiations are important. For this activity, you are going to want to draft up a preparation checklist. This is good for your emotional intelligence because it gives you something to look at each and every time you have one of these meetings and ensure that you are prepared. The things you might include would be:

1. Ensuring your speech is prepared.
2. Making sure everyone knows what is going to be discussed in the meeting.
3. Coming up with responses – more than one option for each potential response.

Your checklist will look different, but this will give you something to alleviate anxiety so that you can know you'll be prepared for each meeting.

Day 27

The time is almost here for your thirty-day challenge to be over! You are probably feeling so much better than at the start. You have the ability to recognize your emotions and come up with your own healthy ways of working through them! Not only that, but you are able to better pick out exactly what's wrong and how to fix the problem.

One important thing to remember is going to be how you can prepare for unplanned events. As an emotionally intelligent person, you have to learn the line between being realistically prepared for something and anxious or scared over when it will happen. For this activity, write a letter to your past-self. Remind the old you that everything has worked out fine so far.

Of course, there are times that you might have wanted a better outcome, but everything that's occurred has unfolded just as it was supposed to. Share your biggest fears, your biggest pieces of advice, and the things that you wish you knew. When you're done, read it over again and remind yourself of how this will help you live happily now. Of course, you'll always want to be prepared for some of the crazy things life has to offer, but at the end of the day, you can never be too worried or scared about what the future holds or else you'll miss out on what's happening around you now!

Day 28

Only three days left! For this day, I want you to come up with your own test in order to find your emotional intelligence score using the ability model. Come up with around five questions per category. They can be small questions, nothing that requires too much response.

Give yourself the test to see how you have really grown throughout this process. Ask someone else to score you as well, to see if the perceptions others have of you has changed at all as well. You could even use this test to interview potential candidates in the future!

Day 29

It's the second to last day and you're probably feeling pretty confident with your emotions. As another review, let's look back at the mixed model to judge emotional intelligence. For this, come up with yet another test to score your emotional intelligence.

The grading skill for this one could be something like choosing from 1 to 5 on how much you agree/disagree like the one we did earlier. Test yourself and go ahead and test someone else as well to see what they think. Maybe you do this in a business meeting or team meeting for your employees. Get a sense of the things that both you and others might still have to work on together.

Day 30

Wow! The last day! It's really inspiring to feel this way, as an emotionally intelligent entrepreneur. This entry is going to be the longest of all. I want you to start by using the trait model of emotional intelligence and think of how this is now your personality. What personality traits do you carry now that help point out your level of emotional intelligence?

Identify the ways that you have changed and how you have grown because of this experience. Compare your newest entries to even the ones that you started with.

Going forward, we encourage you to take this challenge again, as it will only help you get to an even deeper level of your emotions! Share with others, especially those in your business, to help others improve. Remember that this isn't the end – this is the start of an inspiring journey for you and your business.

NLP FOR ENTREPRENEURS

Reprogram Your Entrepreneurial Mind for Better Decision Making, Negotiation Skills and Higher Self-Confidence Using these NLP Techniques to 10X Your Business

Introduction

We all want success; everyone would like to make more money than they could reasonably spend. Unfortunately, for all our best efforts, more people fail at entrepreneurship than those that succeed. It is not hard to see why, though.

The average entrepreneur is bedeviled by a myriad of challenges, loopholes, and blockades. He is typically the sole decision-maker, planner, and visionary in the business, and his viewpoints and positions on business-related matters usually triumph over others'. Unfortunately, most people are not well equipped to handle this load all by themselves.

Therefore, the entrepreneur needs to be in a state of perpetual mental, emotional, and psychological excellence, so as to be in full capacity to handle their business dealings as meticulously and successfully as achievable. Unfortunately, intrinsic factors effectively hinder entrepreneurs' smooth sail to business success.

The four major, personal problems that entrepreneurs encounter are:

1. Poor time management
2. Poor decision-making
3. Low self-confidence
4. Bad communication

These problems make it increasingly difficult for these entrepreneurs to convert hard work and planning into business victory efficiently. Unless they are gotten rid of, or minimized to the barest minimum, productivity continues to suffer.

For instance, many entrepreneurs put a great deal of effort and time into their business, working endless hours every day – including weekends and holidays. Yet, some of these business owners find that the results their efforts are accruing are not congruent with the amount of time they put in. This problem of time management is faced by entrepreneurs across all spheres and sizes of business, although large business owners seem to show a greater proclivity to suffering the strains of poor time management – and more severely – than medium-scale or small-scale business owners. Nevertheless, effective time management is a trait all entrepreneurs must endeavor to have irrespective of their business sector or size. Problems with time management are often caused by factors such as procrastination, distractions, multitasking, failure to prioritize, and ineffectual planning.

Another scourge of the contemporary world of entrepreneurs is the problem of bad decision making. One of the invaluable traits of successful entrepreneurs is their ability to take decisions in the spur of the moment – decisions that very often have the potential to decide the trajectory of their business. In the face of the innumerable everyday hassles that entrepreneurs face in their lines of business, it is vital that they are able to cough out the right major and minor decisions concerning the running of their business quickly and effectively. Failure to make decisions or act on them quickly enough lies at the root of the downfall of many businesses. It is also a major reason why some companies fall short of expectations and/or lose the market to their competitors. Aside from the negative effects that poor decision-making can have on a business, entrepreneurs may suffer the consequences of their bad decisions in their lives; it is not very rare to find a failed entrepreneur exhibiting symptoms of depression.

Low self-esteem and low self-confidence are also factors that impede entrepreneurial progress. Entrepreneurs suffering from low self-esteem usually find it unbearably difficult to respect their workers and customers and seem to over-compensate for their low self-confidence by being overly rude and arrogant. These attitudes often lead to dissatisfaction among workers or team members and a consequent decrease in productivity at the workplace. Hence, such entrepreneurs open themselves up to not only the routine hassles of everyday work, but also the challenge of dealing with co-owners, workers, and customers who perpetually feel belittled and unvalued. This is not the perfect recipe for a successful business outfit.

Even when an entrepreneur has learned to manage time effectively to achieve desired results, has rock-solid self-esteem and confidence to see deals through, and always seems to make the right decisions concerning business matters, poor communication between themselves and team members, customers or clients could still hamper the desired flow of business dealings, thereby impacting negatively on results. Some of the reasons for poor communication are poor listening skills, talking over others, and failing to ask enough or appropriate questions.

The effects of ineffective communication include failure to motivate or inspire team members, poorly presented and understood ideas, poor employee performance, and ineffectual negotiation skills, amongst others. In order to build and sustain a successful business enterprise, entrepreneurs need to be able to communicate clearly through both verbal and non-verbal means. After all, all business dealings with clients, investors, team members, and customers require some sort of communication to run through.

All of these problems that impede an entrepreneurs' path to success can be remedied through the application of Neuro-linguistic Programming (NLP). What is NLP?

NLP is a method of communication and personal development and wellness designed in the 1970s by Richard Bandler and John Grinder to help people achieve certain goals in their lives. The three components of Neuro-Linguistic programming are Neuro, Linguistic, and Programming.

The *Neuro* component describes how every individual uses their unique internal refining system to analyze and understand the multitudes of information they take in through their senses; the *Linguistic* component describes the way the state of mind translates into verbal and non-verbal communication; the *Programming* component identifies one's ability to alter the state of the body and mind.

The concept of NLP takes root in the assumption that there is an interconnection between the body's neurological processes, spoken language, and certain behaviors that have been learned over a period of time, and that these variables can be modified to achieve desired goals and objectives. NLP has also been hypothesized to have a capacity to make ordinary people acquire exceptional skills by modeling the skills of exceptional people. Furthermore, NLP practitioners and experts claim that its methodology can prove useful in the treatment of abnormalities, including phobias, allergy, depression, and near-sightedness.

NLP aims to understand the way people organize their thoughts, emotions, and language. It also tries to observe how these lead to the results that people obtain. In other words, it studies how individuals develop their unique 'maps of the world' according to how they perceive the information they have received from the environment through their senses. NLP teaches not only fluidity in interpersonal communication, but also fluency in communicating with oneself. It literally assists you to communicate better with yourself by teaching you and getting you to master the language of your mind.

Hitherto known as the study of subjective experience, NLP has its roots in the domain of intrapersonal communication and has been used by psychotherapists and specialized NLP practitioners to enable people to understand themselves better and, therefore, make better decisions and live an overall richer and happier life. NLP teaches that you are fully in control of, and can alter, the workings of your mind, to achieve either positive or negative results. Through the help of NLP's techniques, you can learn to gradually reduce and eventually eradicate the negative emotions, feelings, behaviors, and actions that impede your growth and development, and replace them with positive ones that will help plunge your business into an unprecedented success.

There are tons of NLP techniques that can help entrepreneurs improve their thinking, decision making, and performance. These techniques include anchoring, mirroring, Metamodel, framing, pattern interruption, and a whole lot more.

Anchoring is a technique used to put oneself in a particular state of mind. It is useful for oneself or on another person. Anchoring works through the association or linking of emotion with a specific action, a process known as 'laying the anchor.' Mirroring is an NLP technique that you can use to mimic the behaviors of someone you are communicating with. This mimicking, which is usually done subtly, can take the form of copying one's speech, gait, tone, general body language, and speech volume.

The Metamodel technique is useful in developing an understanding of another individual's problems, and to help them understand their problems better. While using the Metamodel NLP technique, you are inadvertently trying to find the root cause of the problem being experienced by an individual with whom you are conversing and to find an effective solution to that problem. The framing technique is employed to increase or reduce emotional feelings. This technique is especially invaluable to entrepreneurs, who typically have to experience a lot of emotions through their engagements with different kinds of people. Pattern interruption NLP technique is another tool used to place words in the subconscious mind of a person you are communicating with. These are just a few of the tens of NLP techniques you can use to bolster your personality and business.

NLP had even been adopted for the treatment of certain mental abnormalities as well as for personal growth and improvement since its inception four decades ago, and its efficacy in bringing about positive results has been supported by scientific research. One study published in the *Counselling and Psychotherapy Research* journal concluded that patients undergoing psychotherapy showed improvement in the quality of life after they were exposed to NLP compared to a group that did not receive NLP therapy. Another research paper, published in 2015, found that NLP has positive effects on patients suffering from psychological or social problems. Though more research is needed in the field of NLP to offer more support to its theoretical framework, the efficacy of its practical application has been proven through improvement in the quality of life of thousands of individuals across the globe.

The application of NLP in your life and business comes with lots of benefits. One of the benefits is that you get better clarity of your vision and purpose. NLP improves offers personal development as it helps you modify your subconscious behaviors to bring about positive results. NLP also gives you more confidence and self-esteem to handle your business dealings optimally and succinctly by helping you to alter and replace your limiting beliefs with more optimistic ones.

In the world of entrepreneurs, you are constantly dealing with people – a lot of people – who come with different personalities, traits, and attitudes. By applying certain NLP techniques, you can learn to manage difficult people, dealing with them in ways that would benefit your business. As an entrepreneur, you are inevitably a leader; your employees, team members, clients, and even customers look to you for support and guidance. NLP can help strengthen your leadership abilities and shape you into a proactive rather than reactive leader. Exposing yourself to NLP can assist you in assessing your present thought, emotional, and behavioral patterns, and creating patterns that are focused on building you to become a problem-solving entrepreneur, thereby increasing your efficiency and performance. Furthermore, NLP techniques help improve your negotiation skills by making you more 'flexible' in communications with clients and customers and potentially increase sales.

NLP has transformed the lives of many people all over the world, turning them into a better version of themselves and helping them to achieve unprecedented success in their respective industries. Tony Robbins, Eben Pagan, and Stefan James Pylarinos, to mention a few, are some of the people who have used NLP to reshape their reality and enterprise. By mastering and applying the concepts of NLP in their lives, they have been able to ascend from humble positions to great heights seamlessly.

Tony Robbins made his first contact with NLP through one of its founders, John Grinder, in the 1980s. He learned several NLP techniques, such as 'firewalk,' which he incorporated into his seminars. By 1991, his infomercials had garnered over 100 million views. He has been named as one of the top 50 business intellectuals by *Accenture*, one of the top 200 business gurus by Harvard Business Press and made the *Forbes Celebrity 100* in 2007.

Eben Pagan learned and has incorporated NLP into his enterprises, which include Cliff's List – an online dating newsletter – and a host of books including *Double Your Dating*, *Advanced Dating Series*, *Meeting Women Online*, and *Deep Inner Game*, and claimed in 2009 that his products and services gross about $30 million per annum. Stefan James Pylarinos is another individual who has learned to channel his knowledge of NLP into his business enterprise. He is currently a 7-figure author and an Amazon Kindle publishing expert, who has built an empire of wealth through eBook retailing.

NLP is a tested and proven method of quickly turning the tides in your business to achieve favorable results. Its teachings and practice can help bolster your decision-making process, improve your self-esteem and self-confidence, better your negotiating skills, grow your leadership skills, and maximize sales. You can also apply the proven NLP techniques that others have used to accomplish great success by mastering the teachings contained in this book. No matter what sector of business you operate in, the size of your enterprise, or the revenue you rake in annually, there is a lot for everyone in this book. The lessons are practical, direct, and easy to incorporate into your daily life. If you are currently struggling with making sales or dealing with employees, customers, or clients, this is the best book out there at the moment that can help put and keep your life and that of your business on track.

By leaning a few NLP techniques presented in this book, you can quickly turn your business stalemate into a checkmate. So, what are you waiting for? Get into this boat and ride your way to phenomenal success!

Chapter 1: NLP EXPLAINED

Background

The foundations of NLP were first introduced in the 1970s in two books co-authored by Richard Bandler and John Grinder, *The Structure of Magic I & II*, which they published in 1975 and 1976, respectively. According to Bandler and Grinder, there exists a connection between an individual's neurological processes, language, and the behaviors they exhibit. The functional basis of NLP is founded on the presupposition that these variables can be altered and reshaped to bring about desired effects or results.

Other major theories of NLP are derived from the works of authors such as Virginia Satir, Milton Erickson, and Fritz Perls, as well as the theories of Gregory Bateson, Alfred Korzybski, Noam Chomsky, and Carlos Castaneda. Of particular interest to Bandler and Grinder were the unique therapy techniques utilized by Satir, Erickson, and Perls, and in the first volume of their book, they claimed that NLP methodology is able to clone those techniques and, indeed, any technique utilized for therapy or otherwise, so that they can be used by anybody. This method of creating models out of an original model is known as codification. In fact, the entire volume 1 of *The Structure of Magic* is dedicated solely to this purpose.

NLP is a method of communicating with the mind. It takes into cognizance that individuals fashion their unique internal maps of the world as they apply a mental filter to the information they receive from their surroundings. NLP helps to achieve resonance with an individual's unique map, so as to understand why and how they do what they do. Away from understanding the thought and behavioral patterns of others, NLP also helps to understand the workings of one's own mind and to communicate vividly with it. Hence, NLP has been described by many as the study of the language of the mind.

Here is an instance to help you understand NLP better. Imagine that you went to an eatery in a foreign country and tried to order a fruit salad in a language you barely understand. After forty minutes of waiting, the steward came with a sandwich. You lividly stormed out of the eatery, frustrated, tired, and most importantly, still hungry. This is potentially very frustrating and might impact negatively on your entire trip. However, the sour experience could have been avoided had you communicated better with the steward. You probably thought you ordered fruit salad, but perhaps in reality, what you asked for was a hamburger.

This instance is similar to the workings of our subconscious mind. Sometimes you feel you are asking for happiness, wealth, and health, but then get stagnation and disease. You begin to think life is unfair, but what you asked for is what you are getting. You simply don't understand the language of your mind.

With NLP, you can learn not only to speak but also master the language of your mind.

NLP has been defined in several ways. One of such definitions describes NLP as the study of communication within oneself and between oneself and other individuals. In this light, NLP has been developed through modeling expert communicators who achieved positive outcomes with their clients. NLP has also been defined as a method of communication, therapy, and personal development, which is aimed at bringing about desired favorable outcomes. Perhaps the most encompassing definition of NLP is that it is a pathway to utilizing the language of the mind to achieve results consistently.

A Brief History of NLP

Although a vast majority of the texts about NLP celebrates John Grinder and Richard Bandler as the founding fathers and originators of NLP, it is worthy to note that several more people were involved in carving out the theories and doctrines of NLP. These remarkable people, including Frank Pucelik, Robert Dilts, Judith Delozier, Leslie Cameron, David Gordon, among others, strove to pave the way for the NLP practiced today.

At the inception of NLP, these individuals, together with Grinder and Bandler, set out on an intellectual mission at the University of California to find out why the techniques employed by exceptional psychotherapists Erickson, Satir, and Perls were so effective on clients. They relied on direct observation of these psychotherapists as they communicated with clients, as well as analyses of their therapy videos to discover the magic behind their communication genius. The process they used to uncover and breakdown the strategies of Erickson, Satir, and Perls is termed modeling, which in essence is creating a copy of what another individual does.

By using the modeling technique, Bandler and Grinder stated in their 1975 book, *The Structure of Magic I* that they could codify the works of individuals who have excelled in their fields and through that codification expose the structure of the strategies employed by those people, thereby making the knowledge available for other people to attain. The authors used this methodology in modeling Virginia Satir, to produce what they termed the *Meta-Model*, a tool for assessing a client's spoken language and discovering the thoughts behind it. Bandler and Grinder claimed that by challenging a client's language, one could be privy to the deeper lying information usually hidden just beneath the *surface*.

Towards the end of the 1970s, the *human potential movement* became more influential and sprouted in its wake an entire industry, which gave NLP concepts and teachings fertile grounds to grow and flourish. Central to the early development of NLP is the Esalen Institute at Big Sur, California, where renowned psychotherapists including Perls, Satir, and Bateson taught in and led seminars. Circa that time, Bandler and Grinder began to market NLP as not only a therapy option but also a system for communication, and attracted businesspeople by using the mantra, "if anybody can do anything, so can you." They started organizing seminars and workshops to teach therapists and students alike the tenets of NLP. In one of such workshops, they made $150,000 when 150 students paid $1,000 each to attend their 10-day workshop. After that initial success, Bandler and Grinder decided to quit academic writing for the more financially promising niche writing, transforming transcripts from seminars into books. One of such books that resulted from this endeavor is *Frogs into Princes*, which sold a remarkable 270,000 copies worldwide. Indeed, certain documents revealed that by 1980, Bandler alone had made a whopping $800,000 from book sales and workshops.

As the days went by, NLP became more popular, evidently through the participation of students and psychotherapists in its training sessions. One of those early participators was Tony Robbins, who learned NLP from Grinder and thereafter incorporated its teachings into his motivational speaking programs. Despite Bandler's several attempts – some legal, others commercial – to cut off other practitioners from using NLP techniques, the practice of NLP continued to grow. As NLP became increasingly widespread in the 1980s, it was greeted with myriads of scientific studies regarding its founding theories and the effectiveness of its practice. The 1990s saw a decline in scientific interest in the theories and applications of NLP, and even more decline was observed in subsequent years.

The combined endeavor of Bandler and Grinder towards the development and sustainability of NLP suffered a major blow when in 1981, Bandler took legal action against Grinder for the latter's purported utilization of NLP and its teachings in commercial activities to personal ends. Bandler won the suit, and as part of the settlement between himself and Grinder, he agreed to give Grinder a 10-year license to use NLP's concepts for financial enterprises, on the condition that he be paid royalties in return.

Years later, in 1996 and 1997, Bandler instituted legal actions against Grinder for a breach of the settlement agreement they had, as well as against more than 200 other individuals for 'illegally' using the NLP brand for personal gains. However, the court ruled against Bandler in 1997, stating that Bandler did not have the right to own NLP and all of its concepts, nor did he possess the exclusive authority to license or certify persons in the practice of NLP. This fallout between the two most famous founding fathers of NLP led to criticism and mockery from the ever-present NLP abhorrers and critics. One of the many criticisms came from Stollznow, who commented in 2010 that the purportedly proven techniques of NLP could not prove effective in settlement of the feud between their developers.

In the late 1990s, NLP garnered wider practice when Tony Clarkson took legal action against Bandler to have his NLP trademark in the United Kingdom revoked. The court ruled against Bandler, revoking his trademark and thereby making NLP more 'open-source.' In the year 2000, Bandler again teamed up with Grinder in a marriage of convenience to agree to be regarded as the co-founders of NLP, and to not instigate any actions intended to impact negatively on either of their ventures concerning NLP. Through all of the legal proceedings that have happened as regards the practice of NLP, membership in, and certification by any society offering NLP services remain unhindered and unrestricted till this day.

It was important to get you up to speed with this background of NLP before we start. It might come in handy for you if you ever have to defend why you have chosen NLP as a tool for self-growth.

Components and Founding Concepts

The teachings of NLP cannot be truly understood without first grasping the underpinning components and concepts that form its foundations. These components are subjectivity, consciousness, and learning.

- Subjectivity

As explained by Bandler and Grinder, individuals go through life and perceive information in a subjective manner, thereby creating subjective versions of their experience. In other words, they create unique maps of the world. These mental versions of experience are organized from information gathered from the five senses – eyes, ears, skin, nose, and tongue – as well as the spoken language. This is why when we recall an event that happened in the past, we tend to "see" images of the event, "hear" the sounds that accompanied the event, "feel" the sensations we felt when we experienced the event, "smell" the odors associated with it, "taste" the flavors of the event, and generally think in some language (typically our most preferred language, or one we are most fluent in). Therefore, in light of the structure and pattern of an individual's subjective representations of their experiences, the definition of NLP as a study of the architecture of subjective human experience is credible, logical, and, in fact, laudable. By taking into account the subjectivity of ours and people's perception of information, we can understand behaviors – why we do what we do –, and by modifying the subjective representations of experiences, we can successfully and consistently alter behaviors both in ourselves and in others.

- Consciousness

According to the teachings of NLP, the concept of consciousness can be divided into two individual components: the conscious component and the unconscious component. The conscious component comprises conscious thoughts, actions, emotions, and behaviors, while the unconscious component includes all of an individual's subjective representations of their experiences.

- Learning

NLP is predicated on the concept of learning through imitation, also called modeling, whereby an exceptional person's skills and mastery in a field or art can be codified and replicated for use by other people.

NLP Modeling Explained

Modeling is arguably the handiest skill in Neuro-linguistic Programming. It is the sum total of the methods involved in the recreation of exceptional strategies employed by individuals to achieve excellent outcomes, for the purpose of allowing other people 'copy' those strategies to achieve similar outcomes. The modeling concept is founded on the notion that any human behavior or strategy can be modeled by carefully assessing, understanding, and mastering the beliefs, skills, and thought patterns associated with that behavior. In other words, it is simply putting yourself in the shoes of the individual whose behavior you want to model. Modeling is like burning a program from a computer, A, onto a compact disc, and then installing that program on another computer, B, that did not have it so that it can begin to run the program too.

It is essential to think of modeling not as an instruction manual, but as a tool that can be used to 'hack' into the strategies of successful endeavors. It is vital, therefore, that before you set out to use modeling, you ascertain what it is you want to achieve, and then open yourself up to the possibility of getting one of several possible outcomes. The goals of NLP modeling include helping you develop skills, behaviors, and strategies that are aimed toward improving your performance, assessing behaviors so that you know which ones are bad or good to keep, and getting to understand other people better so as to create rapport. The processes involved in achieving these goals come in three phases:

a. First phase: Model observation

In this phase, the modeler (you, in this case), attempts to imagine themselves in the state and reality of the individual they are trying to model (also called the model) by employing a term called *second position shift*. Here, you must try to focus on the things the model does (this includes behaviors and physiology), how they achieve these (what thought patterns they have while doing the things they do), and why they do it (their belief systems, assumptions, and presuppositions). You can ascertain what the model is doing by directly observing them; how and why they do those things can be deduced by asking them questions and carefully assessing their feedbacks.

b. Second phase: Yanking out the difference

This phase involves finding out the essential ingredient in the model's strategy. Modeling allows us to take out all of a model's characteristics or elements and assess each one to find out which one makes the difference. By trying out element after element, the model's strategy should fail to work without the essential element. Therefore, the element, without which the strategy does not have value, or does not produce the desired effects, is *the difference*. To arrive at a probable result, you must endeavor to ask quality questions, such as:

- What behaviors does the model exhibit?
- How does the model achieve their results?
- What did the model do differently than other strategies that did not achieve success?
- What is the difference?

c. Third phase: Teaching the strategy

This is the final phase of the modeling process. When you have found out and mastered a model's strategy and all of its elements, you would then be in a position to teach others the vital skill the model is using to achieve their exceptional results.

The above-detailed phases of modeling can be further broken down into simpler steps, for practicability and easier comprehension. These are:

1. Ascertain the exceptional individual you want to model. Ensure that you have seen them perform the skills you want to model, either firsthand or in a videotape. Watch and listen to them as they perform the skills as many times as feasible.
2. Get yourself in a comfortable position, usually sitting, and then try to imagine the model performing the skill. Try as much as possible to imagine yourself getting in sync with them as they perform.
3. Imagine 'getting into' the model's body as they perform the skill. You have to be creative in your imagination, as you try to feel, hear, and see what they feel, hear, and see as they perform the skill.
4. 'Get back' into your body, and as you do that, make sure you are leaving the model's body with the knowledge you have acquired. Now try to re-imagine the performance of the skill, but now with you as the actor.
5. Repeat step 4 over and over until you are satisfied with your performance.
6. Break the chain, that is, try to focus on something else. For example, you could focus on the ceiling or floor, and observe their designs.

7. Repeat all of the steps above and continue to practice until you have mastered the skill.

The above exercise details the steps involved in modeling another person. But NLP modeling can also be used to model your behaviors. Here is an exercise that can help you model a behavior (such as smoking) and replace it with a better behavior (such as drinking a glass of water instead).

1. Identify the behavior you wish to modify (in this case, say you want to alter your smoking habit).
2. Point out the steps you take to accomplish that behavior.
3. Identify and assess the factors that trigger that behavior.
4. Start making little changes to the steps that get you to accomplish the negative behavior. For example, it may be that you are tempted to smoke whenever you see a cigarette. In this case, seeing a cigarette is the trigger, and now you want to change the result of that trigger, which is lighting and smoking the cigarette and replace it with a healthier behavior, like drinking a glass of water.
5. Use the *future pace* technique to change the result of the trigger. You can do this by imaging that in the future when you see a cigarette, you take it, examine it, and then throw it in the bin. Then you smile and drink a glass of water.
6. Test your imagination. Get a cigarette and a glass of water, then throw the cigarette in the bin and drink the

glass of water. Tell yourself that it is ACTUALLY easier and better to drink the glass of water instead of smoking.

NLP has proven to be an effective solution to a wide range of problems and bottlenecks. It has been used by practitioners to remedy or, at least, minimize the symptoms of low self-esteem, depression, certain phobias, and more. It is because of its possible applications in these diverse areas that NLP has garnered the amount of fame and widespread practice it currently enjoys. Over the last four years of its existence, NLP has been used by psychotherapists and other practitioners to bring about better communication, smoother customer relations, and other positive outcomes in the businesses of entrepreneurs. It helps improve your interpersonal skills.

Effective communication is central to the concept of NLP and is a key fixture in most NLP techniques and strategies. Communication is not only words, as the unspoken cues in a conversation, such as an eye movement and body postures can often tell the rationale or reasoning behind spoken words, and therefore form the bulk of communicated language. NLP can teach you to become a master of non-verbal communication, so that you better understand the 'why' behind the 'what' in communications with clients, customers, and team members. Through modeling, NLP allows you to replicate the strategies that successful enterprises have utilized to their benefit and achieve similar levels of success to what they attained. NLP improves negotiation skills so that you can close deals more easily and successfully too.

In this chapter, I have tried to bring you up to speed with the formation and development of NLP as a widely accepted and adopted technique. The core tenets have also been introduced to you. This background is important as we now move to localize NLP techniques to entrepreneurship in subsequent chapters.

Chapter 2: ENTREPRENEURIAL MISSION/MOTIVATION

Getting Motivated

Motivation is the fuel of success. A motivated individual is an individual driven and pushed by the desire to succeed. Unfortunately, with the weight of everyday struggles bearing down on us, it may be difficult to be perpetually motivated. While NLP has been used over the years mainly to offer solutions to psychological anomalies such as phobias, depression, and compulsive disorders like (binge eating disorder), some of its techniques have also proven useful as a means of motivating people.

One of the most common techniques used to induce motivation is modeling. The concept of modeling, including its theory and practical application, has been discussed in the previous chapter. In light of motivation, you can use modeling to model an individual who seems to have the ability to stay motivated by assessing the behaviors and thought patterns that enable them to achieve that level of motivation.

Another NLP technique that is used for motivational purposes is that of 'copying' a skill or resource that an individual has and installing it in another person. Think of the compact disk example given in chapter 1! A motivation strategy can be installed in an individual in one of several ways:

- Using a strategy elicitation technique to copy a motivational strategy from an individual and installing it on yourself or another person,
- Using a strategy that worked for you in the past or that you currently use to get motivated for a task, or
- Developing a motivational strategy of your own from scratch.

Since the first option is inextricable similar to the modeling technique we have learned and tested earlier, we will not delve further into it. The second option tends to be the preferred option for most people as it is considered the easiest of the three. I am therefore going to demonstrate how you can reuse a strategy you used in the past to motivate you to carry out a task in the present. But you cannot truly understand the technique involved in this strategy without first getting familiar with *submodalities*. So, what is meant by the term submodalities?

Submodalities, as the term implies, are the subsets (*sub-*) of the sensations – visual, auditory, olfactory, gustatory, and kinesthetic – (*modalities*) through which we fashion and give shape to our experiences. In simpler terms, submodalities are the bricks with which we 'build up' our experiences. In the early days of NLP, submodalities were used as a way to give color to experiences. However, in 1983, Richard Bandler started to offer an explanation of the nature and architecture of submodalities. He showed how people could use *submodality shifts* to alter their habits, modify beliefs, and induce motivation, and how the root structure of experiences could be revealed using the principles of submodalities.

A submodality as regards NLP can be defined as a distinction or variation in a sensory modality, as perceived by an individual. In other words, submodalities are the subjective 'shades' of the structures of the sensory representational systems. The concept of submodalities in NLP is predicated on the notion that humans fashion experiences using some or all of their five senses. The five senses, including eyes (visual sensation), ears (auditory sensation), skin (kinesthetic sensation), nose (olfactory sensation), and tongue (gustatory sensation), are called the modalities or *representational systems* in NLP.

The representational systems

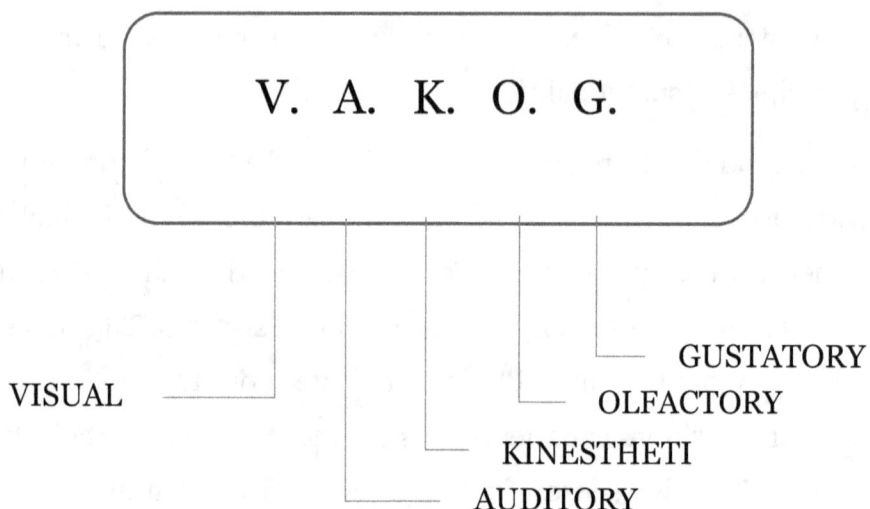

The principle of submodalities comprises the finer details to each of these modalities. For example, a substance could be described as sweet or bitter in taste or described as strong or sour. An image could be light or dark, or low or high in contrast. An odor can be pungent or mild, or pleasant or unpalatable. These distinctions or variations are known as submodalities and represent the structure of the internal workings of our mind. NLP submodalities have been used as a standalone technique, in conjunction with other techniques, or incorporated into therapy strategies to help individuals quit smoking, modify their dietary behaviors, challenge compulsive disorders, scrutinize beliefs and highly held values, get motivated, relieve stress, and address phobias.

Examples of submodalities

VISUAL	AUDITORY	KINESTHETIC
Bright or Dim	Mono or Stereo	Heavy or Light
Distant or Close	Low Pitch or High Pitch	Rough or Smooth
Color or Black & White		Warm or Cold
Moving or Stationary	Low Volume or High Volume	
3D or Flat		
Internal or External		

Submodalities play a very important functional role in the mind, as they help project memories and thoughts from the unconscious to the conscious mind. Even though there are literally tons of submodalities, NLP experts hypothesize that certain submodalities are more vital and can bring about weightier effects than the others. It is of vital importance to understand that submodalities differ between individuals, as a result of the subjectivity of the process through which they are formed in every individual, and the particular sets of submodalities inherent to an individual can often be discovered through inquisition and observation.

When a person alters the constitution of their 'vital' submodalities, they are almost always certain to get an immediate change in the way the emotions attached to those submodalities present themselves. Therefore, submodalities provide a unique panacea for therapy, by which we can understand how the mind subjectively structures events or experiences. The concept of submodalities has gained extensive usage in many NLP techniques, including the Swish technique, Mapping Across, Compulsion Blowout, and in NLP treatment of phobias. Let's quickly dive into the Swish technique.

The Swish technique

An NLP method used to alter an undesired behavior in oneself or in others easily and without the need to be overly disciplined. It involves changing one's identity from the person who does the undesired behavior to one who does not. By altering your reality in this manner, you can quickly transform yourself from who you are to who you want to be. After all, we hardly deal with reality as it is, but through our subjective projections of it. That is to say, we deal with life not as it ACTUALLY is, but as we see it. Therefore, by changing the way we perceive reality, we can change outcomes from undesirable to desirable ones. Here is an exercise in learning and using the Swish technique to change an undesired behavior (such as eating chocolate late into the night):

1. Ascertain the trigger(s) for that behavior. For example, you may feel like eating chocolate while watching a movie late into the night, but this trigger is not there in the daytime. Here, the trigger is the time of the day.
2. Develop a mental image of the trigger. Have a picture of say 1:00 am on the clock in your mind.
3. Identify the vital submodalities in that mental picture. For example, think about what makes the picture less attractive. Try reducing the brightness, changing it from color to black & white, changing its size or shape, or making it more distant.
4. Fashion an image of yourself without this undesired behavior. What would you look like without the habit you are trying to quit? Would you look and feel healthier? Would you have whiter teeth? Would you stop having digestion problems and therefore feel more comfortable on mornings?
5. Identify the vital submodalities in this desirable mental picture of yourself. Make it more attractive by tweaking certain submodalities. Try bringing it nearer, making the colors more vivid and bright, increasing the size of the image, or adding background music.
6. Check if you agree with this desirable mental picture. Do you have any worries concerning how this desirable image might affect your life?

7. Now, bring the two mental images side by side, or make them overlap, whichever works for you, but make the undesired image large, colorful, and attractive while leaving the desired image small, bland, and unattractive.
8. Quickly explode the desired image into a large, attractive image and simultaneously shrink the undesired image into a small, distasteful picture while making a swiiiiissssshhhh sound. Allow this new image to linger for a few seconds to savor its beauty.
9. Break state. You can stare at the ceiling or floor or use any other method you are comfortable with. It is important to break state as you do not want to swish back to the former image.
10. Quickly repeat steps 5 to 9 at least four times.
11. Test. See if thinking about the undesirable image immediately brings the desirable image.

Now that we have a decent understanding of what submodalities are and why they are important in NLP, let's slide back to option two of how to install a motivation strategy via the following steps:

1. The first thing to do is to create a mental image of an action or behavior that you do without much efforts, such as brushing your teeth or taking a shower.
2. Then, create a mental image of the thing you want to be motivated to do.

3. Using table 2.2, fill the visual and auditory submodalities of the thing you usually do effortlessly in the 'Motivated To Do' column and those of the thing you want to be motivated to do in the 'Not Motivated To Do' column.

Visual and auditory submodalities exercise

VISUAL		
Submodality	Motivated To Do	Not Motivated To Do
Brightness (Bright or Dim)		
Position (Near or Far)		
Size (Large or Small)		
Color (Black & White or Color)		
Focus (Blurred or Sharp)		
Distance (Close or Distant)		

Movement (Moving or Stationary)		
Border (With border or Panoramic)		
Associated (Seeing it through your eyes or Seeing yourself in the image)		
AUDITORY		
Submodality	Motivated To Do	Not Motivated To Do
Volume (Quiet or loud)		
Tone (High or Low tone)		
Tempo (Slow or Fast)		
Pitch (High or Low pitch)		
Direction		

(What direction is the sound coming from?)		

The aim of table 2.2 is to enable you to figure out the differences in the submodalities between the task you do with ease and that which you need to be motivated to carry out.

4. Now that you have successfully listed the submodalities associated with these tasks use this table as a template and create a similar, blank table. List the differences in the submodalities between the two tasks, disregarding the similarities.

5. Once you have figured out the difference between the submodalities, the next step is to identify the vital submodalities altering, which can create that feeling of motivation. To do this, you will have to 'match' the submodalities of the task you are unable to be motivated to do with those of the task you feel easily motivated to do. For example, if the motivated image had loud music playing in the background, but the unmotivated image had quiet music or none at all, change the unmotivated image so that it now has loud music playing in the background. If the motivated image was a panoramic image and the unmotivated image had a thick, black border around it, change the unmotivated image to a panoramic image. Every time you change a submodality

in the unmotivated image, observe how you feel about the new image, then remove the change. Do this for each of the differences in submodality between the motivated image and the unmotivated image until you find the submodality that makes the difference.
6. Once you have discovered the vital submodality, apply the change to your mental image of the task you are unmotivated to do.
7. Break state. You can stare at the ceiling or floor or use any other method you are comfortable with. It is important to break state as you do not want to swish back to the former image.
8. Visualize the new image of the task again, and then break state. Repeat this until the new image becomes the primary image you see when you think of the task you were feeling unmotivated to perform.
9. Take a breather.
10. Think of the task you were hitherto feeling unmotivated to do. You should feel differently about it by now. If you are still unmotivated to do it, repeat this exercise.
11. If it still fails to work, try a different set of motivated/unmotivated mental images.

Now let's slide into the third option of installing a motivational strategy, which is making one from scratch.

To create your unique motivational strategy, you need to have a solid understanding of your submodalities. Good knowledge of your submodalities would give you the capability to answer pertinent questions pertaining to the submodalities that motivate you and those that can enhance your attachment to something. As an example, if by making the image of a chocolate bar distorted and small, you can demotivate yourself from eating chocolate, then the opposite should most certainly motivate you. You could also try to identify what auditory submodalities motivate you. For example, if you like a loud, high pitch, female voice behind you telling you to jump at your task and do it, you may wish to try that out – you could get an actual female with these characteristics to do the trick, or imagine it all on your own!

You may also want to incorporate a certain feeling into your motivational strategy. The trick is, if the other submodalities are tuned correctly, the feeling might come naturally. But if it does not, then you would have to use a certain desirable feeling you had some time in the past. Once you have all of the necessary 'ingredients' in their appropriate amounts, installing the strategy is usually easy. All you have to do is keep the feeling, and bring the image to your mind, then tweak the submodalities until you have the desired outcome.

Strategy installation can also be done systematically – following a step-by-step process of instructions. There are at least five different ways in which you can install a new strategy. These are anchoring, accessing cues, repetition, future pace, and metaphor. While you could use any of the five systems to install your brand-new strategy, using a combination of all five has been proven to be more effective in bringing about a positive outcome.

i. Anchoring

Anchoring, as the name suggests, is a method of 'chaining' a number of sequential steps in a strategy together. When a number of steps have been anchored, you can then 'fire the anchor,' meaning to reverse all of the steps quickly. To make this more interesting, you could inculcate physical movement in the anchor by moving parts or all of your body in a forward direction as you move from step to step in the strategy.

ii. Accessing Cues

This method is used to associate specific gestures or body movements with steps in a strategy. They are great to use with anchors. For example, as you move your body forward while taking a step in a strategy, you can look to the right to associate that step with the 'eyes-right' accessing cue.

iii. Repetition

Repetition is an effective way of learning a new habit, skill, or behavior. You can literally repeat the steps in your strategy over and over until you begin to perform them subconsciously.

iv. Future pace

You could also future pace yourself a number of times upon mastering and applying your strategy.

v. Metaphor

Metaphors are effective in associating with a strategy. Try using an appropriate metaphor to illustrate your strategy so that you buy into it.

These techniques will be explained in detail in subsequent chapters. It should be incredibly easy to use any or all of these techniques to get motivated for any task you may wish to perform. However, if you still find yourself experiencing bottlenecks in the understanding or application of the techniques and methods herein, you may find solace from adhering to the following tips, as they are designed to help make your self-motivating endeavor a lot less stressful.

- Prioritize. Sometimes the thought of having so much to do can be overwhelming and may discourage you from attempting to do anything at all. Pen down all that you want to do and then pick the top thing you want to accomplish. It may be tempting to try to do so much at a time – multitasking, if you may – but the drawback to this is that you are unable to give every task your best, as they each take only a fraction of your efforts and resources. Focus on one thing at a time, and only move on to another task when you're done and satisfied with the one in hand.

- Outline specifically. You need to make the outcomes of completing a task as specific and detailed as possible. Your mind is the forerunner of your internal affairs, and if it does not have enough clarity as to the benefits you stand to accrue from performing a particular task, it may shut down positive emotions and stifle any urge you may have to perform the task.

- Get away from harm. Picture the cost of not performing the task. How would it impact on your business, career, or health? Imagine that a year has passed and you still have not performed that task. How negatively has your failure to perform the task affected that future? Now picture yourself in 3 years still living with the cost of having not done the task. Does that future look bright? Is it what you would have wished for? Chances are, the more unpalatable or unfavorable the cost of not performing a task is, the more motivated you would be to get it done. This is called the "away from" motivation.

- Move toward benefits. You have a vivid mental picture of what your life would be if you don't complete the task you are feeling unmotivated to perform. Now try to picture the benefits of performing that task. How would it affect your life, business, or career in the present, in the near future, and in the distant future? Would it pave the way for you to attain better health, fatter paychecks, or larger clientele? The "toward" motivation, a direct opposite of the "away from" motivation, assumes that the greater the benefits you stand to gain from performing a task, the more your motivation to carry it out would be.

- Less is more. You should endeavor to spend most of your time performing your 'big' tasks rather than the small ones that would yield underwhelming results. Chances are, you have already graded your tasks by the degree of influence in your life and business. But if by chance you have not, you can do so by simply putting them through two filters:
    - The cost filter: Ask yourself, "How greatly would my not performing this task affect my life, business, relationships, or career? Is it really worth all the time it requires?"
    - The benefit filter: Ask yourself, "What benefits could completing this task possibly offer? How would these benefits impact my life, business, or career?"

An objective assessment would certainly reveal which tasks have the greatest impact and which ones are simply bugs.

Setting Goals

Goal setting is the cornerstone of all success. It is disheartening than that most people either do not set tangible, specific goals or fail to stay true to them. Whichever is the cause, the outcome remains the same – people who fail to set or stick to their goals end up laboring for those who don't.

In the entrepreneurial world, goal setting has a massive place as regards personal development and business growth. There are many benefits attached to setting goals, and chances are you already know quite a bunch of them. Rather than talk about what you stand to gain from setting goals – which you might already have known – let's take a look at HOW to set goals and stick to them until you eventually achieve them.

There are many models and methods of goal setting employed by people who have attained success in their endeavors. Some of these methods are specific to particular niches and personality types, while others are more general and encompassing. NLP has again come to the rescue to offer effective solutions in the area of goal setting. Perhaps the best NLP models of goal setting applicable to the life of an entrepreneur are the Timeline and Well-Formed Outcome models.

NLP Well-informed Outcome Model

The well-formed outcome model is an NLP technique fashioned from the lives of successful individuals. It involves making an inquiry about your goals and is focused on clarifying your thought patterns and behaviors, on making your goals 'well-formed'. The steps involved in the well-formed outcome model include the following.

1. Clarify the outcome of your goal

It is crucial to have an understanding of the structure of goals. Goals are defined representations of what it is we want in life in our internal environment and, so, must have defined structures as well. Since your mind pretty much controls your emotions and your emotions control your actions, you need to have the correct representations of your goals in your mind in order to be able to achieve them as efficiently as is possible.

The SMART and PURE acronyms are two incredibly useful tools that can help you fashion your goals in a manner that would allow for the optimization of the techniques and methods you employ to achieve them. You need to make your goals SMART and PURE before you can set out to program them into your mind.

- SMART

The SMART acronym is based on the goal setting method developed by Edwin Locke and is described as follows:

- **S** stands for Specific: You need to make your goals as specific as possible, for easier 'assimilation' by your mind. It is much easier to pursue a specific goal that has a definite form than a general one that has tentacles in every direction. While attempting to make your goals specific, you must ensure to ask these invaluable questions:
    o What is it that I want to achieve?
    o With whom do I want to achieve this?
    o When do I want to achieve this?
    o Where would I want to achieve it?
    o What do I require to achieve it?
    o With whom, where, and when do I not want to achieve it?

  The aim of these questions is to give form to your goal, so you can picture it in as vivid a way as possible.

- **M** stands for Measurable: Develop a strategy for measuring your progress towards the achievement of your goal. By tracking your progress, you would be able to stay focused and not detail from the path you have set out to take. Furthermore, measuring your progress gives you the satisfaction of having succeeded thus far in working towards your goal and motivates you to move even further. The caveat to this is, not all goals are measurable. So, from the start, make sure you set out to achieve a measurable goal. You can be certain that your goal is measurable if you can answer the questions of "how much," "how many," and/or "what markers would notify me of progress."

- **A** stands for Attainable: How achievable is the goal you have set out to achieve? Is it extraordinarily huge and illogical for the timeframe? Has it been done by any other person? Although it is a core belief in NLP that one can achieve almost anything one wishes to achieve, it follows logic and reason that you streamline your goals to fit your reality, and. It may be deemed illogical, for instance, for you to have a goal of going to Mars in the next month, while you're currently a small business owner with no affiliations with NASA.
- **R** stands for Relevant: Are your goals relevant to your personal development, business, career, or relationships?
- **T** stands for Timely: What is the timeframe of achieving your goals? By time-binding your goal, you give it a sort of an expiry date, by which you should have attained it.
- PURE

PURE is another goal forming method, created by Roger Terry to help clarify your goals and give them meaning.

- **P** means Positive: You must state your goals as though you have already attained them, rather than stating them as if attaining them is not in your capacity.
- **U** means Under Your Control: Get a goal that is entirely or mostly under your control, not a goal the controlling and influencing factors of which is not in your control. For example, "I want to complete the cycling circuit three times in under an hour" would be a better formed goal than "I want to be one of the first three people to complete the circuit three times," because while completing the circuit three times in an hour is under your control, the skills and strength of the other competitors, as well as the number of competitors that enter into the competition, may not be under your control.
- **R** means Right Size: Do you have right-sized goals? Are they too easy to pull off? Are they too difficult to achieve? What is your track record as per achieving set goals?
- **E** means Ecological: What effects would be attaining your goals have on yourself, other individuals, and your relationships with them?

2. Assess your present condition

Even when your goals satisfy all of the SMART and PURE conditions, you might still end up not attaining them because of your current state. You need to assess your condition objectively to identify what it is that is delaying the attainment of your goals. Are you capable of achieving your goals? Do you have the requisite skills, resources, time, and behaviors to achieve them? Sometimes you need to modify a habit or two in order to be in a better position to attain your goals. If you discover that the factors stopping you from achieving your goals are not within your power to control, then let go of those goals and move on. Assume, for example, that you have owned a small toy shop for two years as your sole business and your yearly net profit is $50,000, having a goal to purchase a million dollar mansion by cash next year might not be achievable, so long as you do not have cash stashed somewhere. In this case, your present condition cannot satisfy the financial demands of buying the mansion.

3. Develop a solid internal representation of your goals

The brain is not as clever as we think it is; it usually cannot discern between real events and imagined or constructed images, as it reacts almost the same way to all of them. Therefore, by creating a strong internal representation of your goals, you help yourself tap into the emotional responses favorable to achieving them. You will have to optimize your use of submodalities in order to create a good internal representation. Use the visual, auditory, and kinesthetic representational systems appropriately to create mental pictures that move you towards attaining your goals. For example, if your goal is to hit the one million dollars net profit mark from your business next year, create a profound mental picture of the goal

– using clear images, crisp sounds, and lucid feelings. How would you SEE the one-million-dollar profit? What sounds would you HEAR when you achieve that goal? Do you hear your employees cheering and congratulating one another? How would it FEEL? You need to be able to use appropriate submodalities to construct images of your goal.

4. Develop a well-formed outcome

This step allows you to assess your progress towards attaining your goals as well as check whether or not they have been completely achieved. These questions should help you in creating a well-formed outcome.

- What are the markers that will let you know that you have achieved your goal? What will you see, hear, or feel?
- Do you need other people to help attain your goal?
- What resources do you require?
- How will achieving your goal impact your life in general?
- What effects does achieving your goal have on your life?
- What effects does not achieve your goal have on your life?

5. Incorporate your well-formed outcome into your internal representations

Now that you have created a strong internal representation of what you want to achieve and developed a well-formed outcome, it is time to integrate your well-formed outcome into your internal representation, to give you a taste of what it would be like to achieve your goal. Play the scene in your mind several times and travel in its glory. Then, start taking the steps necessary for the attainment of your goal. Use table 2.3 to make taking action about your goal easier for yourself. Write out the first three **actions,** you need to take to attain your goal, **how** you wish to perform them, and **when** you need to get them done. Start with the first action you must take. It could be, for example, putting a call through to a potential investor or customer. Don't make the actions bogus, uninteresting, or unnecessarily complex; make each action ' short', practical, and achievable within a relatively short period of time.

Table 2.3: Action plan to achieve a goal

S/N	ACTION	HOW	WHEN
1.			
2.			
3.			

The NLP Timeline Model

Another effective method of planning or setting a goal is by using the NLP timeline model. The concept of timeline in NLP describes time as a continuum, that is, as a 'stretch' of the reality of our experiences, or, more commonly, a line. Everything that has happened in the past, whatever it is that is happening at present, and everything that will occur in the future are all lined up in a straight line in our minds, such immediate reality (in the past or future) is nearer and distant reality (in the past or future) is farther from the focal point (the present). Another way of picturing time is to take a wall clock and stretch it out so that it makes a straight line. As time goes by, we would be literally 'walking' in a forward direction along the clock line, leaving behind the hours that have come and gone. The entire timeline model, as used in NLP, is founded on this concept of time.

Now that we've understood what timeline is and how it relates to time let's run through the process of setting a goal by using the timeline. This process is broken down into the following steps:

1. Have a mental image of the goal you want to achieve. Make sure to fixate on that image for as long as would be necessary to ensure that whenever you think of your goal, that image jumps at you.
2. Ascertain the specific time you want to achieve the goal.
3. Picture yourself accomplishing the goal. Be sure to include the visual, auditory, and kinesthetic submodalities necessary to create a solid internal representation.
4. Now, levitate your body in the mental picture.
5. Picture your timeline stretched out in front of you. Holding the mental picture of your goal in your preferred hand, float along your timeline until you reach that specific date and time by which you wish to achieve your goal.

6. Drop the picture on this time and make sure it fits well into it.
7. Float back along your timeline and land on the present time.
8. Break state. You can stare at the ceiling or floor or use any other method you are comfortable with. It is important to break state as you do not want to swish back to the former image.

You have successfully dropped a goal in the future. Now all you have to do is work towards achieving it. Refer to table 2.3 to kick-start the process.

Chapter 3: CONFIDENCE

Removing Fear

This chapter deals with confidence, but before we even mention it, we need to start from its greatest adversary which is fear. Fear is one of the mind's natural responses to a stimulus that does or threatens to cause harm, pain, or endanger our wellbeing. Many people have one, two, or a few things they are scared of – some people have a fear of needles and other sharp, pointed metals; some fear tight places and corners, some have a fear of height, and so forth.

Research has shown that a sizable number of people suffer from one fear or another. Therefore, fears, in general, are not what you would typically describe as weird or abnormal. They are perfectly normal and might even prove beneficial sometimes. A fear of sharp, pointed metal ends, for example, can help us better protect ourselves from needle pricks, which in their own rights are an exceedingly potent way of contracting diseases and infections.

However beneficial they might be, fears have their downsides. They have a capacity to prevent us from driving hard enough towards the attainment of our goals or reduce our productivity and efficiency at the workplace. In the entrepreneurial world, the commonest kind of fear that cripples entrepreneurs and reduces their vigor and steadfastness in pursuing and achieving business successes **is the fear of failure**.

Failure has become an 'unheard-of' sort of result in the society. Nobody likes to fail or even think about the possibility of them failing in an endeavor. The thought of failure seems overwhelming. But it is a possibility; and because we know it is always there waiting by the corner, we always seem afraid of it popping out its head from the shadows. Unfortunately, when the fear of failure is allowed to grow over time, it becomes suffocating, confining, and stagnating. It hinders you from taking the sorts of activities that can help you and your business grow. It becomes a limiting, self-imposed barrier.

Mostly when people look back on the lives they have lived and the things they have done, they regret not the repercussions of what they did, but the things they should have done but failed to do. In essence, people tend to regret their inaction more than their actions. In that case, it is vital to remove any fear of failure that is hindering you from pursuing your goals. Here are some ways that a fear of failure can harm you as an entrepreneur:

- Fear of failure cripples, limits, and restricts you. By being afraid to fail, you are deeply inclined to playing it safe and avoiding any major risks. You avoid at all cost any endeavor that might have the capacity to break you free from your current level and plunge you into a higher level of success. As a result of the deep-seated fear, you are inadvertently forced to see only the possible harmful outcomes that may result from an action, rather than the benefits you're likely to gain from it. This behavior stagnates your business or at least limits it to minimal growth.

- It makes you resist taking a path that leads to abundance – abundance in wealth, time, and confidence. Though the well-traveled road is usually the easier one, it often leads to a land where there are more people competing for resources than there are resources to cater for them all. People who do not fear failure take the less traveled path, because they know it often leads to a land where there are fewer people competing for abundant resources.

- It hinders you from expanding. Sometimes, the business might be running smoothly and efficiently, and you might be handling your affairs in a decent way. But if you are operating a business that has seemed to reach its peak success, you would need to expand and explore other possibilities. Fear of failure prevents you from doing this. It tells you to stay put in your little comfort zone and reap all of the booties therein. This hampers further growth and sophistication of your business practices.

In addition to the points raised above, the fear of failure can impede your ability to make more money, by cutting you off the pathways that lead to wealth creation and growth. It could also impact your personal space, your life. When you refuse to venture into taking actions and exhibiting behaviors that can improve the state of your business, soon, your business stagnates. Once this happens, you begin to develop certain negative emotions such as regrets, depression, and even more fear. These can have severe negative effects on your wellbeing.

NLP Techniques to Overcome Fear

NLP has described many techniques for quickly and effectively removing fears and phobias alike. Some of these techniques were developed by the creators of NLP and others were developed by contributors such as experts in psychotherapy, hypnotherapy, and commercial self-help ventures. Three techniques for overcoming fear are detailed in this chapter. You can attempt all and choose the one(s) that work(s) for you best. Central to almost all NLP techniques to rid oneself of fear lies the concept of anchoring. To understand these techniques then, you must first gain an understanding of what anchors are and how they are used in NLP.

- What are Anchors?

Anchoring is one of the most commonly utilized NLP technique, largely due to its effective and rapid impact. It allows you to put yourself in any state you desire consciously – states of happiness, confidence, motivation, etc. – quickly. Anchors have a dual application, that is, they can be applied to oneself or other people. They can be used in the immediate as well as some time in the future. Therefore, in essence, anchors, when they have been developed, are always available on demand.

- How Can Anchors be used?

Anchors are specifically created to bring about a positive change in thought, attitude, or behavior. For example, anchors can be used to evoke positive emotions whenever you see or think about something that usually scares you. In order to be able to create powerful, effective anchors, you need to have a solid understanding of NLP submodalities and how to apply them. Powerful internal representations breed powerful anchors. If you do not create strong enough internal representations, your anchors might be loose and largely ineffective. Mostly, people prefer to use the sense of touch to set up anchors, as they tend to be more accessible than visual or auditory anchors. However, you could also create powerful visual and auditory anchors, as long as you perform the anchoring process conscientiously. Let's dive into an example to make the understanding of anchors easier.

We are going to make an example of how to use NLP anchors to rid ourselves of fear of cockroaches.

- First, think of a time when you were in a state of fearlessness.
- If it so happens that there was not a time in the past you felt fearless, then try to imagine what it would feel like to be fearless.

- Create a vivid mental picture of you being fearless. This could be the day you started your business, the day you had your best presentation or any other moment in your life, you felt no fear whatsoever.
- Once you have that image on your mind, add the appropriate visual and auditory submodalities to make it even more appealing. 'Appropriate' in this sense means the submodalities that make the image more attractive to you. Also, notice the way you feel about the image. For example, if the picture you have in your mind is the day you had your best presentation, try making it colorful, then add your favorite background music. Does the image look better? Is it more appealing? What you are doing is trying to achieve as strong a mental state as you can develop.
- Keep the feeling building through your body by fixating the mental image to your mind.
- As the feeling continues to build, using one of your hands, slightly pinch your thumbnail. Continue to pinch the thumbnail as the feeling builds.
- Keep on with this process until you have the most powerful feeling of fearlessness.
- Break state. You can stare at the ceiling or floor or use any other method you are comfortable with. It is important to break state as you do not want to swish back to the former image.

Once you have completed the anchoring process, the next thing to do is to test (fire) the anchor. By firing the anchor, you ascertain whether or not you have created a powerful anchor. To test the anchor you have built, pinch your thumbnail as you did in during the anchoring procedure. Notice what happens to you. Do you have that strong feeling of fearlessness? If you do, then congratulations, you have just created a fearlessness anchor! However, if you do not get the fearlessness feeling, start, and complete the process again. Then test. Still, don't feel it? Try again. Keep trying until you develop a powerful anchor.

Now that we have understood what anchors are and how they can be applied to great effect let's continue on our journey to ridding ourselves of fear.

Technique #1: The three-step fast phobia cure (originally designed by Richard Bandler)

Step 1: Look for a safe environment to reach out to fear.

- Create an image of a movie cinema. Do not be afraid to make full use of your imaginative prowess.
- Move into the cinema and locate the most comfortable, VIP seat available. Sit comfortably in it.
- Create a video of the fear you wish to overcome. This could be a short clip of a reaction you once had or a

possible reaction to the fear, or the result of exposing yourself to it. Make sure the video is colored.

- Now, separate into two, keeping your original form and physique. This is called the *double dissociated state*. Keep a version of yourself seated and float the other version of yourself to the gallery where you can perch and watch both the version of yourself watching the screen and the screen itself.
- As you are watching a seated version of yourself as well as the screen, play the video you have created.
- Freeze the last frame of the video and change it from colored to grey.

Step 2: Associating the fear with healthy emotions.

- Think of your favorite song, one that makes you feel great. Connect the last (now grey) frame of your video to this song.
- Now play the video backward at a very fast rate (double the normal rate, or faster). When you get to the first frame, freeze it and turn it to grey.
- You may repeat step 2 in order to make it as smooth as possible.

Step 3: Dissociate yourself from the fear.

- Now float back from the gallery and rejoin the version of you sitting in the most comfortable seat in the cinema.
- Whiten out the screen.

- When you are ready, watch the video of your fear associated with your favorite music from start to finish in color. Notice your new reaction to the fear.
- If you don't have the desired feeling, repeat the procedure from start to finish.

Technique #2: Overcoming fear with NLP hypnosis

Step 1: Establish rapport with yourself.

While establishing and maintaining rapport with your own self might sound ridiculous, it is a vital first step in this technique – and many other techniques – of overcoming inherent fear. You must be able to develop an interest in your thoughts and emotions and how one leads to the creation of the other. After all, thoughts and emotions are the structures that create our experience. You need to be patient with, and kind to yourself. Encourage yourself. If the methods for doing this do not jump right at you, then use a proven, commonly used technique: treat yourself the way you treat the person you love and care about the most.

Step 2: Reframe your state of mind.

Change the way you visualize a problem by assessing the intentions behind your actions and behaviors that led to the problem. A problem might be a result of inappropriate handling of techniques or methods to accomplish an intention. In this sense, your actions and behaviors are not bad; they were just used poorly. Most fears harbored by individuals come from an episode or two of injudicious use of resources, the poor outcomes of which prevent the individuals from venturing into any further endeavor in that line of action. By changing the way you think and feel about bad outcomes, you can be more open to carrying out actions and less fearful of what the results might be, while making better use of your resources.

Step 3: Trigger the fear reaction.

The motive behind triggering the fear reaction is to allow yourself to identify and assess the signs of your response to the fear stimulus. While in this state, ask yourself pertinent questions such as, "What makes me fear? What if that thing presents itself here this moment?" Immediately you find yourself responding to these thoughts in a fearful manner (similar to how you usually respond to them), break state.

Step 4: Use the double dissociated state technique.

Go over the fourth point in step 1 of technique #1 to put yourself in a double dissociated state.

Step 5: Making a movie of your fear.

- Think of a time when you first had the fear, or when you felt it the most...or the most recent episode. Create a movie of it in black and white and watch it on the screen. Make sure to include sound in the movie and play it at a normal speed or frame rate.

- Watch yourself in the movie, and while so doing, continuously remind yourself that you are safe presently and that the fear cannot get you where you are at the moment. Then watch your other self in theatre also watching the movie. Emphasize that it is just a movie.
- On reaching the end of the movie, freeze the last frame.

Step 6: Reunite with yourself.

Float away from the gallery and into your former self in the frozen frame on the screen. Then, play the movie backward from the end to the beginning, colored, at a very fast rate.

Step 7: Carry out a test.

Upon completion of the reverse running of the movie, test your responses by asking yourself questions that would have elicited the feeling of fear in you. The questions could be, "What makes me fear? What if that thing presents itself here this moment?" If you still feel fear, then run through the procedure again. Repeat the process as many times as would be necessary to bring about the desired outcome.

Step 8: Perform an ecology check.

This is the stage where you evaluate your new responses to the fear triggers. What makes them different from the responses you used to exhibit? How can you ensure that you exhibit better responses in future circumstances?

Technique #3: Removing fear through visualization and anchoring

Step 1: Think about the fear.

The feeling generated by the fear should generally 'come' from a certain direction in your body. Identify this direction. Imagine that this fear is a physical thing, then move it out of your body, and put it back in such a way that it now wobbles in the opposite direction. Make the fear continue to wobble faster and faster, and while doing so, continuously think of the fear.

Step 2: Get to the root of the fear.

You need to find out the reason behind the fear. Certain fears, for example, help prepare an individual for defense or have protective functions. Find out positive ways you can achieve the reason or intention behind the fear, without resorting to the negative emotion of fear. This can prove invaluable if done correctly.

Step 3: Create powerful, fearless states, anchor them, and fire the anchors whenever you feel fear.

Step 4. Get aware of your physiology.

You may exhibit certain behaviors when afraid, such as assuming a certain posture or breathing in a certain way. Try adjusting your physiology, like adopting a new posture, breathing differently, or raising your shoulders.

Step 5: Lessen the weight of the fear.

Lighten your fear. A good way to do this is by making jokes about having the fear and literally laughing to your own jokes. This makes the fearless of a burden and easier to overcome. Do this routine and effectively enough, and you find yourself laughing at the thought of the fear.

Gaining Confidence

Lack of self-confidence is one of the foremost reasons why some entrepreneurs fail in business. Low confidence – in one's abilities, skills, ideas, and solutions – is also a major reason why some would be entrepreneurs give up their dream to focus on other less weighty options such as focusing on a nine-to-five job. Confidence in oneself is a vital – and the perhaps the most important – ingredient in the making of a successful entrepreneur. Without it, very little can be achieved no matter the weight of the opening balance in the checking account.

Confidence in yourself allows you to be able to take the best decisions and impact the workplace more positively. It also increases your satisfaction with yourself and your enterprise. You're the leader at the workplace, and, therefore, by staying confident and calm even in the face of adversity, you subtly urge your team to do the same. However, overconfidence has its own negatives. Having the confidence in your abilities to carry out tasks is one thing, having the actual abilities to perform is another, and as a leader, you should be able to discern between the two. As much as you believe in yourself, be in touch with yourself to know your limitations and when you need to call for help.

Low confidence in yourself prevents you from expressing your true abilities, no matter how good they are. Not being able to express your abilities means you cannot achieve success, and if you do, it would only be a shadow of what it could have been. Lack of success leads to further decrease in self-confidence; it is a vicious cycle that destroys you and your business from within. Here are some other common effects of low self-confidence:

- Low self-confidence hinders spontaneity. It prevents you from acting when you really need to, because you do not think you have the abilities to act or that your action would be praiseworthy. What's worse is, a person with low self-confidence may begin to interpret their low confidence as laziness or passiveness. This mindset severely hurts their potential to succeed.
- It makes you unwilling to test the waters. No amount of knowledge, expertise, or experience will make you try daring and active if your self-confidence is low.
- It affects your ability to create or maintain healthy relationships. When you have low confidence, you perpetually try to impress the people you are relating with, as you don't feel adequate or worthy enough to be in the relationship. Low confidence also increases your sensitivity, such that you get annoyed or hurt easily by

people you are in a relationship with, causing unnecessary conflicts and fallouts.

- Low confidence deprives you the enjoyment of celebrating your victories and achievements because you do not believe you have done enough to deserve the accomplishments.
- Either low self-confidence breeds perfectionism or perfectionism breeds low self-confidence. Whatever the case, there seems to be a strong correlation between the two, and as perfectionism is as unachievable as it is unreasonable, individuals suffering from low confidence are likely to get stuck rather than progressing and excelling. Lack of confidence also restrains you from seeking the help of others, as you feel asking for help dishonors your own self-respect.
- It also comes with a certain lack of motivation to act. If you don't believe in your own abilities to succeed, then what is the need to even try?
- On a personal level, individuals with low self-confidence tend to have a poor image of themselves, even if there is absolutely nothing wrong with their appearance.
- Low confidence people are usually passive or aggressive rather than assertive. Assertiveness is one of the best qualities of an entrepreneur, as it expresses confidence and calmness. Passiveness and aggressiveness in the

business environment only elicit damaging negative responses.

NLP Techniques for Building Self-confidence

Low self-confidence, as we have seen from the points above, is a crucial attribute of successful individuals and a damning scourge of unsuccessful ones. No amount of work can make you as successful as you could possibly be if you lack the confidence to showcase your abilities and value. You need to be confident to command higher prices on your products and services, to demand and secure higher productivity and creativity from your staff, and to assert your authority at the workplace.

Lack of confidence simply derides your efforts and hampers your progress. Hence there is a need to develop your confidence level if it is low. Far from the popular belief that you are either born with self-confidence or lack it for the rest of your life, self-confidence is something you could actually develop. It can be nurtured consciously or unconsciously at any age and in almost any circumstances. Fortunately, there are many NLP Techniques that can help increase your level of confidence so you can always perform at turbo speed and machine efficiency.

Before getting started on the techniques to increase your confidence level, make a comprehensive list of all the times in the future, you think you could be let down by your low confidence. This could be specific occasions, such as an interview or more general events such as meeting with people. Ensure not to rush the process; take your time and make this list as comprehensive as possible, as the results you would get depend on its accuracy. You could also return to this list at any point in the process to alter or modify it as appropriate.

Once you have made your list, use the NLP swish technique to change the negative image of each of the items on the list to a more positive image. Let's quickly run through the swish technique again, in case you might have forgotten how to use it.

NLP Swish Technique

1. Ascertain the trigger(s) for the behavior. For example, you think you would lack the confidence to be successful at an interview because you feel the interviewers might have a problem with your tie. In this case, your tie is the trigger.
2. Develop a mental image of this trigger in your mind.
3. Identify the vital submodalities in that mental picture. For example, think about what makes the picture less attractive. Try reducing the brightness, changing it from color to black & white, changing its size or shape, or making it more distant.
4. Create a mental image of yourself without this undesired behavior. What would you look like without your poor confidence level? Would you look and feel better? Create a vivid picture of a confident version of yourself. Ensure

to spend quality time in this stage to get a strong mental picture, as the success of this technique depends on it.

5. Identify the vital submodalities in this desirable mental picture of yourself. Make it more attractive by tweaking certain submodalities. Try bringing it nearer, making the colors more vivid and bright, increasing the size of the image, or adding background music.
6. Check if you agree with this desirable mental picture. Do you have any worries concerning how this desirable image might affect your life?
7. Now, bring the two mental images you now have side by side, or make them overlap, whichever works for you, but make the undesired image large, colorful, and attractive while leaving the desired image small, bland, and unattractive.
8. Quickly explode the desired image into a large, attractive image and simultaneously shrink the undesired image into a small, distasteful picture while making a swiiiiisssssshhhh sound. Allow this new image to linger for a few seconds to savor its attractiveness.
9. Break state. You can stare at the ceiling or floor or use any other method you are comfortable with. It is important to break state as you do not want to swish back to the former image.
10. Quickly repeat steps 5 to 9 at least four times.

11. Test. See if thinking about the undesirable image brings the desirable image to mind immediately.
12. Do this for the remaining items on your list.

Apart from the swish technique, there are other NLP techniques that you can employ to bolster your self-confidence successfully. These techniques include the *NLP Get Grounded* exercise, the *Mommy, Make it Go Away* technique, the *NLP Whiteout* technique, NLP technique to kill nagging voices, and *NLP Anchoring* technique. We'll now dive headfirst into each of these techniques. As always, it is highly recommended that you try out all of these techniques and then make a habit of performing the ones that work for you best.

NLP Get Grounded Exercise for Boosting Confidence

This exercise is a brief one that has been used in many NLP inspired workshops and lectures to help people increase their self-confidence. It is also exceedingly useful in preparation for social functions or interviews. It goes as thus:

1. Remove your shoes. While this is not exactly mandatory for the success of the exercise, it is recommended that you keep your feet flat on the ground or floor. If you are in an office, however, you may keep your shoes on. It is

not recommended to wear high heels for this exercise as your feet must be as flat as possible.
2. Stand on your feet. The NLP grounding exercise is not one of those techniques that require the practitioner to sit and imagine. You need to be on your feet for this exercise to come through. If you have a problem standing (if you are in a wheelchair, for example), you could sit straight with your feet touching the ground.
3. Point your feet in a forward direction and spread them apart to about the width of your shoulders.
4. Check that your feet are flat on the ground, then grip the ground with your toes.
5. With your toes now gripping the ground, gently rotate your hips inwardly a bit. This might feel a little uncomfortable, but it would all be worth it in the end.
6. Ensure that your shoulders are relaxed and arms are in a loose position.
7. Slightly relax your knees.
8. Keep your legs in an upright position, but do not lock your knees.
9. Breathe out and slightly sink your body.
10. Locate a point about 2 inches below your navel and focus your attention on it. If the positioning is correct, this point should be where you feel the tenseness in your stomach muscles. You should also feel as though this point is the center of your balance and support.

11. While keeping your body in a relaxed state, take deep, slow breaths in and out continuously.
12. Make sure to spend plenty of time perfecting this position. Once the position becomes comfortable for you, make it a habit to get into it for some minutes every day. When you become very familiar with it, try moving whilst keeping your focus on the central point. It may be somewhat weird at first to move around in this position, but soon you would come to terms with it and feel more comfortable in it. Pay particular attention to your breathing as it could change without your notice.

Practice several times until getting into this position becomes very fluid and convenient. You should be able to maintain and walk around in this position in public in no distant time and retain the position even while still. This position gives people the impression that you are grounded, confident, and calm.

Mommy, Make it Go Away Technique

This NLP technique allows you to replace the negative feelings you have whenever you think of an uncomfortable event from your past with positive feelings. This could be an interview, a class presentation, a project defense, or any other experience. For this technique to be put to effective use, you must have a solid knowledge of NLP submodalities – which you do – and a good knowledge of the NLP memory manipulation technique – which you don't...yet. So, let's start with the memory manipulation technique, get grounded in it, and thereafter slide into the Mommy, make it go away technique.

The NLP memory manipulation technique is a technique used to alter memories of events or experiences. In NLP, it is presupposed that when we remember an event, we do so with our five senses – we remember what we saw, heard, felt, smelled, and tasted. Mostly, only three of these five senses (visual, auditory, and kinesthetic) are used for NLP purposes. So, in essence, by remembering an event, we are attempting to recollect what we saw, heard, and felt, but in a subjective manner. In this light, we create internal representations bypassing what actually happened through our internal filters, such as beliefs, education, and values. By manipulating these internal representations, we could always restructure our memories. There are several exercises you can take to alter the content of your memory. Let's get ourselves familiar with three of these exercises.

- Exercise 1
  - Imagine a person who ridicules you, someone who makes you feel unworthy or unimportant, someone who usually gets the better of you in an argument, or someone who belittles your contributions in a group discussion. Create an image of that person in your head.
  - Create an image of you dealing with that person sometime in the future.

- Assess the image and find all of the unrealistic features therein. Turn all unrealistic characteristics of the image realistic. For example, if the person that bothers you is unreasonably tall in your mental picture, shrink them. If they are extraordinarily huge, making them slimmer. Do this for all the other unrealistic features.
- Now, you are going to make some of the realistic features in the image unrealistic. For example, give their face a huge clown's nose. Now observe how the person seems now. Is the person still scary or intimidating? How about giving them really big blue pants? How do they look now?

- Exercise 2
  - Imagine someone whose voice bothers you or has bothered you in the past, someone whose voice intimidates you or makes you uncomfortable.
  - Change their voice. If the person has a stern, commanding voice, what happens when you make them sound like Donald Duck, or when you increase their speech speed until they begin to sound like squabbling mice? You could use the help of a search engine if you have no idea what Donald Duck sounds like.
  - If the person has a really smooth speech, slow them down and make them talk incoherently.

- Exercise 3
    - Remember four or five people who give you a hard time.
    - Imagine the next time you would have to relate with them.
    - Use visual submodalities in your mind to make your encounter with them easier for yourself. For example, you could give them a big clown's nose, make their gait wobbly, give them a terrible haircut, make them wear a dress meant for the opposite sex, or give them features of the opposite sex (if the person is a woman, give her a mustache).
    - Use auditory submodalities in your mind to make your encounter with them easier for yourself. For example, you could make them sound like Donald Duck, make them speak slowly in a funny way, or make them sound like the opposite sex.
    - You could also use kinesthetic submodalities to make them easier to deal with. You could, for example, make yourself feel like laughing hysterically on thinking of them.

These exercises are very easy to use, and once mastered, you could use them to modify almost any memory you are struggling with. Let us now glide into the "Mommy, make it go away" technique proper. Here go the steps:

1. Think of the memory you want to let go. As you think of it, notice that the image of the memory has a definite location somewhere in your mind.
2. Ascertain the exact location of the image – in front of you, by your right, by your left, or behind you.
3. Take the image and move it nearer a bit and back to its original position. By now, you know you can change the position of the image.
4. Imagine that you have a huge catapult (or a slingshot) in front of you.
5. Imagine that the image is perched in the catapult.
6. With all of your strength, pull the elastic band of the catapult all the way back until it reaches its elastic limit. Then, let go.
7. Watch the image shoot off into the distance until it becomes a tiny speck in space.
8. Think about something entirely different.
9. Think of the memory you just catapulted into an abyss. Is the image still in the same position as it was earlier? If it still is, don't be afraid to give it another dose of catapulting. Repeat this step until the image becomes only a tiny speck in space whenever you think of it.

NLP Whiteout Technique

Similar to the Mommy, make it go away technique, the whiteout technique is a technique used to forget uncomfortable memories permanently. Bad memories can affect your present and challenge your ability to make progress. With the NLP whiteout technique, you can push those bugging memories out of your consciousness for good.

1. Think of something that makes you feel uncomfortable. It could be a memory of a time you embarrassed yourself at an interview or gave a terrible presentation.
2. Make the image as lucid as possible.
3. Increase the white balance of the image quickly until it turns completely white.
4. Break state. This step is important so that your brain does not create a loop.
5. Repeat steps 3 and 4 five more times.
6. Remember the memory and notice what happens. Notice that the image either whites out automatically or is completely white and you cannot see it clearly.
7. If you do not achieve the results you want, repeat the process all over again. In the repeat process, try performing the whiteout faster and adding sound effects.

NLP Technique to Kill Nagging Voices

This NLP technique can be used to destroy the voices of hesitancy in one's mind. It is potent in summoning courage and confidence to carry out a task, such as speaking in public or offering your solution at a workshop. The steps are simple and straightforward and are presented in the following lines.

1. Think of a time you wanted to do something, but a nagging voice told you not to.
2. Notice that the voice comes from a certain direction in your mind. Also, try to ascertain whose voice it is. Is it really your voice or that of someone else?
3. Know exactly what the voice sounds like.
4. Change the location of the voice, so that it now comes from a distant place in your mind, and you can only hear it faintly. Is there a change in the effect the voice has on you now?
5. Change some of the characteristics of the voice and see what happens. For example, you could change the voice to that of Donald Duck.
6. Add certain features to the voice to make it seem less important or serious. Try adding background music from one of Charlie Chaplin's films. How does the voice sound now?
7. Repeat the exercise if it doesn't work out at the first try. Do this for all the nagging voices in your head and send them out.

NLP Anchoring Technique to Gain Confidence

We have run through some anchoring techniques in previous sections of this book, so we should be decently familiar with NLP anchoring and anchors by now. Let's look at how you can build powerful anchors which you can use to boost your self-confidence.

1. Remember a time in the past when you had your highest confidence level. If there has not been such a time, then you could simply imagine it. Create a mental picture of you being super confident...the most confident you could possibly be.
2. Once you have that image in your mind, play around the auditory submodalities of the image. If the image has no sounds yet, add relevant sounds to strengthen the state. Notice how the image makes you feel now.
3. Once you have that image on your mind, add the appropriate visual and auditory submodalities to make it even more appealing. 'Appropriate' in this sense means the submodalities that make the image more attractive to you. Also, notice the way you feel about the image. What you are doing is trying to achieve as strong a mental state as you can develop.
4. Keep the feeling building through your body by fixating the mental image to your mind.
5. As the feeling continues to build, using one of your hands, slightly pinch your thumbnail. Continue to pinch the thumbnail as the feeling builds. Note that you could build an anchor on any part of your body...it doesn't have to be your thumbnail all the time. You could use your toes or

knuckles. You also do not have to pinch…a tap, or a slight press can do the trick as well.

6. Keep on with this process until you have the most powerful feeling of confidence.
7. Break state by concentrating on something else.
8. Once you have completed the anchoring process, the next thing to do is test the anchor. By firing the anchor, you ascertain whether or not you have created a powerful anchor. To test the anchor you have built, pinch your thumbnail as you did in during the anchoring procedure. Notice what happens to you. Do you have that strong feeling of confidence? If you do, then congratulations, you have just created a confidence anchor! However, if you do not get the feeling of confidence you are looking for, start, and complete the process again. Then test. Still don't feel it? Try again. Keep trying until you develop a powerful anchor.

All of these techniques are effective in quickly boosting your self-confidence. You may choose to use any one of them or use a combination of two or more; the choice is yours really. One thing to keep in mind is that every technique must be practiced adequately and mastered for effective use. While you are unto mastering these techniques to boost your confidence, you may as well work along with the following guidelines and self-help rules for optimization of the confidence boosting process.

- Your self-talk affects you.

How do you talk to yourself? Do you engage in conversations with yourself in a respectful and courteous manner, or do you self-hate and self-criticize? You are worthy of all the respect you give to other people. Give some of that respect to yourself when you self-talk. Talking negatively or contemptuously can have a huge negative impact on your life, your relationships, and your business. You can build your confidence from within by consciously talking to yourself in a positive, empowering, loving manner. If you would be anywhere near business success, you must learn the art of positive self-talk. After all, if you don't love and believe in yourself, who will?

- Act it before you feel it

In business, time is of the essence. You need to stop waiting to feel strongly confident and start behaving and performing as though you already are. No matter how many times you practice the NLP techniques detailed out in this book, if you do not start acting confidently immediately, you may never really feel as confident as you would like. Acting confident rewires your brain to visualize and respond to experiences in a better, more positive manner. When your brain does this, you get clearer internal representations of what you see, hear, and feel, and respond to them more positively. Hence, your confidence grows.

- Vivify your purpose

If you feel unsure about your purpose, then you might struggle to achieve success. Having a defined vision is the fuel that drives you to perform. If you lack a defined "why" on a task, you are going to lack the motivation required to thrive at the task. Hence, you resort to self-doubt. You must have a clear, concise purpose of creating and developing a business venture, aside from making profits. Apart from making your entrepreneurial journey a lot less bumpy, a clear purpose helps you set better goals and aligns you with better pathways to achieve your goals. Furthermore, as you achieve success at a business that has a defined purpose, you not only accrue more profits but also feel more satisfied with yourself and your actions. This helps boost self-confidence.

- Get rid of your fear of failing

The popular misconception that entrepreneurs are totally devoid of fear cannot be further from the truth. We all have fears. Everyone does, including the most successful entrepreneurs. However, the difference between successful and unsuccessful entrepreneurs is that the successful ones have chosen to act regardless of their fears and phobias. Learn not to take failures as woes or hardships, but as opportunities to learn and develop.

- Exercise the confidence muscle

Just like a muscle that gets built through regular exercise, confidence builds through constant practice. The more you practice being confident, the stronger your feeling of confidence gets. Nobody was born with a confidence ring hanging around their neck; confidence is developed through conscious (and unconscious) actions and behaviors. Rid your life of habits, thoughts, behaviors, and emotions that deteriorate your self-image and self-confidence and imbibe those that exacerbate them. Practice being confident consciously until you begin to act confident unconsciously. In other words, "fake it till you feel it."

Chapter 4: SELF-APPRECIATION AND SELF-ESTEEM

Self-Appreciation

Self-appreciation is the opposite of self-blame. It is saying thank you to yourself for all of your efforts. Self-appreciation is about being grateful for who you are, what you are, and what resources you have – including your physical, intellectual, emotional, and social attributes. In a world that is rooted in high self-esteem, we tend to be forced to express ourselves as being better than average.

Hence, we focus on the outward and neglect the inward attributes of our being. We constantly see ourselves through the eyes of other people and judge our abilities and attributes from their perspective. Hence, our valuation of ourselves is perpetually contingent on the judgments of others. The basis of self-appreciation lies in the reverse direction – to see ourselves for who we truly are and be grateful for how we are.

Self-appreciation must not be confused for self-pity or self-indulgence; it does not mean being self-centered. When people indulge in self-pity, they tend to focus on themselves and immerse themselves in the thought that they are always on the receiving end and are suffering more than any other person in the world. By pitying yourself, you are perpetually playing victim, and as you do so, you slowly but surely lose control over yourself and your fate. Self-indulgence, on the other hand, is a way to escape reality – to focus on other than the matters that are pertinent to your life and success.

Self-appreciation is about caring for what you have, getting in tune with yourself, and having a healthy relationship with yourself. It is valuing what you have and making the best use of the resources available to you in a positive, optimistic manner. As Malcolm Forbes says, "Too many people overvalue what they are not and undervalue what they are." This statement is true to the extent that people seem to value external appreciation in an exaggerated way and use whatever appreciation they get from other people as a means of measuring their own worth and value.

You do not have to become someone or something else to appreciate yourself; you must appreciate what you already have and who you already are. However, self-appreciation does not promote self-limiting, as it is not meant to encourage you to remain the same and never progressing. You could appreciate who you already are whilst still engaging in behaviors that are aimed at making you a better person, as long as you are striving to be a better person for you, and not because you feel under pressure to be someone else. Self-appreciation is being fully aware of your strengths and weaknesses, your abilities and flaws, your beauty and faults, and appreciating yourself all the same. It is loving who you are even though you are not perfect, without pretending that you are something you are not.

When we begin to look inward for appreciation, we tend to find negatives rather than the positive things about ourselves. This bias in our thinking is at the root of the discontent in society and the main reason why we continually strive for improvement and even perfection. A way to get out of this rat race of needless self-criticism is to practice self-appreciation consciously. If self-appreciation does not come easy to you, you could take the following steps to help you out.

- Think of something you appreciate about yourself — just one thing. You could be funny, smart, intelligent, or a good leader.
- Think of one time when you noticed this quality about yourself. Notice how good feelings well up in you.
- Verbally acknowledge this quality in you by saying, "I am so." For example, "I am smart." Say this repeatedly at various speeds and different volumes.
- Savor the feeling by saying each statement for as long as ten seconds and in the best way you can.
- As you repeat the statement continuously, the feeling of self-appreciate eventually begins to slip away. Bring your focus back to the statement and arouse that feeling of appreciation again.

Notice how you feel about yourself now that you appreciate yourself more. The aim of this exercise is to rewire your brain to focus on the positives and shift attention from the negatives in yourself. Self-appreciation should not make you supercilious or narcissistic, but rather stronger and more resilient to the inevitable external forces that sometimes trigger us to focus on our negative ends. A major scourge of self-appreciation is comparison. Society, particularly in this age, has turned us into competitors, making us compare and contrast between ours and other people's skills and abilities. It is hard to love and appreciate yourself in these circumstances. However, a constant reminder to ourselves that we are neither perfect nor meant to be, and that we are unique and wonderful just the way we are can go a long way in eliciting a feeling of appreciation in ourselves.

Self-Esteem

Self-esteem is commonly defined as a person's subjection estimation of their worth or value. It is an individual's personal statement about their belief in their own worth – in simple terms, how much they love themselves. Self-esteem is one of the most commonly discussed psychosocial matter in general, as it is believed to be the underlying factor behind and a major determinant of certain outcomes, such as academic or entrepreneurial accomplishments, happiness, and criminality. In essence, it can be stated that a good level of self-esteem is a belief in oneself and one's self-worth and low self-esteem teeters on disbelief in oneself.

According to research, some 85 percent of the world's population suffer from a variety of low self-esteem. [3] That's quite a high number! It means eight to nine out of every ten persons in the world suffer this scourge. Additionally, it is proven that the victims of low self-esteem are not only uneducated or poor people of society but also some of the more learned and wealthy individuals in the world.

A normal level of self-esteem is a must-have trait for true success. Notice the use of 'normal' rather than the word 'high.' High self-esteem, like low self-esteem, has its own flaws. While low self-esteem cripples your mind and leaves you feeling depressed, too high self-esteem can have serious psychosocial effects on you – one of which is the well-known narcissistic personality disorder – and hurt your relationships. Therefore, it is best to aim at balanced self-esteem, which is neither at the extremely high nor extremely low end of the spectrum.

The entrepreneurial world is one that is constantly demanding and evolving, and as such one that requires that entrepreneurs continually show their flexibility and creativity in presenting solutions. Entrepreneurs who are more confident in themselves and their products tend to thrive in this highly competitive world, leaving those who have little faith in themselves and their products on the fringes. Belief in oneself emanates from having a decent sense of self-worth, believing that one has the right to *be*.

While self-confidence and self-esteem have been used interchangeably over time, it is worthy of note to state that they are two distinct phenomena. Self-esteem is how much you value yourself or your opinion and would often apply to all facets of your life. On the other hand, self-confidence is your belief in your abilities and applies to certain situations.

For example, an individual with good self-esteem may have low confidence in situations that involve dancing. This does not mean they have low self-esteem in general, but that particular situation is one they do not believe they have the requisite abilities to excel in. In general, a person with low self-esteem would have some or all of the following traits:

- They are very critical of themselves
- They often undervalue their positives and overvalue their negatives
- They think other people are better than them
- They tend to use negative words while talking about or describing themselves
- They blame themselves for the faults of others and are not quick to accept praise or take credit for what they have done well
- They have a hard time believing genuinely positive things people say about them

If you notice that you have exhibited any of these behaviors sometime in the past or are still doing so now, then your self-esteem level may need working on. If you do not develop your self-esteem to a good level, some of the effects your low self-esteem would have on you are:

- You may find yourself always dissatisfied about the way you are, and as a result, feel depressed, anxious, sad, or guilty.
- You may have relationship problems, as you find it difficult to express in clear terms what you want from a relationship. You could endure certain things you wouldn't have if your self-esteem were not low.
- Because of your low self-worth, you avoid trying to accomplish anything or shy away from actions that could put you in situations where you would have to relate with other people.
- You could aim for perfection as you continuously push yourself to over-achieve as atonement for lacking self-esteem.
- When you have low self-esteem, you care very little about your health and wellbeing. Hence, you may indulge in behaviors that can put your life at risk, such as excessive alcohol intake.
- Low self-esteem has been identified as a major factor contributing to the disparities in the income of

- entrepreneurs undertaking same or similar business ventures.
- If you are considering starting your own business or have a business idea you wish to inculcate into your current enterprise, low self-esteem might prevent you from pursuing the idea, and instead encourage you to stay put in your comfort zone. People with good self-esteem are much more likely to pursue a business idea that people who have low self-esteem.
- People with low self-esteem are not risk takers. As a result, they are slow in progressing business-wise.

Needless to say, low self-esteem is an enterprise killer and a dream crusher. If you are unfortunately caught up in its grasp, don't fret, NLP has got you covered. Just as it does for self-confidence, NLP has several techniques that are designed to raise your self-esteem to a level you can be happy about. There are many NLP techniques that have been designed to help give you a self-esteem boost. They include the ten-step self-esteem enhancer, the seven-step self-esteem booster, the six-step reframing technique, NLP belief creator technique, and NLP belief disintegrator technique. We will now look into these techniques one after another.

NLP Ten-Step Self-Esteem Enhancer

The ten-step self-esteem enhancer is a 10-step exercise founded on NLP principles and developed to create positive feelings within you that can help you ride smoothly through the day. It is best utilized up your *ante* when your self-esteem and self-confidence levels are low. It is recommended that you run this exercise on a daily schedule – for example, you could run through it twice a day in the morning before work and at night before bed. You could also practice it at any point during the day that you feel low in self-esteem or self-confidence. One thing to remember as you perform this exercise is that it is not a magic wand that can recharge your self-esteem instantly; instead, it is a tool that only gets better through constant use. Let us now run through the exercise.

1. Relax your body, close your eyes, and take deep breaths in and out. Think of a person who you know truly cares about you. Create a mental picture of this person and focus on what makes them beautiful to look at.
2. Imagine that you are sitting behind a desk. With a beautifully designed pen and a finely crafted hardcover book, begin to write your autobiography. Write out all of your experiences from the day you discovered you're being to the present day and the possible future. As you are writing, imagine that that person that loves you is

standing close, separated from you by a glass barrier, and watching you as you write.

3. As you picture this person, start to write about them in your autobiography. Write down all their good features and qualities, as well as all of the experiences you have shared with them. Notice how you feel about this person in general, about their presence in your life, and about the fact that they genuinely love you.

4. As you continue to write and feel, this person is now smiling at you from behind the glass barrier. Their smile is radiant and true, and it leaves you feeling good. Now, dissociate into two. With a part of you still seated at the desk, float the other part to where this person is standing and stand next to them. Now both of you are watching the other version of you that is still writing your autobiography.

5. Look at how beautifully you are seated behind the desk and how well you are writing. Notice how you see yourself from this perspective. Ask yourself, "What do I like about this person I'm watching? What am I capable of doing? What abilities do I possess?"

6. Now step inside the loving person you have been standing next to and begin to see through their eyes. Try to see as they would see, hear as they would hear, and feel as they would feel about you. You and this person are now one. You are now this person who truly loves and adores you.

7. As you see, hear, and feel from this loving person's perspective, ask yourself, "What does this loving, wonderful person think of me? How do they feel about me? What do they think I'm capable of doing?" As you continue to ponder over these questions, try as much as you can not to utter the first answers that come to you; take them as they come.
8. Slowly detach yourself from this person, and as you do so, keep the answers you just got from the questions you asked earlier. Keep them with you, as if they are your own views. Now transfer these feelings to the "you" behind the desk who is still writing. On doing so, so, write about the feelings you now have about yourself in your autobiography. Write about how your new views about yourself are different from the old views you used to have.
9. At this point, begin to write about your future in a positive light. Write about how the feelings you now have about yourself have changed your life for the better. Answer questions such as, "How do I feel about myself now? How has my future changed with the emergence of these new feelings? How much more self-esteem and self-confidence do I now possess? What challenges am I now willing to undertake? What are the positives in this new me that can make me succeed at whatever I want to do?" Make sure to provide an adequate answer to each question proceeding to the next. Commit to inculcating

these new feelings you have about yourself into everything you do.

10. Finish writing your autobiography, and as you round up, imagine that the lights in the room have begun to dim slowly. As the lights slowly go out, gradually return to the present reality. Feel the new positive energy that now runs through your entire body as you now love and value yourself more.

Self-esteem is quite simply a necessity you cannot do without if your aim is business and professional success. It is the foundation upon which you must base your efforts and attempts to create something different. If for any reason this foundation is weak, then you need to deal with the rot with the NLP techniques I have highlighted above. It is important that you fix any underlying fear and esteem issues before you can approach success with assured steps.

NLP Seven-Step Self-Esteem Booster

Another vital NLP technique routinely used to improve self-esteem is the NLP seven-step self-esteem booster. This technique is useful for when you need a boost in self-esteem and self-confidence either to carry out a task or simply to feel good about yourself. You could also use this technique to heal from past experiences that have dealt with your self-esteem a significant blow. Quite literally, the seven-step self-esteem booster is a dose of self-esteem to use whenever you need it. So let's get to it. Try out the following steps to give yourself a surge in self-esteem:

1. Be in the know of your state of mind throughout the day. This is the first step of the process. You must ensure to stay vigilant of how you feel about yourself in every moment of the day. Whenever you become aware that you are getting low on self-esteem or lacking in self-confidence, give yourself a break from whatever it is you are doing and run through the rest of this exercise.

2. Carry out a self-evaluation. When you find out that you are not feeling your best, you would need to carry out a self-assessment to ascertain your exact state of mind. To do this, ask yourself these questions:

- What is the specific problem I'm facing right now?
- How do I feel about this problem?
- Why do I feel the way I do about this problem?
- What is my internal focusing mechanism like? How is my mind focusing on things?
- How am I reacting to things externally?
- Why do I react to things this way?
- How do I self-talk? Am I talking to myself the appropriate way?
- What is my tone of voice like when I'm talking to myself?
- In what ways am I moving my body?
- Why do I move my body in this manner?
- How is my breathing and body posture?

- What are my beliefs about myself?
- How is my mind interpreting the challenges I'm experiencing?
- What assertions about my challenging am I making?
- Have I discovered a new thing about myself that I didn't know before now?
- What factors are preventing me from feeling good in these circumstances?

The goal of this self-assessment is to find out the factors that are stopping you from feeling good in this particular situation. By answering these questions, you gain clarity about why you are presently not feeling your best. Some of these questions require significant reasoning to get answered, so, endeavor to put in the mental work to answer them as objectively and prudently as you can. The more accurately and clearly you can answer these questions, the more confidence you will have that you can get up on top of your present situation.

3. Create a mental picture of a future version of you basking in a good level of self-esteem. This version of you should feel very confident, strong-minded, and capable of handling any task. This future version of you should be able to take care of your present situation with ease. Make sure this future you are not in the distant future but in the near future.

4. Evaluate your future self. Visualize and assess how your future self is handling things and how their methods of

taking care of situations are different from yours. Pay special attention to the confidence with which they're handlings things, and evaluate how they are able to run their affairs so smoothly by asking these questions:

- How is my future self-feeling?
- Why do they feel this way?
- How does their mind focus on things internally?
- How does their mind focus on things externally?
- Why do they focus on things the way they do?
- What tone of voice do they use while engaging in self-talk?
- What are the exact words they use?
- What are their beliefs about themselves?
- How do they move?
- How is their breathing and body posture?
- How do they interpret the events happening around them?
- What does your future self think of their 'present' circumstances?
- How are they relating to other people?
- Are they in a good mood and at peace with themselves?
- How have they attained this level of excitement and happiness? What are the things they had to do to get to this state?

The purpose of these questions is to find out the resources and behaviors are necessary to attain the level of self-esteem and confidence you need at present. The answer to these questions should challenge you to find the intellectual and emotional understanding of what it takes to get the level of selfoesteem you want.

5. Create a picture of your present self (who has low self-esteem) side-by-side with your future self (who is brimming with self-esteem and confidence). Make the picture as clear as possible, and a true representation of both your present situation and your future expectation. Assess the picture and pick out the telling differences between your present and future self. Now separate the picture into two – your present self and future self. Insert the picture of your present self in a glass bubble and that of your future self in an identical glass bubble.

6. Reach for the glass bubble containing the image of your future self and shrink it. Shrink it more and more, until it becomes the size of a bean. Then, make it larger and larger until it reaches your own body size. Continue to shrink and expand the image and as you do that, feel the self-esteem and confidence of your future self crawl through your body and change your present emotional reality. While you are at this, say these to yourself:

- I am feeling good about myself.
- I have confidence in myself and my abilities.
- I am empowered to deal with any challenge that stands in my way.

Now, reach for the glass bubble containing the image of your present self and put it in front of that containing your future self. Then, take the glass bubble containing the picture of your present self and make it bigger and bigger until it reaches life size. Now, poke a hole in the bubble and watch it deflate. As this bubble deflates and shrinks, watch the glass bubble of your future self come to the forefront and overshadow that of your present self completely. Feel the positive energy that rushes through your body as you continue to do this, and watch it transform your present situation.

Again, affirm these statements to yourself:

- I am feeling good about myself.
- I have confidence in myself and my abilities.
- I am empowered to deal with any challenge that stands in my way.

Clone the glass bubble containing the image of your future self to produce many identical glass bubbles. Now, stack them on top of one another. Then, pick up the glass bubbles and insert them into your timeline, past and present. Now you have succeeded in populating your past and present with positive emotions. As you wake up every day of your life, you simply absorb the positive energy you have placed already in it. This should give you the self-esteem you need to get through any day.

The Six-Step Reframing Technique

A third NLP technique we're going to look into and apply to boost our self-esteem is the six-step reframing technique. The six-step reframing technique is used to bring about behavioral change. It can be used to kill a bad behavior or habit and replace it with a better one. The concept of reframing is based on the notion that our mind, just like our body, is divided into different parts. These parts of the mind are responsible for the actions we take. So, with reframing, you can train a part of the mind responsible for a bad action, behavior, or habit to start acting in a certain way. Individuals with low self-esteem have a bad habit of downplaying their abilities and exaggerating their flaws. Reframing can be used to replace this undesirable habit with a positive one. The six steps of NLP reframing are as follows:

Step 1: Identify what you want to change

As a first step, you must identify clearly the behavior, attitude, habit, or response you find undesirable and which you want to change. For example, you may want to change the negative manner in which you treat yourself.

Step 2: Communicate with the troubling part

Try to establish communication with the part of your mind responsible for the troubling behavior or response. Ask the part if it would like to engage in a conscious discussion with you. Note that this communication may be a picture, a voice, or a feeling in your mind. If you do receive a response from the part, thank it for responding. It is important to appreciate a response from the part, as it may already feel bad for having been alienated by you.

Step 3: Ascertain the positive intention

One of the basic presuppositions of NLP is that behind every behavior lies a positive intention. You must find the positive intention-behavior behind this undesirable behavior of yours. Ask the part, "What is it that you want? What is the positive intention behind this behavior you are exhibiting?" The purpose of these questions is to discern between the behavior, the intention behind it, and the way your mind is going about fulfilling the intention.

It is possible, even as humans, for our good intentions to get misconstrued by a person we are trying to help. They might even get angry at us, because they interpreted our actions wrongly. In such situations as this, we may not be willing to render assistance to that person a second time. This is similar to how our unconscious mind works. It is sincerely doing its best to fulfill positive intentions for our own good, but sometimes we misinterpret what it is attempting to do, and even get angry at it for its responses. Just as you cannot be motivated to wake up early by someone who constantly tells you what a lazy person you are for waking up so late, you cannot change an undesirable behavior by shaming your mind. You need to build rapport with your mind to motivate it to change

Step 4: Create other ways

Once you know the positive intention behind your bad behavior, ask the creative part of your mind to create 3 other ways to go about fulfilling the intention.

Step 5: Evaluate the alternatives

Ask the part to assess the alternative options to see if it agrees with them. Find out whether these other ways of fulfilling the positive intention would be as good as or better than the one that created the undesirable behavior in the first place. The part must be willing to try out these new alternative pathways. Do not attempt to push the troubling part into accepting and trying these new options out. You must instead negotiate with it so that it willingly accepts to give them a go. If you find that the part does not approve of the new options, go back to step 4 and create new alternatives.

Step 6: Carry out an ecology check

Once you have successfully convinced the part to try out new alternatives to fulfilling an intention, carry out an ecology check to determine if the new behavior we are trying to adopt will be beneficial to us and the people around us. If your new behavior is thinking positively about yourself and your abilities, check to ensure that it does not, for example, make you start to feel or act over-confident or arrogant. If an ecology check comes out negative for a certain behavior, go back to step 2 and complete the entire reframing process from there.

NLP Belief Disintegrator Technique

This technique is used to destroy or annul negative or limiting beliefs, such as a belief that you don't have what it takes to lead. You may also start this exercise with a minor belief before moving on to a major one. The steps in this process are as follows:

1. Think of a thing you truly don't believe. You don't need to think of anything extraordinary; think of something simple, such as the belief that air is blue. As you think of this belief, notice that there is something related to it. For example, you can tell that the mental image of this belief is located somewhere in space. Is it located to the left or right? How far away is it positioned? Are there sounds attached to the image of this belief? When you have ascertained the position of this image, label it 'position A'. Now break state – think of something different, such as the last time it rained.

2. Now think of a thing you have no idea whether it is true or false, something you may not really care about at all. For example, think of whether the egg came before the chicken or the chicken came before the egg, or any other thing you are unsure about. As you think of this, notice that there is something attached to this thought as well. Where in space is the thought located? Is it located to the left or right? How far away is it positioned? When you

have ascertained the position of this image, label it 'position B'.

3. Now you have two positions in your mind. Think of the new belief you want to generate and note where its image is positioned. Now move this image first to position B, and then to position A. You may experience certain problems in this step. Some of these are:

   a. The image may not move from one side to the other, for example, from right to left. You can solve this problem in three steps:
      i. Move the image from where it is – left side, for example – to the center.
      ii. Move it far away into the distance until it almost vanishes.
      iii. Move it towards yourself and slide it onto the other side – right side, for example.
   b. The image may go back to its original position. You can solve this by:
      i. Nailing the image in place
      ii. Locking it in place
      iii. Swishing (swiiiiiiishhhhh) to secure it in the position of your choice

4. When the image is finally in the appropriate position, make sure it has the same size as the original image. Break state – think of something different. Think of the belief you just created. How does it feel now? Is it still in

position A? Does your mind tell you that the belief is true? If the answers to these questions are negative, go back and retake the steps. Once you have successfully destroyed a negative belief, you can then use the NLP belief creator technique to create a new, positive belief.

NLP Belief Creator Technique

The belief creator technique is the direct opposite of the belief disintegrator technique. If you are struggling with self-doubt and low self-esteem, the NLP belief creator can help you generate new beliefs about yourself so you can feel your best always. For example, you can create a belief that you have the ability to lead. Even if it isn't true, it is still better to hold on to this belief that the opposite belief. Before you start out on creating a new belief, you must erase any trace of doubt from your mind, to maximize the outcome of this exercise. It is recommended that you attempt this exercise several times with a minor belief before trying with a major, life-changing belief. Here are the steps to create a brand-new belief:

1) Think of a thing you truly believe. You don't need to think of anything extraordinary; a simple belief that you can breathe, eat, or sleep will do. As you think of this belief, notice that there is something related to it. For example, you can tell that the mental image of this belief is located somewhere in space. Is it located to the left or right? How far away is it positioned? Are there sounds attached to the

image of this belief? When you have ascertained the position of this image, label it 'position A'. Now break state – think of something different, such as the last time it rained.

2) Now think of a thing you have no idea whether it is true or false, something you may not really care about at all. For example, think of whether the egg came before the chicken or the chicken came before the egg, or any other thing you are unsure about. As you think of this, notice that there is something attached to this thought as well. Where in space is the thought located? Is it located to the left or right? How far away is it positioned? When you have ascertained the position of this image, label it 'position B'.

3) Now you have two positions in your mind. Think of the new belief you want to generate and note where its image is positioned. Now move this image first to position B, and then to position A. You may experience certain problems in this step. Some of these are:

   a. The image may not move from one side to the other, for example, from right to left. You can solve this problem in three steps:

   i. Move the image from where it is – left side, for example – to the center.

   ii. Move it far away into the distance until it almost vanishes.

iii. Move it towards yourself and slide it onto the other side – right side, for example.
    b. The image may go back to its original position. You can solve this by:
        i. Nailing the image in place
        ii. Locking it in place
        iii. Swishing (swiiiiiiishhhhh) to secure it in the position of your choice

When the image is finally in the appropriate position, make sure it has the same size as the original image.

4) Break state – think of something different. Think of the belief you just created. How does it feel now? Is it still in position A? Does your mind tell you that the belief is true? If the answers to these questions are negative, go back and retake the steps.

Chapter 5: PRODUCTIVITY AND TIME MANAGEMENT

Time is perhaps the most valuable resource available to an entrepreneur or business owner. Indeed, the value of time is perceptible and can be appreciated in the popular phrase "time is money." After all, we have only 24 hours in a day to do all that we have to do. For entrepreneurs, especially those who have reached quite a remarkable stage in their business, the length of the day seems increasingly shorter; it is common to see these entrepreneurs struggle with managing time effectively to carry out their daily business activities.

As a business owner, you are your own boss. While this may sound exhilarating, it also means that you have to shoulder the brunt of the responsibilities at the workplace. You have to create and attend meetings, make marketing plans, create an effective budget, set up devices to monitor your sales, engage in networking, and so on. Honestly, all of these tasks could be quite daunting. To come anywhere close to achieving success in your business, you need to manage resources appropriately, especially the resource of time. Since time is not negotiable and cannot be purchased at will, optimizing every passing second of the day is key to achieving success. This especially applies to entrepreneurs who have just started their business or those who are looking to scale their business up. However, notwithstanding your business level or growth, you'd always need to manage your time as efficiently as possible.

It may be impossible or unthinkable to create time, but it is possible to create and develop attitudes that are geared toward ensuring that you make the best use of your time. Perhaps this metaphorical anecdote will help you to understand this point better: A professor once held an empty glass jar and began to fill it with golf balls. He filled the jar to the brim with golf balls, and then asked his students, "Is the jar full?" They responded, "Yes," in unison. Then, the professor picked up small stones and began to throw them into the spaces between the golf balls. When the jar seemed full and could no longer take more stones, he asked his students again if the jar was full, and again they answered in the affirmative. The professor then started to fill the spaces between the golf balls and stones with sand. When the jar could no longer take in more sand, he asked the students for the third time if the jar was full. The students, now obviously confused as to what to answer, kept quiet. The professor then got hold of a water bottle, uncovered it, and started to pour its content into the jar. Again, he filled the jar to the brim.

The lesson to learn in this short story is that time is like the professor's empty jar, containing nothing. The jar represents the total time you have per day – 24 hours. The contents of the jar represent the activities you may spend your time on during the day. The golf balls represent the most important activities you may engage in, the ones that move you towards achieving your goals. They are the big hitters, they have the greatest impact on your set goals and objectives and rank first on your list of priorities. The stones are activities that are both urgent and important, but that does not impact your goals significantly. If left unchecked, these activities can easily take up all of your days, leaving you with no time left to spend on your goals. The sand is urgent activities that are not very important. You can leave these tasks for after you are done with your urgent and important tasks. The water represents the fact that you must reserve time to spend with family and friends. This should be time to unwind, relax, and reflect on everything you have done so far.

In order to maximize our time and get more done, we must start to plan our activities as and when we mean to do them. By planning, we can stack up activities in the future, so we take them on one after another as time goes on. NLP can help you plan better by making you work your plan from the future to the present. The NLP technique that helps you achieve this is called the timeline therapy. NLP Timeline therapy allows us to start our journey from the future so that we can assume better internal states while we work back to the present. When in the present, we can also work our plan forward, so as to ensure its feasibility. A major advantage of working from the future is that it allows us to be motivated enough to see the plan through to the end, which we are less likely to do when we begin from the present. So how exactly do we start to work from the future? The following exercise should show us how:

1. Sit in a comfortable place. Imagine that the future is in front of you and that it is a colorful triangle that keeps expanding. Imagine that your past is a triangle, positioned behind you. For the next few minutes, think of how you want your future to be and what you would be required to do to achieve that future.
2. Now place yourself in that future and imagine that you are now living the life that you want. Notice what you can see, hear, and feel at that moment. Integrate yourself completely into that mental picture and enjoy every moment of the future.
3. Use the double dissociation technique to dissociate from the "you" in the future. Observe the version of yourself in the future and mention three things that have helped you get there.
4. Begin to move towards to present, but don't arrive at the present just yet. Ask yourself what you did to master the three things you did that took you to that future.
5. Now come to the present. Ask yourself what you can start doing now to develop and master the three factors that can take you to the future you want.
6. Imagine that you have already developed and mastered the three factors required to give you the future you want

and imagine all the hurdles and challenges you had to go through to arrive at mastering them.

7. What advice can you take from your future self? See if the version of you that has conquered the present and moved to the future has any vital advice to offer you.
8. Now start from the present and move towards the future, taking with you all of the advice you just garnered from your future self.
9. Lastly, show appreciation by thanking yourself for making time to plan your future.

Sometimes, as an entrepreneur, we get caught in a web of options, many different pathways we can pick and choose from – such as choosing from a number of marketing ideas. This situation can be an effective time waster, as time spent on deliberating and choosing from the multitude of options could be spent on other important things. There is an NLP technique that can help you decide and choose faster in situations such as this, thereby saving you valuable time. This technique is known as the NLP visual squash and can be incredibly helpful.

NLP Visual Squash Technique

The visual squash technique is a simple yet effective NLP technique useful in resolving an internal crisis, such as an inability to make up your mind about something. Here are the steps in the technique:

1. You are going to have to trim your options down to just two or take all of the options two at a time for this exercise.
2. Create a mental picture of each of the two contrasting options and hold each picture in hand.
3. Feel the image in each hand and try to find out the positive intention it is trying to fulfill. What are the options trying to do for you? Create a mental picture of each of the intentions behind the two options. Now replace the pictures you have in each hand with the new mental pictures of intentions you just created.
4. Create a mental picture of the combination of all of the positive intentions of the two original options. Imagine this mental picture hovering over both your hands.
5. With a clapping motion, add the contents of your left hand with those of your right hand, and merge (or squash) them with the mental picture hovering over your hands.
6. When you are ready, place the palms of your hands on your chest and let your body absorb the third mental picture.
7. When you feel you have experienced the change you are looking for, break state, and return to the present moment. You should now have one unmistakable option to deal with.

8. If you have another set of two options, repeat the exercise for them, and when you have one option at the end of the process, repeat the exercise for the final options to arrive at only one.

Everyone has a limited supply of time, energy, and focus. It is relatively easy to lose time, get low on energy, and have depleted focus; so it's best to use them prudently. This is why planning is so invaluable. It allows you to be aware of and make the best use of your resources. Here are some tips for managing your time, energy, and focus on improved productivity:

- Set priorities and handle your top priority tasks first. Remember the golf balls metaphor – know the activities that get you closer to your goals and dedicate most of your time to carrying them out.
- Engage in activities that can increase your energy and focus, such as exercise, meditation, and rest. It is useless spending time on activities if you don't have enough energy or attention to see them through. Aim not only to maximize your time but also to improve the quality of the time you spend on tasks.
- To make the best use of your time, you must be able to discern between the various times of the day. There are times when we are energetic and can carry out the most difficult tasks of the day, there are times when it is best to handle only the less physically demanding activities, and

there are other times when it is best to rest. You must know what time is best for what and act accordingly.

- Start early and finish early. The most productive times of the day span from early in the morning to dusk. Many of the exceptional entrepreneurs of the world have emphasized the need to start the day early and finish in time for a good, long sleep. Make this a habit, and you'll notice a surge in your productivity.
- One of the best qualities of successful entrepreneurs is they know when to outsource and delegate. Even if within your capabilities, you must not complete all available tasks; this eats your time away considerably. It is OK to delegate specific tasks to people who have the abilities to handle them and can do so at rates affordable by you.

Chapter 6: COMMUNICATION

Communication is, quite simply, interacting with yourself or other people. Effective communication is vital for gaining insight into other people's circumstances and can help to know the "why" behind their actions, behaviors, or attitudes. In the world of business, effective communication is required between an organization and its clients to make sales; this is external communication. The organization would also have to have an effective communication strategy in place between the individuals at the helm and other staff; this is known as internal communication. For a business to thrive and achieve high levels of success, it has to put in place mechanisms that ensure that both external and internal communication needs are met. Therefore, there is always a need to strive for better communication, as it not only leads to more customer participation but also brings about the rapport between members of staff, hence improving productivity.

Communication can be verbal as well as nonverbal, and a good grasp of both can go a long way to motivate employees, convince clients, and help make sales. The most important communication skills for an entrepreneur who wishes to succeed in the business world include:

- Conversing

Engaging in a conversation is one of the simplest forms of communication and one we all do on a daily basis – perhaps this accounts for why the art of conversing has been largely underestimated. A simple yet effective conversation with an employee can help build rapport and get you in the know of hitherto hidden issues. Even a seemingly innocent conversation with a stranger can turn into an opportunity to make sales. As an entrepreneur, you must learn to converse in a friendly and calm manner.

- Body language

A large part of our daily communication is nonverbal. Therefore, you must get a grip on your body presentation. The posture you assume in a conversation matters a lot. Sit or stand straight up; keep your shoulders back and relaxed; keep your head high and look the person you're conversing with straight in the eye. Your body language decides to a great extent whether you would be in command of a room or be just another occupant.

- Writing

If you are going to make headway in business, you will need to possess a certain level of writing skill. You don't have to be an expert with a pen, but you do need to be direct and concise when transferring words to paper.

- Presentation skills

You can't escape having to present your ideas, business reports, innovation, or business pitch to a group of people within or outside your organization from time to time. The way you present has a direct impact on how people would react to your presentation. You must be concise, clear, confident, and poised during presentations.

- Negotiation skills

Everything in business is based on negotiation – getting a deal from investors, making sales, and even paying employees. As so much depends on negotiation, the more you hone your negotiation skills, the better you would be at making deals that are favorable to you.

- Mediation skills

Although you may not do much mediating as an entrepreneur, there are times when you need to step up and mediate between conflicting parties. It may be employees or co-investors who can't agree on something; your mediating skills can be applied to extinguish any spark before it becomes a wildfire.

- Debating

There is a difference between debating and arguing; the former requires that you respectfully bring out your opinions and ideas as opposed to other people's opinions. You may need to convince investors, employees, or cofounders that your idea works best in a particular situation; the way you handle the situation will determine what they make of your viewpoints.

- Cross-platform messaging

There are more communication platforms now than ever, ranging from SMS, emails and phone calls to instant messages and video calls. You must learn to use the appropriate communication platform to handle your messaging tasks at all times.

- Listening

Listening is one of the most vital communication skills. Active and effective listening can enhance your leadership, debating, mediation, negotiation, and conversing skills.

Mastery of all of these skills can make you a better entrepreneur and a better, more thoughtful individual overall. As with any skill, you need to practice these skills consistently until they become part of you. When you fail to invest your time into becoming a better communicator, you fall into the pool of the many entrepreneurs whose businesses are failing due to lack of proper communication skills. Here are some effects of poor communication on the business of an entrepreneur:

- Low morale at the workplace: When there is poor communication between those at the headship of an organization and the ground staff, what follows is a general drop in morale. Reduced morale affects productivity negatively, and the situation goes through a downward spiral of negativity and dissatisfaction after that.

- High employee turnover: One of the manifestations of poor communication in the workplace is an increase in employee turnover. It is logical for employees to seek work elsewhere if they feel dissatisfied with the treatment they are receiving at their current job. High turnover rates are injurious to the finances of a company, as it costs money to replace employees continuously.
- Poor customer service: Poor communication affects customer service in two ways: One, the employees may not have adequate instruction as to the tenets of customer relations, and hence lack the knowledge to attend to customers properly. Two, customers may perceive the low morale at the organization and therefore, have an unpleasant buying experience.
- Health issues may begin to develop: Poor communication can cause dissatisfaction among workers. If an individual is left with virtually no way to de-stress, stress can accumulate quickly and lead to the development of chronic mental and physical health problems.
- Dissatisfaction among customers: It is a no-brainer that when morale is low, and customer service is poor, customers may begin to feel uneasy patronizing your

company. Hence, they soon take their business dealings elsewhere. This costs you money, lots of it.

- Poor communication breeds arguments: With personnel uncertain about their roles or not communicating effectively with one another about what needs to be done and how it has to be done, it is likely for them to be caught up in destructive arguments. Once this becomes the order of the day, it becomes difficult to move the company forward.

Poor communication can quickly erode the personnel and financial structure of a business. For a business to thrive and achieve its set goals and objectives, especially in this highly competitive era, there has to be in place an effective system of communication that not only improves communication between the owners of an enterprise and employees but also helps the employees to communicate better among themselves. There are several methods of improving communication in NLP. Of these methods, creating rapport, improving your tone of voice, and using eye accessing cues are the three most commonly used to attain positive results. These methods will now be discussed further.

Creating and Building Rapport

Building rapport with clients, team members, and employees is an important step in learning to communicate better with them. When you are in rapport with an individual, the contrasts between you and the person are minimized while your similarities are emphasized. Rapport allows you to be in sync with a person you are communicating with and allows the conversation to flow smoothly. Rapport can happen naturally between people over time, as we tend to like people who are like us. However, it is also possible to consciously and deliberately build rapport with someone in a bid to communicate better with them. There are two common ways of building rapport with someone; matching & mirroring and matching a person's representational state.

i. Matching and Mirroring

Matching and mirroring are one of the most effective ways of building rapport with a person. It is done subtly, in a way that doesn't seem like you are mimicking or copying the person, as these might have the opposite effect on the person. While mirroring a person, you essentially try to reflect the person's body language back to them in a manner that seems natural and comfortable for the person. Generally, the purpose of matching and mirroring is to build rapport with a person without their noticing what you are doing. You can mirror a person physically or verbally to achieve positive outcomes.

a. Physical Mirroring

In physical mirroring, you mirror a person's body language (e.g. tilting of the head, crossing of the arms or legs), posture (slumping or in an upright position, facing forwards or facing sideways), gestures (like the person's hand gestures while talking), breathing (slow or quick), and voice (the person's tone of voice, the speed of their speech, their volume and pitch). All of this is done in a very subtle manner. For example, if a person you're communicating with sits and crosses their left leg over their right leg, you can mirror that by crossing your right leg over your left leg, as though the person were looking into a mirror.

    b. Verbal Mirroring

Verbal mirroring can be done by mirroring a person's tone of voice as well as their pitch and the speech of their speech. You could make this process even more effective by repeating the person's last few spoken words in your next sentence.

    ii.   Matching the Other Person's Representational State

A person's representational system is exposed by words that have a big I pact on what they are talking about. People who are visually oriented tend to react best to the way things look; auditory oriented people respond best to the way things sound, and kinesthetic people respond best to the way things feel. This is so because the way we express ourselves will always be biased towards the sensory modality we prefer (visual, auditory, kinesthetic, olfactory, and gustatory). Sometimes a person may mix more than one modality, but the person's preferred modality will have the biggest impact on the way the person expresses themselves.

When you sync your words to reflect the preferred sensory modality of a person you're communicating with, you would be able to build rapport more easily and faster than when you mismatch modalities. For example, when a person says, "I don't feel this thing is right," it is evident that this person favors the kinesthetic sensory modality. You could then respond by saying, "I feel the same too," using the kinesthetic modality. This is a good way to build rapport. If you wish to master this art, you must cast aside your own sensory preferences and deliberately evaluate people's words to find the sensory modalities they prefer.

- Visual Language

A person who favors the visual sensory modality often uses words such as "see, vision, envision, look, appear, picture, and show" to convey their messages. For example, a person may say:

"I don't see this plan coming along."

"This method appears to be working well."

"The future looks bright."

- Auditory Language

An individual who prefers the auditory sensory modality uses words that reflect the hearing sensation, such as sound, hear, say, and listen, to express themselves. They may say, for example:

"That sounds like a good idea."

"I paid attention to and listen carefully to your speech."

"I hear you."

- Kinesthetic Language

People who prefer the kinesthetic sensory modality use words such as feel, grasp, let go and hold on to express themselves. Here are some examples:

"I don't feel the need to let go of the methods we currently have on the ground."

"I'm struggling to grasp the lesson in his anecdote."

"I want to hold on to my practices for now."

You can always tweak your statements to reflect a person's preferred sensory modality to connect with the person on a deeper level and build a strong rapport. Again it must be emphasized that you should know your own sensory preferences and make appropriate adjustments so that you do not crossmatch your own preferences on another person's. In case you do not know your preferred representational system yet, you can simply think of something and evaluate your reaction to it. For example, if you think of the woods and you begin the recollect images of the woods as well as everything one might find in the woods, you can be sure that you are a visually oriented person. If you don't really care how the woods look but are rather paying attention to the sounds therein, then you are an auditory oriented person. If you think of the woods and you begin to feel the sensations of walking in the woods, then you have the kinesthetic sensory modality as you dominant or preferred representational system.

Using Eye Accessing Cues

In NLP, eye accessing cues represent movements of the eyes in certain directions that indicate visual, auditory, or kinesthetic reasoning. People tend to move their eyes in various directions while talking, and, according to NLP, we can deduce what representational system the person is thinking in by carefully observing their eye movements. Just as you would use a torch to point in various directions when looking for something within your home, we use our eyes to "look" inside our minds for information we have stowed away. Depending on where the information is stored, we can use the visual, auditory, or kinesthetic torch you look into our minds. You may have found the accessing cues out for yourself when you asked people questions, and they moved their eyes in a certain direction. There are six directions in which the eyes may turn while trying to secure information. They are top right (for visual remembered images), middle right (audio remembered images), bottom right (during self-talk or while making calculations), top left (visual constructed images), middle left (audio constructed images), and bottom left (tactile images) (see figure 6.1).

Figure 6.1: Eye accessing cues

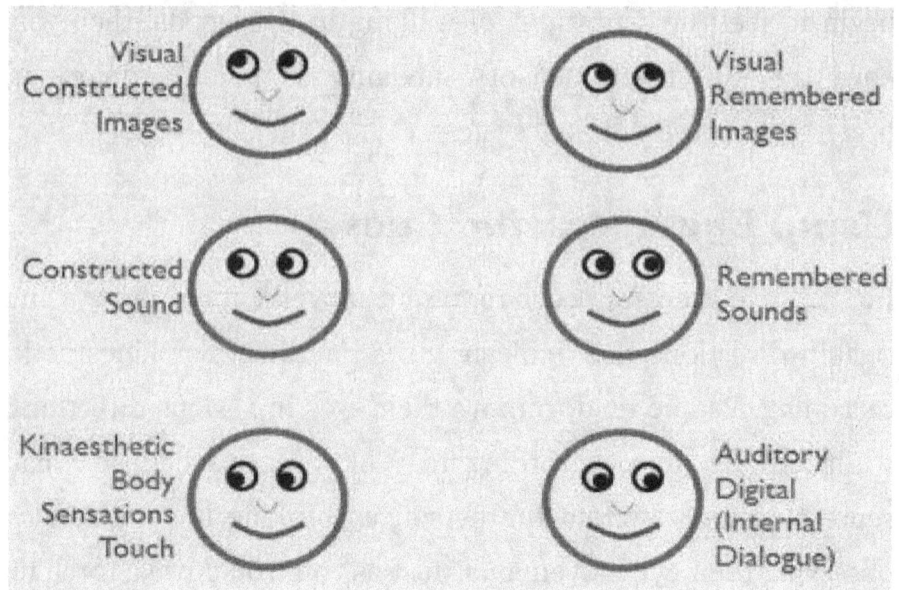

You need to keep this image in your head use it when you are in a conversation with someone. A good way to remember this image is to put yourself in the shoes of the observed person. When you look to the top right, you are trying to remember visual images because "remember" and "right" both begin with an "r." For example, if someone were to ask where you live, your eyes should move to the top right, because you are trying to remember the picture of the place you are living in. However, if you are asked to talk about your dream house, your eyes would probably look to the top left, because you are trying to construct images of your dream house.

In the same vein, if you're asked what your best friend's voice is like, you would look to the middle right as you are attempting to remember your best friend's voice. If you are asked how you would like your dream woman to sound, then your eyes would move to the middle left because you are trying to construct a voice you probably have never heard before. If you are asked how your breakfast tasted, you will look to the bottom left as you would be attempting to bring the taste back to the surface. When you understand what all of the eye movements stand for, you can then start to employ it in your day to day conversations. Here are some tips to help you through:

- Although the eye movements, as described above hold true for most people, it is worthy to note that these movements are completely revered in some individuals. For example, in these people, the top right may indicate visual constructed images and top left for visual remembered images, and so forth. This reversal is usually found in left-handed individuals, though not all left-handed people are like this. So, before you set out to use eye accessing cues in an individual, first ask that individual a question to which you already know the answer. Use the result you obtain from that test question to form your conclusions about that person's eye movements.
- It is possible that a person you are conversing with answers to your questions without moving their eyes to either side and keeping them fixed in the middle. This usually happens when the answer to a question lies in the person's short-term memory, and they don't need to

think much before providing it; for example, "How old are you?"

- You must be as concise and straightforward as possible while searching for eye accessing cues. Avoid questions that may trigger extra and unnecessary thought patterns in people. Keep the questions straightforward and clean. For example, if you want to know the color of a person's apron, simply ask, "What color is your apron?" This would elicit a simple visual response. But, if you say, "Can you tell me what color your apron is?" You may not get a straight visual response, because the question "Can I?" may trigger self-talk within the person and cause them to look to the bottom right. This might be confusing.

A. Improving your Tone of Voice

Your tone of voice has a direct effect on your message and how people respond to it. When you increase your tone of voice, you sound better, and people are more willing to respond to you in a positive way. There are two common methods of carrying out this exercise. As with all exercises, you must practice these exercises regularly to master them and improve your tone of voice significantly fully.

Exercise 1

- With your preferred hand, press on your nose and say the word "nose."

- Continue to say the word until you feel that your nose is vibrating.
- Repeat this exercise with your throat while saying the word "throat."
- Then repeat the exercise on your chest while saying the word "chest."
- Notice the contrast between the sounds of the different words.

Exercise 2

- Take a deep breath in.
- Open your mouth wide and say the letter "r" with a high tone. Prolong the pronunciation while reducing your tone gradually until you run out of breath.
- Do this ten more times.
- Again take a deep breath in.
- Say "ou" (you without the letter y) with a low pitch. Prolong it while increasing your tone of voice gradually until you can no longer increase your tone any further.
- Do this ten more times.

Chapter 7: NEGOTIATION AND SALES

In business, the most important thing is making sales. But sometimes it is also the hardest thing to do, due to the myriad of reasons why customers just won't buy our products and services. It could be that they don't need the product at the time of our advertising it, they may find that the price is too high for the value of the product, or the product may simply not be right for them. Whatever may be their reason, it is clear that sometimes selling a product or service in exchange for money is a Herculean task. But there are always ways around things with NLP. In NLP, a lot of emphases is put on one's state of mind, as it has the potential to impact on a person's outlook and behavior, and hence, the response one gets from customers. So many of us had bought products in the past which, when we got home and evaluated, we decided were not good value for our money and that we didn't really need or even want it. But then, why did we buy it in the first place? The salesperson! They just weren't prepared to let us go without having their product, and due to whatever reasons we could give ourselves, we ended up buying a product we may never use. Such is the power of negotiation in business.

Just as location is important when it comes to real estate, your state of mind is most important when it comes to sales. Do you believe you can sell your product? Do you think that your product or service is providing any sort of solution? Do you think your price is appropriate for the value your product promises? You need to answer all of these questions and be poised to make the customer understand why they need to make a purchase.

No matter what you are selling you must expect that some people will make objections. They will blame the color, price, and structure of your product, or liken it to a product they bought in the past that failed. You must be prepared for these objections and know how to respond to them. You could even use NLP to bring up the objections yourself before the customer does, in order to stop them in their tracks and leave them with no attacking potential. You could say, for instance, "Some say this security device is too costly, but what is the price of making sure you and your family are safe? Is this price higher than the value you place on their lives?" By bringing up a possible objection to the price of your product, you halt any thought processes in the customer in that direction and focus their thoughts instead on the value of their lives and those of their families. This is called a redirection technique. You could also use the redirection technique in another way.

Say you want to sell a car to a customer who would rather have another (that you don't currently have), you could liken their attitude to a weak or ineffectual state, such that they start to dissociate themselves from that attitude and come closer to making a purchase. For example, "Sorry, my friend, if I appear a little blunt, I had this customer some moments ago who just wasn't prepared to buy anything. He complained about everything, like the price of the vehicle, the color, even the tires, but what he should be complaining about really is his wife's grip on his collar. He simply didn't want to buy a car his wife wouldn't like. Now, tell me what manner of slavery that is, when you cannot even buy things because you want to. Sorry for taking your time, my friend, what brand would you WANT?" By bringing up a story of a (fictitious) customer whose wife apparently controlled his buying habits, your client immediately starts to dissociate himself from the other man and tries to act differently.

Negotiation is all about making rapport with your customer. While in deep rapport, you can influence the customer's decision and swag it in your direction. Inculcate the rapport skills we discussed in the previous chapter into your negotiation system and see a surge in your results. In addition to the rapport techniques we have learned, here are some tips to help you negotiate better and make sales:

- Try to establish a situation where everybody wins. Customers often see negotiation as a win or lose situation, where they stand against you in a heated contest. With this mindset, they find it difficult to come to terms with your proposition as they see the whole negotiation process as a competition. You need to reframe the situation and turn it to a win-win scenario by making the customer see the problems they would be solved if they purchased your product or service.

- Refrain from making counters claims. When a customer raises valid objections to tour product, do not immediately start attacking them or telling them why their opinions don't hold water. Instead, listen to them carefully, even agree with them on some fronts, and turn their arguments to your favor. For example, when a male client tells you a certain color is not for men, tell them, "Yes, traditionally this color is deemed not suitable for men, but out of the last ten customers who purchased this product, six of them were men. Maybe it's high time men tried something different."

- Learn useful metaphors and hypothetical situations you can use to sway customers in your direction. From time to time in a negotiation, bring up a hypothetical situation in which your product or service could be used to great effect. Make them understand why your service is the best option in that situation, and why they must not allow an adverse situation to happen.

- Have a handful of useful facts ready every time younger negotiating with a client. Make sure to poke holes in your client's defenses by bringing up indisputable facts that they just can't ignore. For example, "Why do you think the rich hardly have any cases of theft or burglary? It's because they have resorted to using the best security mechanisms available, however expensive they come." Sound authoritative, but not sarcastic or disrespectful. Use a commanding tone, but also be gentle and wise, and always wear a true smile.

Conclusion

Since its introduction in the 1970s by Richard Bandler and John Grinder, neurolinguistic programming has been used by many to improve the quality of their lives or that of the lives of other people. Perhaps the group of people who have utilized the principles and concepts of NLP to greatest effect are entrepreneurs, whom, in the ever-demanding world of business, need to be perpetually sound physically and mentally. Many of the problems bedeviling entrepreneurs and impeding their progress, such as poor time management skills, bad decision making, low self-confidence, and poor communication can be easily remedied with NLP techniques. These NLP techniques have been created and developed over time to solve the multitudes of challenges the contemporary entrepreneur faces, such as are listed above. While some of these techniques were created and structured by the founding fathers of NLP, some others have been developed by NLP enthusiasts, psychotherapy experts, psychologists, and counselors to meet the psychological needs of their patients or clients. Not all NLP techniques are focused on effecting therapy; some are geared towards making an already sound mind, even firmer and more resilient. Others have been specifically designed to allow people to achieve the successes that exceptional individuals have experienced, by modeling the skills and toolset those exceptional people have utilized to their benefit.

Modeling is one of the earliest and most practiced NLP techniques. It allows you to fashion your life and your business after those of truly remarkable people who have achieved the goals you wish to attain. Through modeling, the founding fathers of NLP have themselves been able to create and develop techniques by studying the lives and works of exceptional psychotherapists, such as Milton Erickson and Satir. The works of these people have formed the larger part of what we practice as NLP today.

To achieve any success as an entrepreneur, it is important that you first have a vision, then break that vision down into feasible, achievable goals, which you can start working to attain. Setting goals is a common concept among entrepreneurs, but, indeed, few entrepreneurs have come to grips with the knowledge of setting goals that are not only achievable, but whose impact on the central vision can be easily measured. There are many strategies and methods that you can employ to make your goals workable. Two of the commonest methods are the SMART and PURE acronyms, which, either used singly or in collaboration, can help you fashion goals that will move you towards your ultimate vision.

This book offers theoretical insight into many of the commonly practiced NLP concepts, gives exercises to aid in understanding these concepts, and provides tips, tricks, and recommendations on important subject matters, such as goal setting, self-esteem, confidence, self-appreciation, communication, negotiation, and making sales. Applying the exercises and tips offered herein is certain to plunge you into the success circle and expand your horizon. However, you should not expect this book to be a magic wand; you can simply wave at your challenges and make them disappear. You must put in an effort to practice the resources provided in this book so that you can understand and master them.

Our mind is the central processing unit' build it and you can get yourself across any realm. This book offers you a set of mind-building instructions. You only need to reach out, practice them and make them your constant companions.

Stoicism for Entrepreneurs

How The Practical Advice Of This Classical Wisdom Can Help You Run A Better Business

Introduction

> *"First say to yourself what you would be; and then do what you have to do."*
>
> *-Epictetus*

What do you think of when you hear the word "stoic?" Do you imagine a person – maybe a half-crumbling marble statue in a museum that represents a towering Greek man – with a serious face, unflinching eyes, and a silent demeanor? Do you imagine a man who never shows his emotion, even in the toughest of circumstances?

Sure, today the commonplace usage of the word implies all that; in fact, the dictionary defines stoicism as "the endurance of pain or hardship without the display of feelings and without complaint." This might be the way you are used to hearing the word "stoic." But did you know that the word "stoic" actually belongs to a long philosophical tradition that began in ancient Greece, spread to Rome and then to the rest of the Western world?

Now wait, before you start to yawn, stop for a second. This is not a philosophy that is meant for long hours of study and endless, fruitless pontification. To learn about stoicism you will not feel like you are back in your high school or college philosophy class, so do not worry. This is a philosophy that is all about taking action. It is about taking control of your emotions and obtaining self-mastery. And, most importantly, it is about getting things done.

To just give you a quick taste, think about these words of one famous stoic, Epictetus, with which this introduction began: "First say to yourself what you would be; and then do what you have to do." As these words suggest, this is a practical, concrete, no-nonsense, actionable philosophy that—if applied correctly—can help you in your daily life, as a person and as a successful, busy entrepreneur. And, above all, it can help you decide what you would be and then do what you have to do, which is the secret to building the business of your dreams.

The philosophy known as stoicism all started on a porch of a man named Zeno in Athens, Greece, thousands of years ago. Today, some of the most powerful, wealthy businessmen in our country have been associated with stoicism. Men like Apple visionary Steve Jobs, Microsoft creator Bill Gates, investment expert Warren Buffet, inventor extraordinaire Elon Musk, finance guru Tony Robbins, and start-up mogul Tim Ferris have been described as stoics. So, too, have Presidents from George Washington to Theodore Roosevelt and Barack Obama. Maybe it sounds surprising, but the world's toughest man, David Goggins, a former Navy Seal and an ultramarathoner, also practices stoicism.

Do you wonder why some of the wealthiest people on the planet have turned to stoicism to help themselves do great, seemingly impossible things? Do you want to know how you can take advantage of this concrete, practical philosophic tradition to improve your business?

Using quotations and anecdotes from ancient Stoics—and advice from their modern-day counterparts—this book will guide you through the practical applications of stoicism and how they can help you become the best possible entrepreneur.

In this brief introduction, we will start by telling you about the five most famous stoics: Zeno of Citium, considered the founder of stoicism. Then we will discuss his major followers: Epictetus, Cato, Seneca and Marcus Aurelius. In a quick biographical sketch, we will tell you the major contributions they made to Stoic philosophy. Then, we will jump into an overview of what stoicism really believes, and after that, we will get started with our practical advice for how to harness the power of stoicism to improve your business, no matter what stage it is currently at. The historian Paul Veyne, a great admirer of Stoicism and an expert on ancient Rome, described Stoicism in this way: *"Stoicism is not so much an ethic as it is a paradoxical recipe for happiness."* If this sounds enticing, keep on reading!

Who Were the Great Stoics?

Zeno of Citium lived between 334 B.C. and 262 B.C. He was a Greek philosopher and is considered the founder of the Stoic school of thought. Zeno of Citium forms a bridge between stoicism and an earlier philosophic trend, the Cynic tradition (a philosophy that espouses a total rejection of society – which is connected to our current English, negative definition of the word).

Zeno of Citium was born on the island of Cyprus, off the coast of what is today known as of Turkey. He was the son of a merchant. He worked for his father for most of his life, until he founded the Stoic school of philosophy in Athens. At first, his students were referred to as Zenoans. However, he taught his lessons on a porch, and since the Greek word for porch is "stoa," the lessons he taught became known as stoicism.

Zeno's original adherence to Cynicism influenced the development of Stoic philosophy. In Athens, before starting his own school, he studied with Crates of Thebes, the most famous Cynic philosopher of the time. Thanks to the influence of Crates of Thebes, Zeo lived a minimalist, even ascetic way of life, a quality you will see being extolled by modern practitioners of Stoicism like Tim Ferris and Warren Buffet. This Cynic influence carried over into his Stoic philosophy. He also adopted the Cynics' rhetorical speaking style, which was very blunt and direct. He engaged in scandalous behavior by spending his time with the lowest classes of society and making fun of the privileged elites. This contributed to making Stoicism seem accessible, which ensured its transmission through the centuries.

Zeno's belief in Stoicism shared some views with the Cynics. Both philosophies believed in a single, virtuous good that is the only goal a moral person should try to pursue. One of his most important teachings is that "man conquers the world by conquering himself." He taught that having a lack of passion ("apatheia" – apathy) is essential. If a person can control his desires and his emotions, this will allow him to gain wisdom and be able to apply that wisdom to everyday life. In order to achieve this state, Zeno advocated the cultivation of indifference—to pleasure and to pain—possibly with the help of regular meditation practice.

Another important stoic idea that comes from Zeno is the idea that all living beings should behave according to the laws of nature. This idea, known as "kathekon," has been translated as "proper function" or "appropriate behavior for nature" or "befitting actions." This should be the Stoic's ultimate objective. Finally, Zeno is also responsible for the Stoics' acceptance of destiny, which some have criticized as being a form of extreme resignation or pessimism. However, as we will discuss, this pessimism actually has a major benefit and, in fact, is more powerful than optimism.

When he died, Zeno was a loved and respected philosopher. Thanks to the influence he spread amongst the people of his time, a tomb was built in his honor, and his stoic teachings continued on through his pupil Cleanthes of Assos. Today, we do not have any of Zeno's writings, although we believe he wrote a book, *Republic,* that was written as an imitation or a critique of Plato's famous work. All of his quotations and anecdotes survive thanks to the large number of followers, such as Epictetus (see below) who wrote about him in their own works. Few people know this, but another philosopher from the time, Chrysippus, is actually credited with developing most of the philosophical doctrines that are currently understood as stoicism.

The next important stoic who will play a major role in this book is **Epictetus**. Epictetus was born in about 55 C.E. in what is today south-western Turkey. He was sold into slavery as a boy, and grew up in Rome. His owner was Epaphroditus, who had himself once been a slave of the famous Emperor Nero. Epictetus was able to study stoicism—which had been developing for more than four hundred years since the establishment of Zeno's popular school in Athens. The afflictions he suffered as a slave left him physically impaired, but that only strengthened his commitment to studying and living philosophy. Thanks to this experience as a slave, Epictetus inspired people of all different class backgrounds, including the most disadvantaged, to adhere to Stoicism as a possible way for gaining emotional freedom in difficult circumstances.

After gaining his freedom, Epictetus went to Greece where he founded his own school of Stoic teaching. He believed that a Stoic teacher had the duty to help his students live the philosophy, which would lead to a life led "according to nature." He also believed in the importance of *apatheia* like Zeno.

President Theodore Roosevelt was known to carry copies of Epictetus' writings with him while he undertook his incredible journeys, like his exploration of the most dangerous rivers of the South American Amazon. Decorated United States' Admiral James Stockdale attributes his ability to survive as a POW in Vietnam to Epictetus' wisdom and teachings.

Next, we introduce you to **Cato** (the younger) who was born in 95 BC in Rome and died in 46 BC. His parents died when he was young, and he grew up surrounded by tragedy (his uncle was assassinated when he was only four years old). As a statesman in the late Roman Republic, he constantly used his speech-giving skills to preach values of tenacity and integrity. Cato was famous for resisting bribes and rejecting the flourishing corruption of the times in which he lived.

Thanks to his unflappable moral standards, Cato captured the imagination of many artists and writers, including the medieval writer, Dante, who placed him in a prestigious spot in his epic *Divine Comedy*. Later, in the 18th century, Joseph Addison wrote a play called *Cato: A Tragedy* that helped preserve the Stoic legacy. General George Washington so admired Cato that he staged a performance of Addison's tragedy during the Revolutionary War in order to inspire the troops and improve their sagging morale.

Cato was beloved by public servants like Washington, as well as the other founding fathers who carefully read and studied his works; President John Adams was also a great admirer. The founding fathers saw him as a symbol of liberty that inspired them while they fought for freedom from Great Britain's more powerful empire. President Barack Obama has also been compared to Cato; President Bill Clinton once described Obama as "a man cool on the outside, but who burns for America on the inside."

Cato never wrote an autobiography, so his teachings are less known today than the other Stoics. However, he left three important lessons that we will discuss more fully throughout the book: that we should learn from pain, insist on uncompromisingly high standards, and keep fear in its proper place.

The next Stoic who made a major influence on the philosophy is **Seneca,** a Stoic associated with the Roman Empire. Seneca lived from 1 B.C.E to 65 C.E. He was born in Cordoba, Spain, but lived his life in Rome, where he studied rhetoric and philosophy. He was known as a successful politician and dramatic person. In many of his writings, he reflects on the danger of ambition and the power of emotion—topics about which he knew a lot, thanks to his powerful role in the Roman empire. (He was an adviser to Emperor Nero). Because he came much later in the Stoic tradition, Seneca is better known for expounding on and passing down Stoic ideas and teachings, rather than creating his own new terminology.

Seneca wrote in Latin and his works have been central in preserving the understanding of Stoicism in the modern era. In fact, in the Renaissance, his works were discovered by philosophers and artists and influenced their work at that time as well.

Finally, we come to **Marcus Aurelius.** Known as "the Philosopher," Marcus Aurelius was a Roman emperor from 161 AD to 180 AD. The last of the "five good emperors" who presided over the end of the empire's peaceful era (Pax Romana), Aurelius was also the author of *Meditations,* a collection of personal philosophical writings that are the most significant basis for our present-day understanding of stoicism. In *Meditations,* he discusses the influence of earlier Stoics, such as Epictetus; but scholars believe he most likely had never gotten to read works by other stoic forefathers such as Seneca. It was thanks to his stoical framework that he was able to acquire the necessary self-mastery that enabled him to thrive in the unbearably challenging role of emperor of the world's most powerful empire. Former President Bill Clinton is said to read *Meditations* every year, and James Mattis, Secretary of Defense, took the book with him when serving abroad in the military.

Even the former Prime Minister of China, Wen Jiabao, is a devoted reader of Marcus Aurelius.

Beyond the original teachers, stoicism is and has been embraced by world leaders, from kings and presidents, to cultural figures to entrepreneurs. At seventeen, George Washington was introduced to Stoicism and talked to his men about Cato during the Revolutionary War. Thomas Jefferson is said to have had a copy of Seneca on his nightstand when he died. Great economists, like Adam Smith, were stoics, and the political genius John Stuart Mill, celebrated stoicism as "the highest ethical product of the ancient mind." Even President Barack Obama has been described as a stoic.

Stoicism also inspired contemporary psychotherapy, known as cognitive behavior therapy or CBT. CBT openly credits stoic philosophers for its values and practices. The quotation of Epictetus' "It's not the events that upset us, but our judgments about the events," was an early mantra taught to CBT patients. Many famous psychotherapists, such as Paul DuBois, have assigned patients homework from classical stoic texts as part of their treatment.

The fact that stoicism has not only survived but *thrived* for thousands of years, and that so many world leaders and mental health professionals have embraced its principles, speaks volumes to its tremendous power. Most likely that power derives from the fact that Stoicism is not a religion (although people have described it as a religion for the non-religious). Instead, it is a living, breathing set of practices that were developed according to the people who practiced it, in order to meet their changing needs. This means that it is a philosophy still being generated and, thus, in order to survive, needs our new contributions. In order to make sure it does not fall out of view, we must adapt it to our present moment, to ensure it remains useful and usable. After all, the core principles of Stoicism are too valuable for us to allow them to fade away. This means that as soon as you begin practicing Stoicism, you are also free to adapt it to suit your needs. (Just make sure you first learn the principles carefully!)

In the next section, we will discuss briefly each of the main ideas of stoicism—a philosophy that is committed to the idea of *practice*. It is not a dry, dead philosophy that you'd find in a dusty book written by someone who never lived outside of a university library. Think of it more like the warm-up for your workout in the gym or an intense yoga class. It is made to be practiced hand-in-hand with your life and work, to help you live the best possible life.

A Brief Summary of Stoicism and Its Values

Stripped down to its most basic essential components, we can say that the Stoic person aims to find the truth and to do what is right. However, of course Stoicism is more complex than that.

Although Stoic *ethics* is the most famous branch of stoic philosophy (that we will be focusing on here), stoicism is actually made up of three branches of study: ethics, physics and logic.

This helps us to remember that Stoics were not abstract thinkers but, in fact, studied the entire world around them. So, just to briefly mention the other two branches: Physics refers to the s study of natural science or metaphysics. Logic refers to rhetoric and knowledge, which today would translate into psychology and social sciences, as well as public speaking and communication.

The philosophy of stoicism is focused on the pursuit of virtue, which stoics believe is the true source of happiness, instead of the acquisition of material wealth, power or human attachment. But what is truly good? How do we know what we are supposed to pursue? The first group of things to value according to the Stoics is: temperance (i.e. self-control), justice, courage and wisdom. These personal or spiritual qualities that are part of one's character are referred to as virtues. The second group of things to value include wealth, beauty and personal gifts (such as strength, good vision, hearing or eyesight, intelligence, etc.), good birth (this concept is slightly outdated today, although no one can deny the benefits of being well connected), power and honors. Socrates, one of the earliest and greatest Greek thinkers who influenced the Stoics, believed that for these things to actually be of any real benefit, they must be used properly, and with wisdom. This means that for the second group of goods to be truly *good,* a person must also have the first group of goods. This is because the virtues are what guide our actions. And what are virtues for? They are the qualities that allow us to choose the things that are right for us and to act in such a way that we always pursue the good option.

For the Stoics, the most important thing a person can do in his life is to improve his character in accordance with virtue. This means that he must behave with extreme self-control, act with justice towards all of his fellow men, and be courageous in his decisions and his behaviors. This kind of behavior will, according to the Stoics, result in a good and happy life.

The words of Epictetus elegantly speak to this understanding of philosophy. He writes, "Philosophy does not promise to secure anything external for man, otherwise it would be admitting something that lies beyond its proper subject-matter. For as the material of the carpenter is wood, and that of statuary bronze, so the subject-matter of the art of living is each person's own life." Seneca also had words of wisdom in this regard, claiming that self-knowledge is the most valuable knowledge of all. He writes, "believe me, it is better to have knowledge of the ledger of one's own life than of the corn-market." This is particularly apt saying for someone who is interested in becoming (or perhaps already is) a successful entrepreneur. In our culture, we often value people for how much knowledge they possess about *things*—especially where money is concerned. However, the

Stoics tell us to keep in mind that our own life has a ledger—a balance book—and this is the hardest and most valuable thing to master.

Because of this emphasis on philosophy's power to transform a person, Stoicism is the ideal belief system for someone interested in self-improvements, like a current or aspiring business owner or entrepreneur. Stoicism is a simple but profound set of beliefs, and it is made up of a series of sayings, guidelines and exercises that anyone can follow as part of their daily routine. The daily routine actually becomes a part of the stoic way of life, not just an accessory, as we will discuss.

So if these principles apply to improve our individual behavior, what does Stoicism have to say about the world around us? Stoicism acknowledges the uncertainty and precarity of human existence. The Stoics believe that we cannot control events outside of ourselves and thus, cannot rely on them for happiness. Included in this definition are our physical bodies, for although we can do our best to take care of ourselves, eat well, get exercise, and seek medical treatment, we can only go so far with that—as any person who has ever lost a loved one to an illness knows. Furthermore, we do not decide how we look or what strengths or weaknesses we might have, or even if we are born able-bodied or disabled. All we can count on is our minds and how it reacts to the chaotic world around us—and within us. As Epictetus observes: "For good or for ill, life and nature are governed by laws that we can't change. The quicker we accept this, the more tranquil we can be. Freedom comes from understanding the limits of our power and the natural limits set in place by divine providence. By accepting life's limits and inevitabilities and working with them rather than fighting them, we become free." So the Stoics encourage you to recognize who you are. This means understanding both what you are great at and what you struggle with. Then, you can make the most of your gifts and learn to work with—not against—your natural limitations.

Beyond our individual selves, the Stoics remind us that we are part of a larger family and society. This means that every choice we make will have repercussions on other people, whether we know it or not. No one can possibly be self-sufficient. This interdependence is celebrated by the Stoics, because a network of cooperation helps forge strong communities, which is the bedrock of human culture—the foundation on which great societies are built. However, this interrelatedness also creates the biggest challenges, because it requires that people learn to separate what is in their control from what is in the control of others. Stoicism, therefore, is very focused on giving instructions for how to deal with these inevitable, complicated and vital interactions.

Stoicism does have a few core beliefs that are easy to understand and to follow. One of its central principles is to remember how very short our life is. Seneca described this truth in this way: "It is not that we have so little time but that we lose so much. ... The life we receive is not short but we make it so; we are not ill provided but use what we have wastefully." Apple CEO Steve Jobs famously reflected on this principle, telling people, "If you live each day as it was your last, someday you'll most certainly be right."

If death is one of the few certainties of life, everything else in the world is unpredictable. In the face of the uncertainty of life, stoicism tells us to be strong and self-controlled. The Greek word for self-control is, *sophrosune,* which sounds completely foreign to us, but the Latin, *temperentia* sounds just like the old-fashioned English term "temperance." Today we might translate it as "moderation," but the important thing to remember is that all these terms have the same implication: a disposition towards controlling a person's most intense desires and, when he feels those desires, to do so in a more controlled and moderate way. One of the key terms of stoicism is the concept of self-mastery, not to avoid emotions but to control them. (This is why the dictionary definition of stoicism, cited above, refers to the lack of visible emotions.) So why do we need moderation? As stoicism warns us, the reason for most people's unhappiness is that they constantly rely on their emotions and their senses, when they should only be depending on clear logic and reason.

Most importantly for us here, Stoicism doesn't concern itself with complicated hypotheses about the world, but with helping us overcome destructive emotions and act on what can be acted upon. It is built for action, not endless, fruitless debate. The Stoics focus on the banal, every day and the mundane issues every person faces. Therefore, stoicism, as a philosophy, enables us to become stronger, by recognizing that all people—ourselves included!—are imperfect. Stoicism does not need a university degree in Philosophy to be comprehended. It does not even require extensive study, research, writing and discussion. However, it will not be enough to just quote the Stoics to look good at parties or download Stoic apps on your cellphone. It simply needs to be lived, practiced and experienced. Epictetus summarized this stoic belief in the following quotation, that will be an excellent conclusion for this chapter: "Don't explain your philosophy. Embody it."

Chapter Summaries

In the chapters that follow, we will take you through the main teachings of Stoicism, using the Stoics words as a guide. Each chapter will focus on a different topic, with activities and practices geared towards helping you as an entrepreneur improve your life from a Stoic perspective. We will also incorporate advice from contemporary successful Stoics, that can guide you towards achieving your business goals.

Chapter 2: Stoicism and Journaling: Plan, Reflect and Achieve Success

Chapter two introduces you to the essential Stoic practice of daily journaling. As Seneca once said, "A person who is not aware that he is doing anything wrong has no desire to be put right. You have to catch yourself doing it before you can reform." Chapter two explains why morning and evening reflections together make the perfect bookend to a stoic day, and gives you advice about how to start your own journal to achieve a clear vision and to glean important lessons from what you have done. The Journal reminds us of the importance of daily improvement and gives us a clean slate every single day, encouraging us to live in the present as the stoics encouraged.

Chapter 3: "Stoic, Prepare for the Worst!" Negative Visualization and the Secret to Overcoming Obstacles, Adversity and Failures

Negative visualization is a pillar of stoic philosophy. By mentally confronting our worst fears through the development of a mental training ground, we can immunize ourselves against them. Beyond the mental comfort, negative visualization also prepares us for the "worst case scenario" and encourages us to have a safety net for whatever life might bring. This chapter will explain why for the businessman, this is essential.

Chapter 4: Get to Work, Stoic. How to use Stoicism to Increase Motivation, Cultivate Discipline, and Enhance Productivity

Chapter 4 is the most stoic of all the chapters, because it is all about action. This chapter gets into the nitty-gritty about how you can to increase your motivation, cultivate the strongest possible discipline and optimize your productivity by delegating, automating and letting go. It ends by giving tips about what a stoic leader should do after: take ownership of any results, good or bad, and persevere through any challenges—which is what actually makes us stronger than our successes. As Epictetus once said, "Give yourself fully to your endeavors. Decide to construct your character through excellent actions and determine to pay the price of a worthy goal. The trials you encounter will introduce you to your strengths."

Chapter 5: The Stoic in the World: How to Stoicism Can Improve Self-Confidence, Communication with Others and Make You a Better Negotiator

Chapter 5 discusses how introspection and extrospection work to put you in the strongest possible position as an entrepreneur. By knowing yourself and others, as used in Stoic philosophy, you can bring the knowledge together for the benefit of your business. After all, knowing yourself is key to one of the foundational business skills: negotiating.

Chapter 6: Practical Examples about How a sense of interconnectedness can help you relate to employees, partners, clients and improve your well being

Introducing the concept of *sympatheia* or interconnectedness, chapter 6 offers advice about how to make the most of your relationships with employees, business partners, and clients. What do you do when an employee performs poorly? How do you react when a business partner criticizes you? How do you win and keep clients? After giving you advice from the Stoic perspective, the chapter also takes a deeper look at negotiation and selling tactics for the stoic entrepreneur. The chapter then concludes with actionable advice about your individual wellbeing. As we will discuss, stoicism can actually show you how to conserve precious energy, decrease damaging stress, and sharpen your time management skills. This chapter contains **a series of exercises, including a stoic week that you can use to lead your employees through at work.**

Chapter 7: Conclusion: What The Stoics Can Teach Us about Obtaining and Maintaining Success in Business

Finally, chapter 7 will wrap everything up and provide a quick, handy summary of everything that we have discussed throughout the entire book, so feel free to use it as a reference guide while you are working through the application of each of the different principles.

Who Should Read This Book

Now that we've introduced you to the major stoics and what they believed, we hope you are starting to get the feeling that stoicism is for you. But just in case you still have any doubts, let's talk briefly about who should read this book. In a word, anyone who considers themselves an entrepreneur—or who hopes, someday, to become one. Obviously, entrepreneurs are a naturally diverse group of individuals. An entrepreneur could be a CEO of a major corporation or a creative developer inside of an established one. An entrepreneur could be a visionary who is planning a start-up, or it could be a self-employed freelancer who is hoping to grow her business. They are always thinking about how to improve themselves and the world around them. And let's not forget, young people are sometimes the truest of entrepreneurs. A child selling lemonade at the side of the road with a handmade sign, or the middle school kid who turns his iPhone into a DJ setup to turn his friends' gathering into a party—and then markets himself to the rest of his school, is an entrepreneur.

Do any of these descriptions apply to you or the people you know? One thing all these different kinds of entrepreneurs have in common is that they are passionate people who are not content to accept the status quo. They like to think, and they think fast. Their thoughts are original, and they welcome change and novelty—but only insofar as it advances their chosen, deeply held beliefs. Even if this doesn't quite apply to you yet, do you wish that it did? Stoicism will teach you to embrace these values, and to shed the misguided values that are not serving you in your entrepreneurial journey. Because stoics recognize the world for what it is—uncertain, ever-changing and full of valuable lessons—they make the ideal businessmen: guided by ideals but grounded in reality.

So whether you're an entrepreneur within a company, are already running a company and want to break through to the next level, are self-employed and hoping to expand, or are just nursing the smallest seed of a startup idea, turn to an ancient, time-tested philosophical practice and see what results come to you.

How to Use this Book

With so many different kinds of readers, we recognize that everyone will interact with this book as he or she needs. But here is some guidance as to how we envision our reader's journey, so that you can decide how to make the most of it. First, let us say that you should feel free to read this book cover-to-cover. Also, each chapter is contained within itself, so if you see a topic that grabs your interest, feel free to read them in any order you choose. However, even if you do read it all at once the first time, in order to get the best results from this book, we recommend that you go back and read it again slowly a second time, if not more. Focus closely on one chapter every week or even every month. Use the "Practical Advice and Tips for the Stoic Entrepreneur" section to form new habits, picking one at a time until it is fully internalized for at least one week (or even more). Only then when you are confident that you have mastered all the activities and principles should you then move on to the next chapter.

We believe that if you carefully follow all the "Practical Advice and Tips for the Stoic Entrepreneur," and apply them methodically to your daily life, you will see incredible, measurable results in your business, no matter what your background is and no matter what your goals are. Stoicism can help you as an entrepreneur whether you are a business of one or the head of a large organization, and whether you are in the planning phases or a seasoned executive looking for a new direction. So let's stop the introducing and go get started!

Chapter 1: Stoicism and Journaling: Plan, Reflect and Achieve Success

> *"When you arise in the morning, think of what a privilege it is to be alive, to think, to enjoy, to love."* –Marcus Aurelius

For the Stoic philosophy, the single twenty-four hour day is the most important unit of time. This becomes clear when we reflect on what Seneca once wrote, "Begin at once to live, and count each separate day as a separate life." This appreciation for a single day means that practicing the stoic way of life must begin the moment you open your eyes, before your feet even touch the floor. After all, Seneca tells us, "As each day arises, welcome it as the very best day of all, and make it your own possession. We must seize what flees."

When you first wake up in the morning, Marcus Aurelius urges people to reflect on their life with gratitude. He tells you to think about the simple, most basic elements of what it means to be a human: to think, to enjoy and to love. Acquiring an appreciative mindset, that is focused on the truly important things, will be key to fully embodying the stoic way of life and reaping the countless benefits. A good way to imagine your mind is as your personal, impenetrable fortress, inside which you can escape from the tumultuous, chaotic world around you. As Marcus

Aurelius writes, "'Men seek retreats for themselves, houses in the country, sea-shores, and mountains... But this is altogether a mark of the most common sort of men, for it is in your power to choose to retire into yourself.'" This comes in handy during the busy day of an entrepreneur. You probably will be too busy to take a regular retreat at a beach house, but no one is too busy to start the day with some quiet, guided reflection.

So, start the morning with a feeling of gratitude for your life, within the fortress of your mind. However, it is not enough to just let these ideas pass through your mind as you go through your morning routine – it would be far too simple to get carried away into your regular habits, and forget all about the Stoics. If you want to truly become a Stoic, you need to find a way to make this morning reflection a habitual part of your existence that keeps its values front and center. For this reason, Stoics recommend taking up the habit of daily journaling.

Before we explain to you the *how* of Stoic journaling, we'll take a minute to reflect on why: for stoics, journaling is not just something to do. For Stoics, journalism *is* stoicism. The daily practice of mindful, written reflection is a central facet of stoicism. Sure, some of the stoics journals were published (like Marcus Aurelius' *Meditations*). Today, modern-day stoics like Tim Ferris also publish their writings online for millions of devoted followers. That's fine for them, and helpful for us, as we can benefit from their wisdom. However, you should not start this habit with an eye towards getting a fancy book deal, starting a viral blog, or even updating your social media and collecting as many "likes" as possible. Journaling should be for yourself. It should allow you to access your most private fears and thoughts and goals. Essentially, it should be a gateway that allows you to access the depths of your true self. This is impossible to achieve if you are constantly thinking about who your readers might be or how many clicks your post will get. Always remember: YOU are your most important reader. So write for yourself. After his experience with journaling, Seneca remarked, "I am beginning to be my own friend." Then, he reflected: someone who is able to be a friend to himself is able to be a friend to everyone around him. So do not think you are being selfish by keeping your self-reflections private; in fact, eventually you might want to share them. But before you get to sharing, remember that by improving yourself you are becoming a better friend, father, boss, community member etc., to those around you.

If you have never done it before, the next question that will come into your mind is: So how do you start a journal? In the "Practical Advice and Tips for the Stoic Entrepreneur" section below, we give you some challenges and exercises to try in order to commit to the daily practice. Here, we go over some other foundational details that will help you begin journaling in no time. And, more importantly, it will get you so committed to journaling that it will become an automatic habit both at the beginning and at the end of your day, every single day.

First things first: What kind of journal should you use, paper or electronic? The most important way to answer this question is to ask yourself, what kind of journal would I be most likely to use? Honestly, at the end of the day, all that matter is that you write. Do not waste hours searching for the *perfect* journal. You do not want that to become an unnecessary distraction. But if you want it, here's our advice:

We prefer a physical, paper journal. It could be a basic notebook without any special features at all. Many companies sell pre-printed goal journals that aim to get you to fill out every aspect of your life, including your daily schedule, all of your thoughts of gratitude, short and long-term goals, and more. They might even provide you with inspirational quotations. These companies often break up time into thirteen-week chunks (one quarter of a year). This matches up with Benjamin Franklin's famous virtue challenge, in which he strived for self-improvement by working on himself for thirteen weeks. (Although he claims he did not ultimately attain true perfection, Franklin remarked that he benefitted greatly from the act of journaling itself and—like a true stoic—he believed that going through the *process* was the really beneficial part, rather than obtaining his specific, lofty goal).

If you want to try a commercial goal journal, go ahead. If you are a beginner, they provide excellent structure, and the daily, weekly and monthly planning features are very much in alignment with Stoic principles. However, if you want to skip all the bells and whistles, a basic lined notebook is absolutely fine. In fact, the Stoics would probably be more impressed with your simplicity! A handwritten journal is great because the very act of physically writing words on the page has been proven to make important neurological connections in our brain: Scientists have shown that we remember better when we hand write concepts, as opposed to when we type them. A handwritten journal will also help you avoid temptation, if you are thinking about immediately sharing your raw journal notes online. At the very least, if you want to turn them into a blog one day, you'll have to type them up—and this will give you a chance to reflect on whether that is the best course of action (and edit as necessary!). The paper journal also provides a nice break from the world of screens, if your business requires you to spend a lot of time online, as is the case with most people's businesses today. Finally, a physical journal will help you stay focused, as it will not be sending out competing notifications that tell you to check your email.

Of course, you can also journal online. This has its own advantages and disadvantages. The major advantages are that you can access it anywhere (if you use an online program). Another huge advantage is that after you have written for a while, you can use the search function to look for any trends over time: what words keep coming up in your journal? Maybe you are repressing a deeply desired goal! Or avoiding fear. Are you constantly journaling about money as a source of anxiety? Is there an employee whose name keeps coming up who is constantly frustrating you? This repetition can give you data to analyze as you plan your next step. You can also use the word count tool to keep track of how much you are writing. Do you start the week with a flood of words and get stingy as the week goes on (or get maybe burnt out)? Or does it take you a few days to warm up to writing? Before you get too excited about the online journal, do not forget that the disadvantage is that you can easily become distracted by the rest of the internet. Once you have truly mastered the stoic principles, you will not have a problem for you to remain completely focused on the task at hand. But since you are still at the very beginning, if you want to journal online, consider turning off your wifi or putting blockers on sites or programs that tempt you. The online journal might also cause you to be tempted to turn your diary into a public document, which we do not recommend at this early stage in your stoic development.

So, whether you decide to use a beat-up old notebook, or your fancy new laptop, what do you do once you start your journal? First, one thing is certain: you will not be successful if you do not have a clear objective in mind. As Seneca wrote, "If a person doesn't know to which port they sail, no wind is favorable." Therefore, when you start your journal for the day, you must start with a clear plan. A good way to approach this is to ask yourself: where do I want to be at the end of the day? How will I know I have been successful? What keywords do I want to use to shape my metaphorical travels today? If you are running a business, large or small, you obviously have countless things to do in one short day, which makes a plan even more important for you. Say you know you need to hire a new employee, upgrade your software, consult your accountant and meet with potential new clients. How do you use journaling to help yourself prioritize?

Start with five minutes of free writing. This means you should put down whatever comes to mind, without thinking about it too hard. Nothing is too trivial: what you ate for breakfast, what song you heard on the radio, think of these first sentences as "clearing your throat." Now tune in to what is around you. Is it noisy or quiet? What about your desk and your chair? Are you comfortable? Are you breathing regularly? Are you already looking around for your next cup of coffee? Do not judge yourself, just write it down. There will be plenty of time to make adjustments once you have gotten some data down.

Now, once you have started to let the ideas flow and are getting past the first few moments of throat clearing, ask yourself what issues are starting to come up to the foreground. Once you have gotten a clear handle on what is surfacing in your mind, you can start to figure out how that information can be used to help you with your day. Ask yourself: Are you unable to meet with potential new clients because you can't find the time, in between handling your taxes and technology and a hundred other competing things? Okay, so maybe you need to prioritize hiring one or more new employees to help you out. Then decide to center your day around that objective. At the same time, you can't let your taxes be forgotten. Plan yourself a few fifteen- or twenty-minute blocks of time to get done the absolute essentials—but only after you have dedicated some serious time on advancing your job search. (When you develop a more keen sense of your daily schedule, you will also start to realize what times of the day you do your more optimal work, such as early morning, and will be able to designate those times to the crucial, complex objectives, while keeping up with less intensive, creative work during the times when you might be less sharp, for instance, right after lunch or at the end of the day.)

Do not forget, your first job in the journal is to plan for one single day, but there will also be medium- and long term goals that you still want to achieve, so note those down and see what smaller steps you can take to advance them. If your day is already feeling crowded, you can commit to a time when you will be working on those goals later in the week—and then keep your promise to yourself! Remember, as another stoic, Publius Syrus, once said, "Would you have a great empire? Rule over yourself." So you have to start treating the promises you make to yourself as seriously as the promises you make to your employees or clients.

Remember, a stoic knows what he wants from his day. He has a clear destination, a set plan of attack and measurable goals. And, in case you do not feel like you are not ready yet to trust the principles of an ancient tradition to guide your modern day business, just remember that psychologists have proven the benefits of the Stoic way of life. Making a specific psychological commitment to an activity, and developing a concrete game plan, actually increases the likelihood of its achievement.

So, once you have got your plan down on paper (or on the screen), then it becomes the time to execute it. Here, we can go by the wise words of Marcus Aurelius, that should be an inspiration to you as you live out your plan. He writes, "Every hour focus your mind attentively---on the performance of the task in hand, with dignity, human sympathy, benevolence and freedom, and leave aside all other thoughts. You will achieve this, if you perform each action as if it were your last." The only other thought you should allow into your mind is the brief mental notes about what worked and what did not about your daily plan. Maybe you forgot to budget at lunchtime and ate at your desk, which made your work slower. Maybe you left your door open and a colleague came in to chat with you, and you did not tell them you were busy. Maybe you gave yourself way too much time for your taxes, and then you were left with a random block of time with no goal. Do not worry about it, for now just make a mental note. During this initial phase, you are collecting as much data as possible for the new experiment that is your stoic life and work. This necessarily takes time; it simply cannot happen overnight. However, do not worry, because it *will* happen with patient, thoughtful, consistent reflection.

Remember, Epictetus tells us, "Progress is not achieved by luck or accident, but by working on yourself daily."

Aside from reflecting on your schedule, you will also want to note how things are going for your business itself. Did you score a new client at your meeting? Awesome—make a note and move on. Did the client seem uninteresting? Okay—make a note and move on. Remember, one of the central stoic principles is to set goals but to detach yourself from the outcome. As Epictetus once said, "Some things are within our power, while others are not. Within our power are opinion, motivation, desire, aversion, and, in a word, whatever is of our own doing; not within our power are our body, our property, reputation, office, and, in a word, whatever is not of our own doing." We will be discussing control and the body later, but for now, just make notes about what you are experiencing. Maybe you forgot your lunch at home and just ate snack bars and then could not focus well. Okay. Maybe you were exhausted after the team meeting and needed an extra cup of coffee. Okay. That's your body today. Maybe you were late for the meeting because of a traffic accident. Okay. Maybe it's raining and you got your suit wet. Okay. Just keep yourself focused on yourself and what you can control.

With all your data from the day you just lived, you will be heading into your evening reflection with a rich stash of information available for you to analyze objectively. There is nothing more valuable than your own lived experience—and most importantly, it is *yours*. Why would you throw away a free resource? Making use of this knowledge is exactly what will set you apart from your competitors and make you a great business person.

So even if you are completely exhausted, do not just sit down in front of the television at the end of the day. Go and get out your journal once again. (And if you *are* exhausted, that is all the more reason to reflect on your schedule and figure out how to improve it so you are *not* exhausted tomorrow!) If you have written in a physical journal, maybe try to use a different color pen to write with and make markings right on top of the morning reflection. Act as if you were a stern, objective teacher. Star the places where you met your goals and circle the ones where you fell short of your objectives. Do not be too hard on yourself for the things that are outside of your control or too celebratory either. Your only job is to be fair. Find the good, the bad and, most importantly, extract the lessons you learned: were you exhausted after your meeting? Maybe go to bed earlier. Were you late for the meeting because of an accident? Do not forget to budget extra travel time. Did it rain on your new suit? Plan to check the weather every morning and bring an umbrella or, even better, make sure to keep a spare one in your car and a fresh change of clothes in your office.

Remember, one of the principles of stoicism is *apatheia*. This might sound like the English word *apathy*, which in casual speech means to not care. Instead, for the Stoics, *apatheia* means not eliminating but mastering one's emotions so that they do not make you deviate from your chosen life path. Most importantly, it means reframing the events of the day in the most helpful, positive way possible. At the end of the day, you must remember there is nothing you can do to change what happened. You can only change what you do going forward. Reframe any negative events and remember, that if you learned from them, they are not failures or setbacks but important building blocks for the future. The only failure would be to keep doing the same thing that does not work. As expert investor Warren Buffett once said, "You know ... you keep doing the same things and you keep getting the same result over and over again." Even though failure is an inevitable part of human existence, we can make the conscious choice to learn from those failures, even the most humiliating. A bad day does not have to become a terrible week. Use your journal to wipe the slate clean and stop the domino effect of cascading negativity when one single thing goes completely wrong. Seneca teaches us, "a gem cannot be polished without friction, nor a man without trials." So take your trials, and use them to polish you and your business into the diamond they both are.

Practical Advice and Tips for the Stoic Entrepreneur

How to Handle the Temptations of Technology: Stoicism, Self-Mastery and Digital Technology

In today's hyper-connected, social media world, it is harder than ever to live with clear intentions. How can we hope to develop and to execute a plan while social media sites like Facebook and Instagram use cutting-edge psychological research to try to distract us for as long as possible? After all, their business depends on it! When we casually surf the web, clicking from link to link with no specific objective, even though we might find many dead-ends, our brain is wired to hold out for the eventual "pay off" (whatever interesting link or article we might be searching for). Worse than that, because humans are social animals, our brain has an urgent need to monitor the "vital" information of how our social group perceives us. Social media allows us to monitor how much our friends are thinking about us, and it also shows how much we are thinking about them. This creates a feedback loop that exploits a vulnerability in human psychology. This powerful loop can cause us to waste precious hours of our day—and over time, these hours add up to huge amounts of time that we have just given away to these corporate giants, padding their bottom line and hurting our personal and economic wellbeing.

Fortunately stoicism gives us the wisdom to defeat this powerful potential addiction. First, by planning out our day and sticking faithfully to whatever we have planned, we can decide how much time social media gets from us. If you have designated to spend fifteen minutes, make it fifteen minutes, not sixteen. You get to decide. (And, of course, if your business requires you to use social media, then by all means, use it – just be mindful of the impact it might be having on you and make sure to take occasional breaks.) If your business does *not* require social media, one option is that you could quit cold turkey. This is the approach that is recommended by experts in habits and social media: to stop using it completely for thirty days, during which time you need to cultivate other habits and in-person relationships. Particularly, from a stoic perspective, we would recommend reading books of great people in history to inspire you, and spending time in nature, another habit that scientists have proved actually works to increase productivity by giving your brain time to decompress.

If going cold turkey sounds too drastic for you, and you want to try to maintain and moderate your social media presence, there are free tracker apps that can help you limit yourself if you have not achieved self-mastery yet. Better yet, use social media like a tiny reward to reinforce your good behavior, and give yourself whatever limited amount of time *after* you achieve a goal for the day.

The other reason why social media is a potential pitfall for the stoic is that stoicism teaches us to avoid thinking about and being conditioned by how other people perceive us. If you're going to walk the stoic walk, you're going to have to stop being so concerned with how many "likes" you get. Every time you leap to grab your phone to see how many "likes" your latest post got, think about the words of Seneca, who once said, "We should not, like sheep, follow the herd of creatures in front of us, making our way where others go, not where we ought to go." And ask yourself...*would he be collecting likes?*

If you need further convincing, consider the thoughts of Arianna Huffington, the founder of the Huffington Post and Thrive Global, who is also a practicing stoic. She carries around the following quotation from Marcus Aurelius wherever she goes, and has another copy on her desk and on her nightstand: "People look for retreats for themselves, in the country, by the coast, or in the hills. There is nowhere that a person can find a more peaceful and trouble-free retreat than in his own mind...So constantly give yourself this retreat, and renew yourself." She believes that this quotation "perfectly illustrates the current moment—right now that first retreat he's talking about is mostly digital. That's how we get away from ourselves—by retreating into technology and social media. But the only way to find peace and thrive is to take breaks from the world and make time to regularly renew ourselves by reconnecting with ourselves."

If the issue of technology is a major challenge for you, consider writing the Marcus Aurelius or Seneca quotation on a post-it note and hanging it above your work area or even on your bathroom mirror. Or, better yet, make it the background of your phone, so that you are forced to see it every time you want to go to participate in herd behavior.

Stoic Journaling Exercises for Success

Journaling and morning reflection: Once you have set limits on your major distractions, now it is time to get to the hard work of scrutinizing your life. Use your journal to write about your personal experience (do not think too much about others or about world events in this exercise). Each day's entry will be like a deposit in the bank that will add up to a valuable amount of data to allow you to analyze, using the tools of stoicism. This constant reflection will allow you to improve your business in the present—and the future. (If you already keep a journal, great. Keep going. Just make sure to avoid tangential reflections on other people or the world for now – we will get to the issue of "extrospection," or reflecting on other people, in a future chapter.) So what should you be writing? Remember what we discussed above, and try to think about your life as the Stoics would: calmly and with detachment, and with an objective eye towards self-improvement. Your writing can be a place where you voice your concerns privately, but then you should also take care to intervene and remind yourself of your objectives of self-mastery.

Evening Reflection: the evening reflection goes hand in hand with the morning reflection. If you do not do one, the other one will not have the same power. Think of them as bookends of your day. The evening is the perfect time to look back and reflect on what you have done in order to learn from your mistakes and strategize for what comes next. As you review your day in your mind, ask yourself the following questions: did I follow each of my principles in word and in deed? Was I professional and compassionate with all the people who I encountered? How did I better myself today? How did I better my business, my community and the world? Have I fought my vices and cultivated my virtues? (As you do this, you will naturally want to plan your next day. That is no problem, once you have completed the first portion of the activity. Write some notes for yourself for tomorrow, to set your next morning reflection off on a great foot.) One of the most important elements to focus on, is to think about how you reacted to any negative events or setbacks. Did you let them derail you? Were you able to accept them and move on? Better yet, were you able to learn from them? This might not happen immediately, but it is important to be moving in that direction. We will talk about this issue more in future chapters.

Finally, at the end of every single day, do not forget to remind yourself to practice *apatheia*. This day is finished and now there is nothing you can now do to make it go any differently. Whether good or bad, accept everything that has happened, and reframe it so that it can become a valuable lesson for the next time.

Advanced challenge: Kevin Rose, a major player in Silicon Valley and an aficionado of Stoicism, tries to incorporate a daily practice of surrender into his routine. He writes, "One thing I practice daily is surrender. I try to surrender to the earth as everything unfolds around me, not judging it, but accepting things as they are. This, of course, is easier said than done. One of my favorite quotes is from philosopher Alan Watts: "To have faith is to trust yourself to the water. When you swim, you don't grab hold of the water, because if you do, you will sink and drown. Instead, you relax and float.""

Long-term challenge: Write a journal entry every day for one month, weekends included. Read the morning entry every single evening, and make notes as needed to evaluate your strengths and weaknesses. In each entry, try to write down one area of your business you want to improve the next day, no matter how small. If you keep improving one tiny thing per day for months, you will be surprised at how your business changes.

At the end of the week and of the month, do a quick overview of the past seven or thirty days to be ready to move forward strong. Some contemporary Stoics recommend a yearly ritual as well to celebrate 365 days of commitment to self-improvement and to provide a powerful overview of how far you have come.

Remember, your journal can also be an excellent place for you to make notes on this book as you are reading and to collect the most significant Stoic quotations you find within its pages or out in the world beyond. You can also use it to create your own glossary of the new terms you are learning to make sure you are incorporating them into your world view.

Bonus challenge: Now might be a good time to read Marcus Aurelius' philosophical journal, *Meditations,* to see the original stoic journaler in action. Many of the most successful politicians and entrepreneurs today are regular readers of Marcus Aurelius. Try joining them and see what happens!

Maximizing your schedule: Use Where You have Been to Help You Shape Where You Are Going

The goal of this activity is not to cram in as much as you possibly can into every single minute of every single day. Instead, the aim is to achieve the ideal, optimized weekly schedule to allow yourself to be as productive as possible in the long term. (Remember, it's a marathon not a sprint!) First, however, in order to do this, you need data. After you have spent one week doing your morning and evening journaling, look back over all of your notes. Ask yourself: When do you work? Are you checking your phone? How long are each of your meal breaks? Are you getting any exercise, preferably outdoors and with friends? Do you remember to drink plenty of water? If you do not have enough information about all these components of your schedule, consider taking an entire week in which you write down everything you do. Be super detailed in your analysis. This will give you a baseline to increase productivity. Then, build an ideal schedule, with everything divided into fifteen- to thirty-minute blocks. When you work, only focus on that single thing. There are free online time trackers that can be useful in keeping detailed notes about what you do, especially because you can use them to identify problematic trends by searching across days, weeks or months.

Remember: Schedule in meals, rest, and outdoor activity. Even schedule in time to talk to your friends, have quality time with your family, and go on social media, if that is important to you. Make sure and actually relax during those times. The mind is like a muscle that, if well treated, can be primed to perform at the highest levels. Or if it is overworked, on the contrary, it can easily fall prey to injury, which ends up costing you in the long run. Do not forget, as Seneca said: "We must indulge the mind and from time to time allow it the leisure which is its food and strength. We must go for walks out of doors, so that the mind can be strengthened by a clear sky and plenty of fresh air." In order to prepare yourself for the greatest daily challenges facing an entrepreneur, you will need to make sure your mind is in top form.

One small parenthesis here: there is a debate in contemporary Stoic communities about whether or not the Stoic should actually seek to optimize his or her environment, in order to make life easier. On the one hand, they argue that it is necessary to eliminate distractions in order to get to the things in life that matter. On the other hand, some argue that a true Stoic would not make things easy and should struggle through all the challenges of his outside world. (After all, he will not be able to control them all indefinitely, so he should learn how to do so.) Greg Sadler of modernstoicism.com weighs the evidence for each of these points and he ultimately concludes that because it is truly difficult to become a Sage (a fully realized Stoic), in the meantime, people should do what is best in terms of making a conducive environment for Stoic productivity. The important thing is that they recognize that it is only possible to control so much: a person can budget a perfect hour of creative work, and then the internet might crash, or the gardeners might start mowing right outside his or her window. But if you can make it easier for yourself, especially in these early stages, do it. There will be plenty of other areas you can use to develop and test your Stoic mettle, as we will discuss in future chapters.

Now that we have worked towards crafting our ideal day, week and month, and we know how to use it to optimize our time and constantly learn from ourselves, in the next chapter we will turn to one of the most challenging and rewarding parts of stoicism: the way we should handle the future. We will discuss the benefits of "worst case scenario" thinking, to make sure you anticipate any potential failures well ahead of time. This will allow you to put a security plan into place and master any lingering anxiety you have about taking necessary bold action.

Summary: The Chapter In Brief

Chapter two takes on the Stoic practice of journaling. Journaling is not just something that stoics do, it actually *is* stoicism. Morning and evening reflections together make the perfect bookend to a stoic day. It forces you to start every single morning with a clear vision of what you want to achieve. It makes you put your objectives foremost in your mind and push everything else to the side. Then, at the end of the day, it gives you the valuable perspective that derives from whatever lessons you happened to have learned, whether they are good or bad. And the best news? No matter what happened during one day, the next day, you have the privilege of waking up with a clean slate and starting the process over again—and again. And again. When you have done your journaling for a few weeks, do not forget to look back and spend a week optimizing your schedule. That way, you can identify productive and unproductive patterns, do your most important work at the time of day during which you are most creative, and make sure you are giving yourself the necessary rest to achieve your fullest potential.

Chapter 2: "Stoic, Prepare for the Worst!" Negative Visualization and the Secret to Overcoming Obstacles, Adversity and Failures

"When you are going to perform an act, remind yourself what kind of things the act may involve. When going to the swimming pool, reflect on what may happen at the pool: some will splash the water, some will push against one another, others will abuse one another, and others will steal. Thusly you have mentally prepared yourself to undertake the act, and you can say to yourself: I now intend to bathe, and am prepared to maintain my will in a virtuous manner, having warned myself of what may occur. Do this for every act, so that if any hindrance does emerge, you can think: I did not prepare myself only to undertake the act, but also for this hindrance that has occurred, and also to handle this hindrance virtuously and keep my will conformed to nature — and this will be impossible if I become vexed."

-Epictetus

All across any social media site today, you will see a culture of optimism popping up everywhere you look. Instagram gurus will tell you to think positively, so that you can attract only the best energy into your life and work. Optimism is such a popular trend, and of course the people who practice it claim to be happy (because that is the whole point, after all!). However, we should ask ourselves: is it *really* the ideal mindset for preparing you for success? The Stoics would say, "no." If you want to know how to prepare for, and deal with, the obstacles, adversity and failures that will inevitably come with being a successful entrepreneur, you will need to master the technique of negative visualization and understand why it can help.

Consider this quotation from Epictetus, as he prepares himself for the simple act of going swimming in a pool (do not worry, we will talk about more challenging, business-related activities later). As he does this, he goes through in his mind all the different negative things that people might do to him while he is there: he starts with small things, like getting splashed, then moves to medium things like getting jostled by someone, and finally he considers truly rotten things like facing abuse or theft. Running through this potential catalog of bad experiences does not make Epictetus anxious. In fact, it helps prepare him to make the most of his swim. By preparing himself to go swimming and making a mental contingency plan for any negative outcomes, he feels most ready to maintain his composure, thus allowing him to respond in accordance to his principles (i.e. virtuously).

In this exercise, Epictetus is thinking about all the possible things that *others* might do to him, that is the things that are outside of his control. Making this distinction is crucial for the stoic philosophy. He once wrote, "The chief task in life is simply this: to identify and separate matters so that I can say clearly to myself which are externals under my control, and which have to do with the choices I actually control." In the swimming pool, he cannot decide who splashes him, who pushes him, who abuses him and who steals from him. What he can do, is decide how *he* acts in response: he can choose to keep his calm composure, to maintain his virtue and to respond accordingly. After all, Epictetus reminds us, "We cannot choose our external circumstances, but we can always choose how we respond to them."

The key to successfully enacting this plan is to keep your rational mind in charge of your emotion. This allows you to stay completely calm and self-controlled. The negative visualization is exactly the Stoic tool that makes this possible. As Marcus Aurelius explained, "The first rule is to keep an untroubled spirit. The second is to look things in the face and know them for what they are." The Stoics use negative visualization in order to cultivate an ability to scrutinize a situation and understand every single aspect of it before they spring into action.

What is negative visualization and why is it beneficial?

> *"What is quite unlooked for is more crushing in its effect, and unexpectedness adds to the weight of a disaster. The fact that it was unforeseen has never failed to intensify a person's grief. This is a reason for ensuring that nothing ever takes us by surprise. We should project our thoughts ahead of us at every turn and have in mind every possible eventuality instead of only the usual course of events."*
>
> -Seneca

Have you ever witnessed up close the response of a person who experienced a terrible tragedy? Maybe a wife betrayed by her husband for decades. A businessman cheated by his longtime partner. An athlete sidelined by an unexpected injury. Have you ever heard them cry out, "I never saw it coming!" This quotation from Seneca speaks to that lack of preparation and warns against living with your head in the clouds.

Although many gurus today will tell you to only think positive thoughts in order to attract positive outcomes, the Stoics tell us that pessimism is actually conducive to a happy and fulfilling life. Contemporary philosopher Alain De Botton goes so far as to suggest that "Serenity ... begins with pessimism." This might sound completely foreign to our current societal attitudes. However, De Botton understands what the Stoics meant: By disappointing ourselves in a safe context, we can prepare ourselves for whatever the world might throw at us. De Botton advises, "We must learn to disappoint ourselves at leisure before the world ever has a chance to slap us by surprise at a time of its own choosing. The angry must learn to check their fury via a systematic, patient surrender of their more fervent hopes. They need to be carefully inducted to the darkest realities of life, to the stupidities of others, to the ineluctable failings of technology, to the necessary flaws of infrastructure. They should start each day with short yet thorough premeditation on the many humiliations and insults to which the coming hour's risk subsequently subjecting them."

However, negative visualization is not just about inoculating yourself against potential disappointment and stopping there. In fact, it can actually turn your life into the life of your dreams by helping you to understand that all these catastrophic things that you are envisioning have *not* actually happened to you. No matter what you are facing, you are comparatively lucky! Psychologists who study "anxious" people have discovered that the act of rehearsing all the possible negative consequences has a concrete, scientific benefit: it allows people to prepare their nervous systems, which means that when they do swing into action they will not be *over*-active and cause crippling panic attacks. This kind of foresight also helps encourage advance planning, which means that when the worst actually happens, you will be that much closer to a solution than people who never even entertained the possibility. So, if you can get the benefits of this "anxious" behavior without the pain of anxiety, why wouldn't you want to do it?

There are countless benefits of negative visualization. They include the ability to understand anxiety and to master it. Spending time contemplating the unknown allows us to train our mind and to protect it against uncertainty—like a vaccination that introduces small doses of a pathogen into the body. The constant exposure to negative images and ideas actually works to numb your mind to them. Think of negative visualization as a free mental training ground. Remember, according to Tim Ferris, "What we fear doing most is usually what we most need to do." This means that negative visualization can give us a roadmap that points to exactly what is holding us back and shows us the way forward. Furthermore, by creating realistic expectations, we avoid crushing disappointment. Finally, negative visualization makes us more grateful for what we do have. The end result is that it creates a healthy environment where it is possible—even easy!—for us to be our best self.

How to Practice Negative Visualization

Negative visualization is a simple exercise that can remind us not to take the good things in our life for granted. In order to perform negative visualization, you just need to imagine that bad things have occurred or that good things have not happened. In order to prepare yourself to get all the benefits of this challenging practice, you need to find a quiet spot where you will not be disturbed. (When you get good at this, you will be able to do it anywhere, even in crowds. For now, as you are learning, make it as easy as possible.) Then, pick your worst fear. For example: imagine going bankrupt, the death of a dear friend, losing your spouse, or even experiencing a traumatic injury. Or, when you are about to start a new situation, imagine all the ways it could go wrong—we call this worst-case scenario thinking. For example, while you are on a boat, imagine that the ship is sinking and that everyone on it will drown (only do this if you are very tough). If you have stage fright, you might imagine your next presentation, and your Powerpoint slides do not work, and you lose your voice, and everyone starts laughing at you. Or imagine that you were born to a different set of parents and never met any of the people you love. In the case of your business, you can imagine that you lost all your clients, that you got caught in a terrible scandal, or that your office was vandalized. This will help you remember that everything you have is borrowed, another essential Stoic belief.

As you start to have these thoughts, try to feel them deep inside your entire body, all the way inside your skin and bones. Notice how they make you feel. Are you tensing up your muscles? Is your face making a pained expression? Do you forget to breathe deeply? Would someone watching you know what troubles you are experiencing inside of your mind? Now is the time to put your *apatheia* in action. The goal is not to avoid having emotions but to avoid being *controlled* by them.

Now, once you have mastered your emotions around the negative scenario, ask yourself what are the consequences if the worst really does happen? What is truly at stake for me and my business? Then, the next step is to ask yourself: am I ready to accept the consequences? How can I set up a plan to make sure to protect me from these possible consequences? More simply put: what is my safety net?

Then, when it comes time to prepare for your presentation, ask yourself: what would I do if my Powerpoint slides do not work? Can I bring a back-up copy? What about printouts? Can I present from memory? Or, when you are deciding on renewing your office security plan or insurance policy, spend some extra time discussing all the ways in which the plan or policy has you covered. With these simple precautions in place, you will be that much more confident when it comes time to tackle the actual challenge or traumatic event.

Stoic challenge: Practice Poverty

Tim Ferris, an American entrepreneur and blogger, recommends going even further and practicing poverty. This is his favorite stoic exercise that allows him to fully experience worst case scenarios in a safe environment, rather than just playing them out in his imagination. He gets inspiration from a quote from Seneca that says, "It is precisely in times of immunity from care that the soul should toughen itself beforehand for occasions of greater stress, and it is while Fortune is kind that it should fortify itself against her violence. In days of peace the soldier performs maneuvers, throws up earthworks with no enemy in sight, and wearies himself by gratuitous toil, in order that he may be equal to unavoidable toil." Tim Ferris recommends going beyond just mental rehearsals or journaling. Instead, he suggests setting at least three days in a row per month in which to fast, for example from Thursday evening to Sunday evening. If you are looking for a more advanced challenge, he recounts that a successful friend of his actually simulates poverty by living in poor conditions for an entire week. He sleeps in a sleeping bag in his own living room and tries to consume no more than $15 of food for the entire time. He does this once every financial quarter. This allows him to "better able to make decisions that are proactive and big picture, and less out of obligation, or guilt, or fear of missing out because he knows that even if he misses a particular deal, even if a cutting edge project or experiment, or his pushing the envelope fails, that he can make do and in fact, often thrive with next to nothing." Ferris notes that the experiment will serve to improve your mental and emotional state and although it feels unpleasant at the time, ultimately, will be freeing. Aside from these extended scenarios like camping out or fasting, Ferris also does other things to cause himself pain and stress in a safe, controlled context, for instance, taking ice baths and suffering cold exposure. This allows him to develop a tolerance for the unavoidable challenges that life throws at everyone. He concludes, "The more you schedule and practice discomfort deliberately, the less unplanned discomfort will throw off your life and control your life."

Another way to "practice poverty" is to simply live a minimalist lifestyle to begin with and avoid getting enslaved by the attraction of riches. Emperor Marcus Aurelius supposedly sold many of the luxurious furnishings of his palace in order to pay down his empire's debt. He realized he did not need all his fancy luxuries, and that they were more of a burden for him and his people than a value. Today, we can see a similar mentality in some of the world's richest men. CEO Warren Buffett is worth approximately $65 billion, but he still lives in the exact same house he bought in 1958 for $31,500. Buffett does not do this because he is cheap. He does it because he knows what matters in life. He became successful precisely because of his commitment to prioritizing: for him, a standard house was better than a mega-mansion, because it allows him to focus his time on his work, rather than interior decorating. Maintaining this lifestyle actually gives him a kind of freedom to pursue what he truly loves. It also gives him a kind of insurance policy that he will always be able to be happy and satisfied even if there is a devastating financial crash—or if he experiences a debilitating injury and can never work again. Buffet understands that the more things people want and the more they have to do to earn or protect that lavish lifestyle, the less enjoyable their lives actually are, and the more constrained. Billionaire entrepreneur Mark Cuban also shares Buffett's frugality and tells people to cut out anything in their monthly budget that is not strictly essential. He claims, "The more you stress over bills, the more difficult it is to focus on your goals. The cheaper you can live, the greater your options."

Beyond just their everyday life, living frugally is a strategy that is celebrated and adopted by many entrepreneurs. The richest man in the world, Jeff Bezos, created Amazon around a frugal mentality. While some companies provide every possible luxury for their employees, Bezos argues, "I think frugality drives innovation, just like other constraints do. One of the only ways to get out of a tight box is to invent your way out."

Scheduling a Pre-mortem with your Team

A post-mortem is a traditional meeting in a business context where people get together to discuss how a project went, to evaluate whether it met the metrics for success and where to place the credit or the blame. This is similar to an autopsy, the moment went scientists figure out the cause of death (Latin: morte). Well, once the body is dead, the time for improvement has past, so the Stoics would suggest, instead, scheduling a post-mortem with your team: that way you can try to figure out all the potential pitfalls that a project might face *before* they happen.

As a leader, it might be hard for you to stand in front of your team and expose your fears about a brand new project. But would you rather do that *before* they come to life—and hurt your bottom line—or after? As Seneca reminds us, "We are more often frightened than hurt; and we suffer more from imagination than from reality." So use this exercise as an opportunity to vanquish your fears, to block your imagination and to show your team what a fearless leader you are.

Do this exercise once you have mastered negative visualization, so you can explain it to the group. Gather them together and ask them to play devil's advocate as they outline all the steps of the next project. For each one, ask them to identify the worst case scenario. Tell them to be creative but not absurd. Then ask them to write up a game plan for how to tackle these cases. What extra resources might you need to have? How much extra money? Will you need the help of an outside consultant? Could a partnership be beneficial? Go ahead and look up some of that contact information now, so you will not be rushing around trying to scramble and find the person when you already desperately need him.

Important note: If your business is doing well, do not be tempted to skip this exercise. Remember, Seneca, who enjoyed great wealth as Nero's adviser, warns us: "It is in times of security that the spirit should be preparing itself for difficult times; while fortune is bestowing favors on it is then is the time for it to be strengthened against her rebuffs." The last time you want to be practicing negative visualization is in the wake of a failure. Do it when you are riding high on success or even on an average day. It just might bring you down to earth—or remind you how good you have it.

Dealing with Adversity

So what happens when you have prepared for the worst and the worst still happens anyway? Sure, you can be an expert at negative visualization, you can even build the most intricate safety net imaginable, and you will still eventually come up against a disaster you never fathomed. Such is life.

This is the time when the stoic philosophy offers the most inspirational pearls of wisdom. First, remember you are in control of every single one of your choices, no matter how bad a situation you might face. As Epictetus said, "You can bind up my leg, but not even Zeus has the power to break my freedom of choice." Let a moment of adversity be the time when you recommit to living in alignment with your values and virtues.

Second, when working in a team, it is likely that the failure was caused by a combination of factors. It is rarely caused by one single weak person or one bad decision. As you are assessing the reasons for the failure in order to learn from it and grow, keep in mind Seneca's admonition: "Let philosophy scrape off your own faults, rather than be a way to rail against the faults of others." In simple terms, this means that you should use your training and experience as a way to look inwards at yourself, to identify your weaknesses and to improve them. This philosophical practice is not for casting the blame on others and refusing to look at yourself.

Third, never forget that we are made strong by our trials. Epictetus famously said, "Difficulty shows what men are. Therefore when a difficulty falls upon you, remember that God, like a trainer of wrestlers, has matched you with a rough young man. Why? So that you may become an Olympic conqueror; but it is not accomplished without sweat." So get up, dust yourself off, and figure out what comes next! If you need a little encouragement, take to heart the words of billionaire investor George Soros who says that "Once we realize that imperfect understanding is the human condition, there is no shame in being wrong, only in failing to correct our mistakes."

Furthermore, if it *is*, in fact, another person who has caused the adversity, this is an excellent opportunity for tapping into the best of Stoicism. The popular blogger, Tim Urban, had this to say to one of his readers who asked him the simple question, **"How do you be a good person?"** He suggested that she keep in mind the following, in order to be a kinder, more empathetic person:

"Every stranger, co-worker, friend, acquaintance, customer service representative, driver, waiter, customer, client, neighbor, and person on the internet you come across:

- Has a family who loves them and vice versa

- Has hopes and dreams and regrets and frustrations
- Has as many thoughts going through their head at all times as you do
- Is dealing with random health problems, trying to make ends meet financially, and is probably tired
- Might be supporting one or more other human beings
- Might be just a little sad all the time about a tragedy in their past
- Might be the most important person in someone else's life
- Is just trying to figure out how to be happy"

In today's fast-paced world, where communication is often anonymous and frequently aggressive and careless, keep these thoughtful guidelines in mind. Urban's suggestion about how to be good touches on the concept of "sympatheia," or interconnectedness amongst human beings. We will discuss that more in Chapter 6. For now, just think about these salient points whenever you encounter adversity that is caused by another person, whether by his careless error or overt malice.

Do not forget, your journal is the most valuable tool to help you achieve these difficult objectives. (Are you still writing in it twice every day? Do not stop! Keep making deposits in that bank of knowledge!) Use it to describe whatever challenges you are facing. As you write, see if you can achieve a stoic mindset and extract the best possible lesson from any negative outcome, no matter how big. Then, remind yourself exactly what is and what is not in your control. For instance, you might even divide up a single story according to what is and is not in your control: I went to the store (in my control), but it was closed (not in my control). So I didn't have dinner (in my control) and at bedtime I ended up eating a bunch of junk food (in my control). Then look back at what you wrote and see if you can pinpoint the exact moment you went wrong—for instance, in this case it was letting the closed store derail your plan for healthy eating. Do not dwell on it, just make a note and try to plan to do better next time. You can write down: check the store schedule before going, find another open store, always make sure to shop *before* I run out of groceries, have a healthy take-out place in mind for when I can't shop, etc.

The first three chapters helped prepare us to get us into the stoic mindset. Now, in the next chapter we will tackle the essential topic of how to use stoicism to get ourselves into action—which is the foundational principle of stoicism. Together, you can harness motivation, discipline, and productivity in order to get your business into the most dynamic, impactful shape possible.

Summary: The Chapter In Brief

Along with journaling, one of the cornerstones in stoic philosophy is negative visualization (*premeditation malorum*). This practice, which involves mentally confronting our worst fears, can help lessen anxiety by immunizing us against it. Beyond the mental comfort it provides, negative visualization also allows us to prepare for an event in advance to make sure we have a safety net for whatever worst-case scenario life might throw at us. For the business person, this is essential because of the countless responsibilities you will certainly have to juggle. At its most basic, negative visualization increases happiness because it stimulates appreciation and gratitude for what we do have. It reminds us not to sweat the small stuff. The chapter also recommends scheduling a post-mortem with your entire team before embarking on any major projects, in order to stem any potential pitfalls and prepare a backup plan. Finally, it reminds you that adversity is an inevitable part of a successful, daring life, so take the challenge for what it is and make it part of your process of growth, development and improvement.

Chapter 3: Get to Work, Stoic. How to use Stoicism to Increase Motivation, Cultivate Discipline, and Enhance Productivity

> *"The chief task in life is simply this: to identify and separate matters so that I can say clearly to myself which are externals under my control, and which have to do with the choices I actually control. Where then do I look for good and evil? Not to uncontrollable externals, but within myself to the choices that are my own..."*
>
> *-Epictetus*

Stoicism is a philosophy that values action, but what happens when you are plagued with doubt to the point where you are unable to make decisions? (Think: Hamlet's "to be or not to be...") This can hinder every aspect of your business, sapping you of your needed motivation and halting your productivity. For Epictetus, good and evil can only be found in the decisions we make, which means that by lacking the willpower and confidence to make decisions, we lose the opportunity to live a virtuous life.

As we discussed in the previous chapter, the power to make choices is a cornerstone of Stoicism. (Recall the striking quotation by Epictetus, who said, "You can bind up my leg, but not even Zeus has the power to break my freedom of choice.") In fact, stoics go so far as to believe that our choices are literally the only thing that matters—because they are the only thing fully under our control.

So once we decide what to do, how do we pass to the action phase and actually get things done? Luckily, the Stoics have a lot to say on the topics of increasing motivation, cultivating discipline and enhancing productivity. After we look at some stoic wisdom on that topic, we will consider their perspective on what is supposed to happen afterward: taking responsibility for whatever outcome occurs and persevering in spite of the odds.

Tips for Increasing Motivation

Stoicism is a unique philosophy because it stands for decisive action, and not for passive contemplation. A stoic cannot simply wait for inspiration to strike him, he must be his own inspiration. One of the best examples of this philosophy is summed up in the pithy statement of Epictetus who once said, "First say to yourself what you would be; and then do what you have to do."

Often the biggest challenge we face when actually getting down to work is the distraction of the world around us. Our cell phones and computers blast notifications about every single news event on the entire planet. Our friends text us at all hours of the day. Advertisers want to grab onto our wallets. Quite simply, a successful entrepreneur does not have time for these distractions. Usually, these distractions end up making us feel bad. We learn about devastating global tragedies we have no power to stop, or we feel inadequate compared to the perfect picture that marketers try to sell us. As Marcus Aurelius teaches us, the answer to this problem is to look internally: "If you are distressed by anything external, the pain is not due to the thing itself, but to your estimate of it; and this you have the power to revoke at any moment."

In order to face these distractions, we recommend creating a plan for your day, with set routines and rituals to help you get through. Using your journal as a guide, you can start to automate your daily activities, so you no longer have to struggle to decide when you will answer your millions of work emails: you will just sit down and answer them during the scheduled time. (And, of course, remember to delegate the ones that are not important.)

Perhaps the greatest bit of stoic wisdom surrounding the issue of motivation is this simple thought from Marcus Aurelius about the brevity of life. How true is it when he writes, "You could leave life right now. Let that determine what you do and say and think." Or, in the wise words of Seneca, "While we wait for life, life passes."

Tips for Cultivating Stoic Discipline

Every single one of the previous activities discussed in the earlier chapters can and should be part of your stoic discipline.

After trying them all out, you will be able to see which ones work best for you. Then you can adapt them to your personal lifestyle and business goals. In this section, we discuss the value of discipline itself, regardless of what it is being directed towards. These principles can be effective for tackling any challenge in your life, whether it is getting into better physical shape, finally finishing a challenging home improvement project or learning a brand new foreign language. Of course, we will want to focus on the business aspects here, but keep these other possibilities in mind, too. After all, the more disciplined you are in general, the better off you will be. If you are a paragon of precision in the office and then come home and cannot manage to cook yourself a healthy meal or go to the gym, you will eventually suffer in your work life too! Remember: No one ever lived their best life without a conscientious fitness regime, including diet, exercise, stretching and proper rest.

If you need more motivation to cultivate discipline, we leave you with this powerful quote about why action, self-mastery and control are the most important tools for living a happy, virtuous life. Seneca writes: "Putting things off is the biggest waste of life: it snatches away each day as it comes, and denies us the present by promising the future. The greatest obstacle to living is expectancy, which hangs upon tomorrow and loses today. You are arranging what lies in fortune's control, and abandoning what lies in yours. What are you looking at? To what goal are you straining? The whole future lies in uncertainty: live immediately."

Tips for Enhancing Productivity

Of course, there is no sense in living immediately if you are just flailing around. Only act after you have cultivated a strategic plan for what comes next—based on where you want to go. Do you want to be in charge of every single tiny aspect of your business? If you answered yes, you might be a perfectionist and, quite possibly, also a control freak. If this is the case, then this advice is especially for you.

When running a business, the most important thing to do is as little as necessary. Not as little as possible, but as little as necessary. Why is this? Because what is truly needed for your business is your big-picture vision. You are not running a business because of your photocopying skills (although maybe they are great) or because you can write a great email. Do less. Automate what you can. That is what technology (and a skilled personal assistant) is for. Delegate what you can't. Then you will be able to focus on what is truly important and maximize your efficiency.

If you are not quite at the stage where you can afford secretarial or administrative assistance, do not despair. Your time will come. In the meantime, use these activities to cultivate another important stoic practice. Visualize the process you are undertaking and see all the interconnectedness even of something incredibly small. Maybe you are photocopying handouts for your upcoming budget presentation. Imagine your prospective clients looking through those handouts and realizing what a talented speaker you are (you can also imagine that they hate the handouts as part of a negative visualization and then inspire yourself to make them even better). Maybe you are sending out fifty Linkedin connection requests in order to meticulously build up your network. As you tediously hit the "send" button over and over again, try to imagine one of them reaching the person who will connect you to the client of your dreams. Then the repetitive act of clicking "send" will not seem so tiresome but instead will feel like an interconnected part of a bigger journey. As you go through this process, always remember what is under your control and keep your eyes on the big picture.

The Importance of Taking Responsibility for the Outcome

Anyone who has spent any time in the real world knows that it is true that we are all interconnected. Even the smallest decision of whether to angrily honk your horn at a careless driver can have repercussions that go beyond what you can immediately see. This sense of interconnectedness gives us a responsibility to think about the consequences of every decision we make. It is particularly true for you as an entrepreneur, as you constantly have to assess those around you to make decisions that will impact their lives and your company. You must decide: whom should you hire? Whom should you partner with? To whom should you entrust your finances? With whom should you sign a lease? And, when something goes wrong, the natural question to ask is: whom should I blame? Naturally your mind might go to the interrelated web of circumstances that led you to a bad business partner or an unscrupulous accountant or an unfair landlord. Stoicism tells us to focus on someone else: yourself.

More precisely, since we want to remove ourselves from the mindset of blame and praise, stoicism tells us that you should take responsibility for whatever happens that is within your control. Seneca has wise words about how stoic philosophy can help us achieve this. He reminds us: "Let philosophy scrape off your own faults, rather than be a way to rail against the faults of others." With these words in mind, do not be afraid of standing in front of your team and acknowledging your responsibility for a major failure. If you have laid the groundwork, then you perfectly understand where you wanted to go and why. Therefore, you will be able to understand your part in the failed journey, if not immediately then with some time for reflection. Most importantly, you will be able to right the course as quickly as possible and to lead your team back on the correct path (or to change the path based on what you experienced and learned). Learning from your mistakes makes you a tough leader, not a weak one, but first you have to acknowledge that those mistakes were yours to begin with.

How to Persevere In Spite of the Odds

When something goes wrong in your personal business, it can be heartbreaking. You put everything you have into a project—your time, your money, your passion—and you bring others along with you for the ride. When you hit a bump in the road, Stoicism offers trenchant advice about how to handle it. Marcus Aurelius once wrote, "Everything that happens is either endurable or not. If it's endurable, then endure it. Stop complaining. If it's unendurable... then stop complaining. Your destruction will mean its end as well. Just remember: you can endure anything your mind can make endurable, by treating it as in your interest to do so." From this perspective, no matter what the situation, the course of action is the same: stop complaining. All you need to do is to work on your mindset, and go forward. Seneca said something similar, but in much fewer words. This could be a good mantra to post above your workspace or on your night table: "It does not matter what you bear, but how you bear it."

Remember, perseverance does not mean stubbornly doing the same thing over and over again regardless of what happens. Yes, it is important to have a vision and to stay committed to it, but a stoic must also always be observing his surroundings and his reality. Sometimes persevering means pivoting to another idea when the original plan proves faulty. Flexibility and adaptability are important qualities in a leader as well—and show a connectedness with the reality that the Stoics argued was essential to living a virtuous life.

Practical Advice and Tips for the Stoic Entrepreneur

1. Write down post-it notes with your goals, and cover your mirror with so you are forced to look at them every day. Put the most important ones in the center where your face should be, so that you can recognize you are blocking out your true self by not striving towards these fundamental goals as soon as possible.

2. Find one thing every day that you can do *less* of, whether by automating it or delegating it or simply letting it go. Remember, a tiny daily change adds up to a lot. Are you answering every insignificant email? Wasting time on social media? Shopping for bargains that cost you more in time than they save you for money? Stop, stop, stop.

3. Look back over your journal. Is there some issue or challenge that you keep putting off? Time's up! Commit yourself to do it immediately—or pay the consequences. (Research shows that penalizing yourself for bad behavior is very effective in motivating people to get things done. Pick something that really hurts: tell yourself you will have to give up your favorite tv show or skip taking the elevator and

climb the stairs every day at the office. There are even online sites that will do this for you, for instance, donating money to a charity you hate, if you do not live up to a self-commitment!)

Summary: The Chapter In Brief

Chapter 4 takes the stoic principles and tells you how to start living them in your everyday life. No more delays. Once you have figured out what is under your control, it is time to make big decisions and take concrete action. This chapter detailed how to increase your motivation, cultivate strong discipline and enhance your productivity. Then it gives some tips about what to do after you have taken action: taking responsibility for any outcome and keeping on with your work, even when things do not go right. Remember it is all just training for future success.

Chapter 4: The Stoic in the World: How to Stoicism Can Improve Self-Confidence, Communication with Others and Make You a Better Negotiator

> *"If you hear that someone is speaking ill of you, instead of trying to defend yourself you should say: 'He obviously does not know me very well, since there are so many other faults he could have mentioned'."*— **Epictetus**

This quotation by Epictetus makes a perfect start to chapter five, because it combines the two interrelated topics we will cover here: how to combine honest self-reflection (introspection) with fair evaluations of others (extrospection). First we will discuss how each of these ideas is to be used in Stoic philosophy, and then we will conclude by exploring how you can bring them together for the benefit of your business. By understanding yourself and knowing how to analyze those around you, the end result will be that you will become a better negotiator.

The brilliance of Epictetus' quotation lies in the set-up. It starts by referring to a common problem or fear, the fear of negative judgment from those who surround us. The usual knee-jerk defense in response to such negative rumors would be to undermine the person's authority by saying, "He obviously does not know me very well." Epictetus starts to follow this logic, but then he quickly turns the tables in the last part of the quotation, when he adds, "since there are so many other faults he could have mentioned." Now, our critic's authority has, in fact, been undermined, but not because he was *too* critical of us, but because he was *ignorant* of all our flaws that only we have access to. Genius!

Building Self-Confidence and Self-Awareness (introspection)

Stoicism is fundamentally an introspective practice. Introspection, defined as the *"Observation or examination of one's own emotional state, mental processes, etc.; the act of looking within oneself,"* is at the heart of all the practices we have discussed so far in this book. As we discussed in chapter 2 on journaling and chapter 3 on negative visualization, the stoic looks inside himself constantly, day and night, week after week. As we discussed in chapter 4, he takes responsibility for the outcomes of his choices and always works diligently on his self-improvement.

The benefit of this self-awareness is, first and foremost, self-confidence. If you know what you are, then you know exactly what you can do. You can walk into a meeting in front of the richest venture capitalists in the world, and tell them exactly why they should trust you with their hard-earned money. And you can have the confidence to walk away from a deal if it does not seem favorable—or if it is not in line with your values. Furthermore, if you know who you are, you know *why* you do what you do. The famous and talented Elon Musk, one of the most successful entrepreneurs the world has ever known, rates daily introspection as one of the most important things a person can do. He says, "I think that's the single best piece of advice: Constantly think about how you could be doing things better and questioning yourself."

Of course, it will sound paradoxical, but one of the key tools for introspection is actually to look to another respected person. As Seneca suggested, "Choose someone whose way of life as well as words, and whose very face as mirroring the character that lies behind it, have won your approval. Be always pointing him out to yourself either as your guardian or as your model. This is a need, in my view, for someone as a standard against which our characters can measure themselves. Without a ruler to do it against you will not make the crooked straight." This "ruler" could be a peer or a mentor—perhaps it is the very person who inspired you to go into business to begin with. It also could be a person from the past (like a Stoic) or a celebrity. So keep your mind open to learning about new people, read biographies, and you will find your ideal "ruler." At the same time, make sure not to follow anyone blindly or singularly; after all, even the most perfect of idols can fall, like some of the apparent business greats of the twentieth century (we could mention Bernie Madoff and Elizabeth Holmes, just to name two).

The Benefits of an Awareness of Others (extrospection)

The Stoics teach that you should only worry about what you control, and in the opening quotation from Epictetus, we talked about the idea that *you* are your own toughest, truest critic. So where does that leave other people?? The dictionary defines extrospection as "the observation of things external to one's own mind...Extrospection is ordinary sense perception or reasoning concerning the things so perceived." But if stoicism is so focused on the self and its improvement, why should we also practice extrospection?

Well, because stoicism is a practical, pragmatic philosophy, concerned primarily with action. Therefore, in this interconnected world it is impossible to just focus on the self. We have to remember we are connected to every other thing on the planet, living and nonliving. In order to make informed decisions, you can't just go inside yourself completely, except during the precious daily moments of meditation (so make them count!). Instead, you need to interact with the world around you, for several reasons.

1) Through
    the consideration and observation of things external to th e self, we are more likely to gain a valuable perspective on

what to do in our lives and in our business. This might mean studying the great businessmen and women we admire, the heroes of the distant past, or even our colleagues and friends.

2) Extrospection gives us perspective about our role in the larger picture, which helps avoid a tragic self-centered disposition. When we observe the world around us, we realize how small we are, and how similar we are to our fellow men and women. This makes our perception of tragic, unique suffering much more proportional.

3) Extrospection gives us both something to strive for—and something to avoid.

4) Extrospection helps us evaluate possible friends, colleagues, and business partners. As Seneca reminds us, "Associate with people who are likely to improve you. Welcome those who you are capable of improving. The process is a mutual one: men learn as they teach." Berkshire Hathaway CEO Warren Buffett, probably the most successful businessman of contemporary history, suggests a similar approach: "It's better to hang out with people better than you. Pick out associates whose behavior is better than yours and you'll drift in that direction." This means we must truly study those with whom we wish to spend time. Ask yourself: do they align with my values? Remember, no one is perfect, so

consider: Will they help me improve myself? Can they learn from me?

Finally, when evaluating people, keep in mind what Seneca said: "There is no genius without a touch of madness." The people you might admire most will also likely have some flaw. Since you are (or want to be) an entrepreneur, the same can probably be said about you!

How to Deal with Anger and Disappointment

When dealing with others as a result of extrospection, you will inevitably have positive experiences and negative ones, too. The Stoics teach that we should neither get carried away by the good or by the bad, so remember not to let your feelings run away with you, even if you think you have found the ideal business partner or employee. Always keep in control of your emotions.

Negative emotions tend to be harder to deal with, so we will spend more time talking about self-mastery in this regard, specifically in terms of the powerful emotions of anger and disappointment. Marcus Aurelius had wise words of inspiration to help discourage anger. He writes, "Keep this thought handy when you feel a fit of rage coming on—it isn't manly to be enraged. Rather, gentleness and civility are more human, and therefore manlier. A real man doesn't give way to anger and discontent, and such a person has strength, courage, and endurance—unlike the angry and complaining. The nearer a man comes to a calm mind, the closer he is to strength." Today, we could rewrite his passage and say that it applies to either men or women, because anger is unbecoming in both sexes. Always try to keep in mind your ultimate goal and remember that it will not be reached by flying off the handle and acting rashly. In fact, you are more likely to destroy all your hard work if people see you as unpredictable; a trustworthy leader knows how to be calm in a storm.

Moreover, if you have been practicing your negative visualization, you will be well prepared to face disappointment, because that is one of its primary benefits: to consider the worst possible outcome of a situation, so that your expectations do not come crashing to the ground when they are not met. Try this practice when imagining a new working relationship: imagine that an employee has done the worst job imaginable, and then think about what plans you have in place as a safeguard against such possible mistakes. This should be a good first step to relaxing you. Remember, when you have finished the visualization, shake off any remaining negative feelings, so that your working relationship with the person stays neutral and controlled.

The contemporary philosopher Alain de Botton, who has written extensively (and critically) about Stoicism, suggests that learning to disappoint yourself can be a powerful way to deal with anger. He refers to a quotation by Seneca that says, "What need is there to weep over parts of life? The whole of it calls for tears." De Botton argues that the Stoics help us put things into perspective. For example, he writes, "We may be irritated that it is raining, but we are unlikely ever to respond to a shower by screaming. We aren't overwhelmed by anger whenever we are frustrated; we are sent into a rage only when we first allowed ourselves to believe in a hopeful scenario which was then dashed suddenly and apparently without warning. Our greatest furies spring from unfortunate events which we had not factored into our vision of reality." De Botton sees Stoic pessimism as a safeguard against anger and, in fact, a path towards happiness. Optimism, on the other hand, is actually what ends up getting us to travel down a dark path because it led us to be foolish in our expectations, to hope for more than what was smart or realistic. He writes, "The person who shouts every time they encounter a traffic jam betrays a faith, at once touching and demented, that roads must always be (mysteriously) traffic-free. The person who loses their temper with every new employee or partner evinces a curious belief that perfection is an option for the human animal." So really, from this perspective, optimism is a form of self-delusion, while pessimism is the kind of pragmatic realism that can make us stronger and better able to engage the world around us.

Stoic Negotiation Tactics

If we have looked into ourselves and examined others, we are ready to bring ourselves into contact with our potential negotiators. But what can stoicism tell us about how to succeed in business negotiations, one of the most challenging but vital aspects of entrepreneurship?

First, we must carefully prepare ourselves for the encounter. This is done bit by bit in the daily work of stoic practices, but make sure to intensify the practice when you are getting near to a major negotiation. Enter into the negotiation with a clear goal. Know what you will accept and what you will not. Have clear boundaries and commit to respecting them to the letter. Remember Seneca's words, "If a person doesn't know to which port they sail, no wind is favorable." So keep your destination in front of your mind.

Second, try to put yourself in the mind of the person with whom you are negotiating (notice we did not write "adversary"—more on that soon). This can be easier if you have been practicing extrospection and have had a chance to observe him, his colleagues or his employees. If not, try an online search to see what you can find out. Maybe you have mutual acquaintances. Be discrete, but make sure to do your homework. Then, on the morning of the negotiation, wake up and remind yourself, as Marcus Aurelius counseled, "Begin each day by telling yourself: Today I shall be meeting with interference, ingratitude, insolence, disloyalty, ill-will, and selfishness..."

Third, when you enter into the actual negotiation, let the other person speak longer and, preferably, first. The more information you have gathered about him, the easier this will be. And, if you have not managed to get too much background on him, by letting him talk during the negotiation, you gather valuable data. On the subject of speaking up—and staying quiet—Cato had these smart words; he wrote, "I begin to speak only when I'm certain what I'll say isn't better left unsaid." If you keep your cool, speak knowledgeably and with confidence, and keep your destination in mind, you will be likely to get what you want.

Finally, in the next chapter we will be discussing the concept of interconnectedness, but we will preview it here, as it is relevant to negotiation. The Stoics tell us to always remember that everyone is interconnected, like threads in a woven cloth or parts of a single body. If you keep that in mind, then the best piece of stoic advice for negotiation is to not see the other person as an adversary. Instead, think of him as a fellow human, all part of the interconnected web of life. Think of him as a fellow businessman who has his own goals and dreams and his own bottom line. Can you find a mutually agreeable solution that does not compromise either of your values? Can you find a workable compromise that will lead to future collaboration and growth? That would truly be "winning" in the Stoic sense.

Practical Advice and Tips for the Stoic Entrepreneur

1. Are you still doing your morning and evening journaling exercises every single day? If you have

stopped, make sure to pick them back up immediately. There is no better defense against all the challenges of the modern world than self-knowledge.

2. As part of your journaling, try to write objective sketches of the people around you in your business life: colleagues, competitors, potential clients. Limit yourself to what you objectively know about each one of them. Do not let your emotions or biases enter the picture. Imagine these people were being studied by alien scientists: how would they each look to someone who only saw them from the outside?

3. Get angry (but only for five minutes). Psychologists recommend a habit in which you experience a difficult emotion for a short period of time in a contained setting. This is similar to negative visualization, but instead it concentrates specifically on whatever emotion is troubling you today, whether anger or disappointment or fear. Set a timer, close your eyes, and think of something that triggers that emotion in you. You may yell or gesture or do anything that comes naturally to you. You might punch a pillow or let out a stream of foul language. Then, when the timer goes off, you must stop and return back to your normal calm state as quickly as possible. Think about how that intense experience made you feel. Did you like the feeling of your blood pressure and heart rate

skyrocketing? Did you like the surge of adrenaline—maybe only for a second. As the feeling subsides with deep breaths, notice how much better you feel after you let the feeling go. Next time you encounter that emotion in your daily life, try to recognize the signs more quickly and revert to the slow, deep breathing rather than exploding and letting your emotions take over. Remember, that by rationally communicating your feelings (telling someone, "I feel angry") rather than swallowing them and hoping they disappear, you will be better positioned to obtain self-mastery.

Advanced practice: after mastering this controlled anger, remember the suggestion of contemporary philosopher Alain De Botton, "One of the goals of civilization is to instruct us in how to be sad rather than angry. Sadness may not sound very appealing. But it carries—in this context—a huge advantage. It is what allows us to detach our emotional energies from fruitless fury around things that (however bad) we cannot change and that is the fault of no one in particular and—after a period of mourning—to refocus our efforts in places where our few remaining legitimate hopes and expectations have a realistic chance of success." Therefore, after mastering your anger, try this exercise again, but with sadness: do a negative visualization with the goal of conjuring up all the tears within you, and let them freely flow as you imagine all the things you cannot change and all the terrible things that could happen to you. Feel where your body experiences sadness, and then breathe into those spots. When the timer goes off, practice returning to a perfectly calm state and continuing on your day. Try this every day for a week or month and see how much lighter you feel in your daily existence.

4. In the days leading up to negotiation, try to practice this exercise several times a day: do a negative visualization in which you imagine every step of the negotiation. Visualize the room you are in, what you are wearing, what you are going to ask for, and what they will want in return. Now imagine each part of this process going terribly wrong. Imagine the room being 100 degrees hot, imagine the other person refusing to listen to you, or being greedy or rude. Feel your body react and then take deep breaths until you return to calm and to composure.

5. If you are really nervous about negotiation, ask a trusted friend to do a practice round with you. If you have done exercise 2 above and created a character sketch about the person with whom you will be negotiating, let him read it and ask him to get into character. Practice negotiating until your body and mind are completely at ease with the interaction.

6. After the negotiation, do not forget to write down what happened, good and bad. Then make notes

about where you would like to improve and save them for review before the next negotiation takes place.

Summary: The Chapter In Brief

Chapter five discusses how introspection and extrospection work to put you in the strongest possible position as an entrepreneur. By knowing yourself and others, as used in Stoic philosophy, you can bring them together for the benefit of your business. One key way that this will help you is in your ability to manage your anger and disappointment. Finally, knowing your strengths and weaknesses — and those of your fellow businessmen! — is key to one of the foundational business skills: negotiating.

Chapter 5: Practical Examples of how Interconnectedness can help you relate to employees, partners, clients and improve your well being

> *"All things are mutually woven together and therefore have an affinity for each other,"*
> *- Marcus Aurelius*

One of the most powerful changes in mindset that you can bring to your new or established business, is a recognition of what Marcus Aurelius calls "interconnectedness" or *sympatheia* (which sounds quite like the English "sympathy" but has a more subtle meaning). In this chapter we will talk about how to deal with different kinds of people in business and different business relationships, such as employees, business partners and clients. However, the underlying principle that unifies each one of these groups is this crucial notion of interdependence. Just like threads in a piece of fabric, each one of the people you interact within your business is part of your business, whether it is the parking lot attendant, the customer service representative who helps you troubleshoot a difficult task, or your closest, oldest confidant. Each one of those people is like the different parts of the body, each with his or her own function and objective, but each integral to the health of the organism. Whenever you encounter difficulties with someone, remember this principle of *sympatheia,* and your interaction will become all the more meaningful and potentially even healing.

How to Deal with Poor Performance in Employees

If you have any employees at all, even if yours are the most diligent, you will eventually have to deal with the unpleasant reality of their poor performance. How you handle their poor performance will have powerful repercussions throughout your business; it will send a message to the other employees and, without exaggeration, it will ultimately determine if your business is to succeed or to fail.

Although sometimes it can be extremely frustrating—or even traumatic—when an employee messes up, the first thing the Stoics tell us to do is to avoid getting angry, as we know that anger is one of the most powerful distractions for the human mind. It clouds our best judgment, and it makes us behave against our core values. Seneca wrote a lengthy essay on anger. In it, he provides some helpful tips for how to avoid getting angry when an employee does not perform. He tells us: "the best plan is to reject straightway the first incentives to anger, to resist its very beginnings, and to take care not to be betrayed into it: for if once it begins to carry us away, it is hard to get back again into a healthy condition, because reason goes for nothing when once passion has been admitted to the mind, and has by our own free will been given a certain authority, it will for the future do as much as it chooses, not only as much as you will allow it. The enemy, I repeat, must be met and driven back at the outermost frontier-line: for when he has once entered the city and passed its gates, he will not allow his prisoners to set bounds to his victory." Here, it may be helpful to remember philosopher Alain De Botton's comment about the power of pessimism and the danger of optimism when dealing with other people. He writes: "The person who loses their temper with every new employee or partner evinces a curious belief that perfection is an option for the human animal." So always repeat to yourself that perfection is an illusion and imperfection is the human condition, and you will be well on your way to dealing with employee mistakes calmly.

Hopefully, you are able to take this advice and avoid letting anger into your mind and suppress your rationality. However, if you have not yet learned this form of self-control, make sure you do not engage the employee in an angry, emotional state. Step away if necessary. Once you are calm, you must carefully evaluate the situation. Ask yourself: What kind of mistake did the employee make? Was it her first mistake of this kind? Did she do everything in her power to get help before the problem occurred? Did she report her problems to the necessary supervisor? If so, she probably can learn from her mistake. In this case, it is your job as an employer to ensure she has the proper support so that it does not happen again. This might mean installing "guard rails" within your company to make sure employees are being helped at crucial phases, without, of course, having their work done for them. This is what hedge fund manager Ray Dalio does with his employees at Bridgewater, when necessary. As this process unfolds, make sure not to get angry at the employee, which according to the Stoics is our duty. If we can better the employee through teaching him and creating new procedures (that do not put your budget at jeopardy, of course), it is your duty to do so. This pedagogical approach will not only improve the individual but ultimately benefit the company—and even society—as a whole.

However, if you evaluate the situation and find out that the employee was trying to hide some sort of weakness or was being lazy, it might be time to terminate the relationship. Similarly, if he knew he was having problems but refused to ask for help, or has committed repeated errors of the same kind, it might also be time to let him go. Remember, your organization is like a body and each part contributes to its success—or could prove to be a fatal weakness (what the Greeks called an Achilles heel). As the boss, you have to evaluate whether rehabilitation of the employee will be possible and efficient—or perhaps they belong in a different role inside the company, if their talents aren't being used to their fullest in their current role. This is an ideal solution, but make sure you are not just relocating them to avoid a painful conversation. You may want to get additional information from other colleagues and supervisors, always being careful to weigh the advice and account for potential biases. But, if after you have conducted a thorough, rational investigation, you find out that they do not have anything to offer the company in any department, then do not be afraid to terminate a poorly performing employee. Being kind and looking the other way ultimately hurts the company, the other employees and you. Whether or not you believe it, it even hurts the employee himself. It is better for him to look himself honestly in the mirror and figure out what line of work he should really be in—and the sooner, the better!

Once you have dealt with the problem, the organism should be able to heal itself quickly. Furthermore, if you are transparent about your processes, about employee performance reviews, transfers and terminations, no one will be afraid for their own job, because they will know exactly what to expect. Remember, leadership guru Brené Brown encourages those good leaders to avoid fostering a workplace where people gossip, because no one thrives in an office full of backstabbing and scheming colleagues. Remember that the enemy to corruption is light, so shed light on what you are doing as the head of your organization—and remove those who seek to keep the organization in the dark. They are always doing so for their own best interests, never yours.

Finally, one last word of advice: if you do a thorough job in the hiring process, you will be much less likely to encounter employees performing poorly. This means to create a hiring process that is transparent and in-depth, with multiple kinds of interviews and tests that are evaluated in a standard way across the company. If you do your own hiring, you can spend time asking the candidate questions about his values and assessing his sincerity and his alignment with company values. If you have hiring managers, make sure *they* are in alignment with company values. Have a strict, well-defined rubric that covers all the areas a candidate must address during his on-site visit. If you trust them, ask them to draft a set of guidelines that you can revise together to make sure you're on the same page. More importantly, ask the hiring managers to do blind reviews of the candidate and forward them to you without comparing their results with other hiring managers. Before the candidate's visit, spend time with the hiring managers in formal and informal situations to make sure they know what to look for in an ideal (preferably stoic!) employee. And unless your company is over 1,000 employees, make sure you spend at least fifteen minutes with a top-level candidate before he gets the formal offer. If you have been doing your stoic exercises carefully, you will be able to assess their potential fit, in even the briefest of meetings.

How to Improve Relationships with Business Partners

So how does stoicism help you when dealing with colleagues? Business partners cannot be treated like employees because they do not answer to you. Instead, they must work with you in the most efficient possible way, for the benefit of all considered. In many ways, the same advice about employees above applies to business partners, in terms of understanding the symbiotic relationship between all people. Quite literally, you and your partners are interconnected, and your success is interdependent.

But what happens when you face inevitable disagreements? You probably picked your business partners because of their fast thinking, independence and innovative attitude—which means you are likely to disagree at some point. Here, Marcus Aurelius has some great advice about what to do in case of such a disagreement. He writes, "If someone is able to show me that what I think or do is not right, I will happily change, for I seek the truth, by which no one was ever truly harmed. It is the person who continues in his self-deception and ignorance who is harmed."

The good news is, since we are all interconnected, it does not matter who is right—all that matter is that you get to the truth, however long it might take. Of course, sooner is better, so when dealing with business partners and disagreements, keep an open mind and an open heart. If multiple smart, disinterested, and fair people disagree with you, you should take extra caution before dismissing their advice. Ask yourself why do you think they are telling you these things? (This same advice holds if an employee gets the courage to tell you he thinks you are wrong. Obviously he is taking a big risk in confronting you.) Ask yourself: is this someone whose opinion I value on this matter? If so, give him the benefit of the doubt and listen—it just might change the course of your business!

On the other hand, if you are sincerely convinced that you are truly right, based on careful evaluation of all possible evidence, then Marcus Aurelius has a different piece of advice. He advised that people should be" kind and good-natured to everyone, and ready to show this particular person the nature of his error." For the Stoics, improving a single individual actually benefits the entire society, and so being a good mentor is a highly virtuous endeavor. It may take a lot of time and effort, but keep in mind all the benefits it is generating, some of which might be hidden to you in the present moment. In any case, do your best, but try not to get too caught up in teaching others to follow your ways. Remember, if it were really that easy to teach someone the Stoic way of life, the world would be a much better place, so possibly the best advice in dealing with querulous business partners is Marcus Aurelius' suggestion: "Waste no more time arguing what a good man should be, be one."

Negotiation and Selling

Chapter 5 looked at how stoicism can help you improve your negotiation strategies, and here we will go a little deeper into the topic and also think about how stoicism can help you make a sale. Here are a few of the ways that Stoicism can help you in your dealings with other vendors or clients. First, the regular daily practices should significantly increase your confidence. This means that you know that you are going into a negotiation prepared with a clear goal in mind. Second, thanks to the self-awareness you gain from doing twice daily journaling meditations, you should know your best strengths and your major weaknesses. This means that you can present yourself or your product in the most flattering possible light and downplay any limitations it might have. Third, since you will have learned to control your passions, you will be able to play it cool no matter what the other person says or does to you. Fourth, because you will remember that everyone is interconnected, you will behave respectfully and justly to everyone, because the person to whom you are selling or with whom you are negotiating also has his own bottom line, his own principles and his own ideals. (Even if you cannot see what they are at the present.) Finally, thanks to Stoicism, you will have learned detachment from the outcome. This means you recognize that as soon as you start to desire a specific result, you always lose, even if it may sound paradoxical. Obviously, if you do not get what you want, you lose. However, even if you *do* get what you want,

Stoics believe you lose anyway, because the thing you have obtained will change or you yourself will change. This does not mean to be resigned to accept whatever might come, but to strive to follow nature in your business as in everything, which will ultimately lead to the proper result.

How to Improve Your Relationship with Your Clients

Especially when starting our business, our clients are the people we crave most to bring into our life. After all, with no clients, there is no business. Or, when your business grows, if your client base does not grow sufficiently, you will fear to have trouble bringing in Venture Capitalists. In these early growth phases, we must be extra attentive to only be associating with those people that bring out the best in us. Do not be tempted to just accept *any* client who pulls out a checkbook. If you do that, you will increase your likelihood of problems later on, when inevitably something goes wrong—or when your values simply clash with your clients. If you are operating in accordance with nature, which according to Seneca is the motto of the Stoic school, you will experience serene interactions with your clients who are themselves operating in accordance with nature.

However, as we all know, the world of business is a competitive place, and you will likely find people like Seneca did, who are corrupt and greedy. In that case, hopefully you will be doing your daily journaling and negative visualization exercises, which will help you realize when you find the right and the wrong client. Moreover, if it happens that you are dealing with a difficult client, always remember, as we said above, other people do what they do because they think it is for the best. This is one of the things a practicing Stoic must learn to accept. If a client behaves badly towards us—or passes us up for another business, or even betrays us—we must remember, that reflects poorly on *him*. If you have been practicing negative visualization and "pre-mortems," then you should have a plan in place to deal with whatever worst-case scenario a bad client throws at you.

How Stoicism Can Foster Optimal Wellness

Stoicism is an ideal philosophical practice for limiting harmful stress and anxiety, for learning to control your energy, and for finding balance and managing your time. In fact, its profound connection with mindfulness has led people to call it the Western form of Buddhism. One of the first things to remember when thinking about wellness and Stoicism, is that the body is not considered to be under our full control. Obviously, the Stoic discipline would advocate that we do our utmost best to take good care of ourselves. This means we should always strive to eat only healthy foods, to get plenty of vigorous exercise and fresh air and, when we are sick, to seek competent medical treatment (and to follow our trusted doctor's advice!). However, it also recognizes that we can only go so far with our choices about our bodies. As much as we can try to alter our appearance with diet, exercise, cosmetics and clothing, we do not decide how we look when we are born, what strengths or weaknesses our bodies might have, or even if we are born able-bodied or with a severe handicap.

So just remember, every person will have to find his or her own way of dealing with stress, restoring energy, and striving for a balanced life—the Stoics do not spell out a diet or exercise regime. They just establish some basic guidelines for a simple, healthy life that is built around using the minimum necessary. As you try these techniques, do not get angry with yourself if you do not have the desired reaction immediately. Practice having patience with your body as you do with your mental self, and with those around you.

Decreasing Stress: If we practice daily, stoic philosophy is like a built-in de-stress program. Every element of Stoicism teaches us how to decrease stress, because once we truly accept that not everything is in our control—and can distinguish between what is and what is not—a lot of natural stress just melts away. Maybe you were waiting for a major delivery, and a snowstorm hits—let it go! Maybe you were hoping to make a major sale, and the client stopped returning your calls. Did you do everything in your power to convince him to buy from you? Yes? Then let it go. Furthermore, the practice of negative visualization will expose you to stressors—the images of terrible things happening to you and to your loved ones. However, it does so in a controlled environment so that you can react more effectively and with more self-restraint when it comes time to face something that you tried to imagine. Remember, a true Stoic is never surprised, which is a major advantage, because being surprised is one of the worst stressors a human can face.

Increasing Your Energy

One of the great benefits of Stoicism is the way it teaches you to let go of every little thing that does not matter. This means that you can conserve the energy you have previously been wasting on trivial things, and dedicate it to the truly important issues and people in your life. Furthermore, the stoic rituals of evening and morning journaling have been shown to help increase energy in several ways. First, it increases energy because it helps favor restorative sleep: once you have your plan for tomorrow and have let go of today, you will be more likely to fall asleep quickly and sleep more deeply. Second, it increases energy because it gives you a clear plan of action, so you stop wasting valuable energy on making decisions—something psychologists have shown to be very taxing in terms of brain capacity. Third, its emphasis on spending time moving in nature has been proven to be a natural anti-depressant, with just thirty minutes of outdoor time a day having a major boost on people's mood and energy levels.

Finding Your Balance

Stoicism is committed to living in balance with nature. For the founder of Stoicism, Zeno, nature is simply "the way things work." Sounds simple enough. This means that following natural laws is the true meaning of wisdom. Marcus Aurelius wrote: "Philosophy requires only what your nature already demands," which sounds easy enough (until you set out to do it without a proper guide!). Seneca said it like this: "Let us keep to the way which Nature has mapped out for us, and let us not swerve therefrom. If we follow Nature, all is easy and unobstructed; but if we combat Nature, our life differs not a whit from that of men who row against the current." This actually teaches us the true advantage of being balanced and of not excessively striving—although we may fear that by backing off and doing less, we will lose to our competition. Remember that for the Stoics, those who live out of balance with nature are like people rowing their boats upstream, while you will be letting the current take you where it rightly needs to go—and therefore will get there faster and with much less effort.

So, how do we achieve the desired balance that comes from living in accordance with nature? Let's go back to the basic tenets of Stoicism. Above all else, you must only focus on what is within your power. This means to accept your limitations and strengths for what they are. Epictetus had some wise words on this point; he wrote, "If you try to be something you're not or strive for something completely beyond your present capacities, you end up as a pathetic dabbler, trying first to be a wise person, then a bureaucrat, then a politician, then a civic leader. These roles are not consistent. You can't be flying off in countless directions, however appealing they are, and at the same time live an integrated, fruitful life." So think about what is your ultimate goal. Then, plan out the steps to get yourself there, and go through them one by one—do not be a dabbler. Luckily, if you are in harmony with yourself, you will be naturally inclined to pursue a limited number of desires, and you will be free from greed—which is often the feeling that pushes people beyond their natural limits and disturbs their balance.

Making the Most of your Time

The truth is, there are only twenty-four hours in the day, so we have to try to spend them as wisely as possible. Seneca had beautifully accurate words on this point. He wrote, "People are frugal in guarding their personal property; but as soon as it comes to squandering time they are most wasteful of the one thing in which it is right to be stingy." So, are you one of those people? Do you agree to do anything someone asks you because you fear they will not like you or will not give you their business? (If you need some help learning to say no, especially if you are a woman or a minority, Berkshire Hathaway CEO and investor extraordinaire Warren Buffett is very direct on this point: "The difference between successful people and really successful people is that really successful people say no to almost everything.") Do you waste time on tiny minutia, like saving a few pennies here and there? Do you let your mind wander, chasing after pointless worries about things that were not—and will never be—in your control? Do you waste your time on friendships long past their expiration date? Amazon's phenomenally successful founder Jeff Bezos has this to say about friendship: "Life's too short to hang out with people who aren't resourceful." If the answer to any of these questions is yes, then time management is still a major problem for you at this point in the book. In that case, we advise you to review your daily journals and spend a little more time reflecting on your schedule. (See exercise three below for some more helpful tips.)

Practical Advice and Tips for the Stoic Entrepreneur

1. Since seeing things objectively is one of the most important qualities for a Stoic, practice being objective with your employees—and get them to try to be objective with themselves. Schedule a sit-down, face-to-face meeting with each one of your employees. In preparation, ask them to write up a brief, objective summary of their yearly performance, as they feel it would be written from a disinterested outsider. Ask them to evaluate themselves as if they had only observed their performance through a pane of glass. You do the same: imagine your company

was being audited by an external Human Resources firm. Think about how they would describe the performance of every person who works for you. (You can also write one about yourself!) Then during the employee meeting compare the two reviews, and see where you differ in significant ways. Try to brainstorm with them about why that might be. If there are major discrepancies, be sure to schedule a follow-up meeting in order to revisit the issue after a few weeks or months.

2. Plan a retreat with all of your partners, somewhere out of the usual office setting, and preferably out of town and in nature. Ask each person to bring a small, inexpensive gift for the team that symbolizes the way they view the relationship and / or their hopes for it in the future. These gifts could be a small animal, like a lion, that symbolizes courage, pride and resilience, or a hearty plant that reminds the team of its roots. Taking an afternoon to recognize one another, celebrate your interconnectedness, and just take your mind off work for a short period of time, can do wonders to unite a team and bring out the best everyone has to offer.

3. Wellness: time to stop wasting time! Go back to your original journaling exercise where you developed your ideal schedule. Now that you have learned more about the Stoic mentality, ask yourself if the items in your daily schedule are truly in alignment you're your nature. Can

you delegate unimportant tasks? What can be automated? What can be discarded? If you are struggling to have healthy meals, try a shopping service or online ordering. Remember, a busy schedule is not necessarily the best schedule (and probably is not). Have you scheduled in enough time for exercise and outdoor time? Can you add in a little more, maybe just five minutes per day? How is your sleep schedule? Have you been maintaining important social relations? Have you trimmed away all the friendships that are not serving you? (Remember, time spent on something is time taken away from something else, so be prudent in your choices.)

4. Stoic words of wisdom: now that you have gone through nearly the entire book, go back through it (or through your journal if you have been taking notes on the book) and select your favorite quotation. Use it for the basis of your next morning or evening meditation. (Now that you have almost completed the book, you may want to refer back to the quotations and intersperse them into your meditations on a regular basis in order to stay connected to what we have learned here.)

5. Bonus challenge: While you are looking through your daily diary entries, consider if anything you have written might be worthy of sharing with the broader public. Ask a trusted friend to look them over and offer his opinion. In

the "further reading" section there are references to popular podcasts; there are also countless blogs and even an active Reddit forum on Stoicism. Look through these options and consider reaching out to the hosts or authors to see if they are interested in interviewing you or featuring you as a guest or even a regular co-host. After all, now you have experienced the power of stoicism in your life for at least several months—which means you have taken it more seriously than the majority of people out there who just quote a little phrase here or there to look smart at a party! (Note: this activity is only to be completed *after* reading this entire book! Do not get sidetracked with publication until its already done.)

One Last Week of Exercises – For Your Entire (Soon-to-be) Stoic Team

Now that you have read the entire book and have taken the time to master each of the stoic teachings and apply them to your own life, it is time to show off your leadership skills and teach your employees to think—and work!—like a stoic.

Look ahead at your next month's calendar. Do not delay any more than that, but scan through your obligations and pick a week that looks conducive to a large, intensive group undertaking. (But do not worry, if you have a lot of employees on the road or clients visiting, etc., all of the exercises can be done individually and remotely. They are designed to help your employees clarify their thinking but *not* take up huge amounts of time.)

Depending on the kind of leader you are and how you communicate with your employees, you may announce the stoic week in an email or in an actual meeting. You may also decide to reveal all seven days at once, or keep them on their toes and give them the challenge just moments before it starts. You know your team best, so you will know what works and does not work for them. (Note: if you have different ideas for a stoic day, feel free to try them out. By now you know the main principles, and should feel confident experimenting with them. Remember, stoicism is a growing, changing practice and it needs you to contribute in order to thrive for future generations.)

Day 1: Monday – Teach your employees to start the week off with a morning reflection. Use your experience with your own reflection to guide them in this new endeavor. You can recommend paper or electronic journals, but make sure your employees know that their words are totally private. (You can ask them if they want to raise any related points to you personally, to everyone in a company meeting or on an online collaboration channel, but it should be completely optional.) Give them a few prompts as they start to write, such as: what objectives do you want to achieve today? How do you want to feel at the end of the day? What do you need to do in order to make this day a success? How will you know this day is a success?

But also make sure to encourage them to "clear their throat" to see what emerges when they let themselves be free. Then give them time at the end of the day to do an evening reflection where they evaluate how their day played out and strategize for a successful tomorrow. Ideally, they will want to continue this practice on their own. If you designate ten or fifteen minutes at the start and end of every day, you will be well on your way to helping them for a habit that will make them happier and more productive employees. Try it. It might just be worth way more than twenty or thirty minutes it costs.

Day 2: Tuesday – Prepare your employees to think about the worst case scenario with some negative visualization exercises. Remember, that the key benefit is to train their rational mind to remain in charge of their powerful emotions, allowing them to stay calm and self-controlled if and when something goes awry at work. If they regularly practice negative visualization, your employees will hone their ability to scrutinize a problem and understand every single aspect of it. Tell them to focus on their biggest project at work, and to imagine every single part going wrong. Ask them to think about how it makes them feel. Then, ask them to write down two or three things they could do to prevent or improve this worst-case scenario. Allow them time during the day to create a back-up plan. Remember, you are investing in your own future by giving them this valuable time right now.

Day 3: Wednesday – Teach your employees to reframe their negative perceptions. Using the results of the journaling and the negative visualization, ask your employees to come up with as many silver linings as they possibly can fathom. Ask them: what went "wrong" in their day? Then challenge them to separate the parts that were under their control and the parts that were external to them. How did they handle the parts under their control? Remind them that is where the true good and evil of any situation lies. Another reminder: this is all training for a future experience. Every single person makes mistakes, but the truly successful people learn from their mistakes and change their future behavior. Make sure this exercise does not become a blame game amongst employees by insisting that everyone recognize his or her responsibility. Tell them that these writings will be kept private, so no one fears creating a climate of suspicion.

Day 4: Thursday – Increase productivity! Tell your employees to look through their schedule and then prepare a short analysis of how they are spending their time (a good preparatory activity for this day is to have them use a time tracking app for a week – there are many free ones available online). Ask them to meet with you or their immediate supervisor (obviously, this will take longer if you have a lot of employees, so plan accordingly) to review how they are spending their time. See where they can cut out, automate or delegate items that are less important. Try to see if they have been putting off a meaningful project because of busywork. Or better yet, see if they can find it themselves. Remember, you are teaching them to be resourceful, so that you can better spend your time elaborating your company's developing vision.

Day 5: Friday – Take responsibility. Today is the end of the work week, and it is time for your employees to look inside themselves in relation to their whole team and to figure out their role in the complex team dynamics. Have the contributed as fully as they should have? Why or why not? Have they behaved with dignity and in alignment with company values? Why or why not? Make sure this is not perceived as a punishment or an attempt at spying. Just ask them to reflect on these stoic principles and to make sure they are acknowledging their responsibility for what is under their control and the choices they make.

Day 6: Saturday – Take a break! Remember, the Stoics are about productivity, efficiency, motivation and action. But this is only possible if you fully disconnect on a regular basis. This might sound totally counterintuitive, but the boldest move you could make for this Saturday activity is to tell your employees to unplug. Tell them not to check their work email for a whole day. (Did that make you nervous? Relax! Do a negative visualization. What could possibly happen in just twenty-four hours without email...?) Encourage them to take a walk in nature, to go for a bike ride, or to take a swim with their friends. Tell them to spend time on self-care, talking to family, eating a good meal, and connecting to what they truly love. Trust us, they will thank you for it on Monday!

Day 7: Sunday – Time to look back on the whole week. As your employees to write another journal entry (hopefully by now they are enjoying the process). Ask them how the stoic week changed their life. Did it meet their expectations? Did it change some aspect of their work life or their home life? Why or why not? Did a certain principle resonate for them? Was one principle harder for them to work with? Why do they think that is? Consider using the results of this activity in a group meeting, again, only if people feel comfortable sharing. If they do, you will have a rich source of information about the people around you, that can only improve your leadership abilities. If not, make sure they know that this is okay and that there will not be any negative repercussions from you.

Bonus: Collect your favorite stoic quotations from this book and use them as the basis of a daily email message to your team. This will help make these principles even more concrete and powerful. Ask your employees to comment on them with one another or to discover their own quotations to help them succeed.

Summary: The Chapter In Brief

Using the umbrella concept of *sympatheia,* chapter 6 offered advice about a range of different business relationships, including employees, business partners, and clients. It also took a deeper look at negotiation and selling tactics for the stoic entrepreneur. Then, it had with practical advice about individual wellness and how stoicism can teach you to conserve energy, decrease stress, and improve your time management skills.

Finally, it concluded with a series of exercises, including a stoic week to lead your employees through at work.

Chapter 6: Conclusion: What The Stoics Can Teach Us about Obtaining and Maintaining Success in Business

> *"There are two of the most immediately useful thoughts you will dip into. First that things cannot touch the mind: they are external and inert; anxieties can only come from your internal judgment. Second, that all these things you see will change almost as you look at them, and then will be no more. Constantly bring to mind all that you yourself have already seen changed. The universe is change: life is judgement."*
>
> *-Marcus Aurelius*

If you have read the book all the way through to this point (thank you! And congratulations!), you are probably able to understand this quotation by Marcus Aurelius by yourself and what it means from a Stoic perspective. But in case you want one more quick explanation, remember that for the Stoics, it is not an actual event that makes us happy or miserable, but the way we interpret it. As Epictetus puts it, "Men are disturbed not by events but by their opinion about events." So as you go through the stages of your business, whether as a sole proprietor or as the CEO of a fledgling startup, it is crucial not to just react to outside events. If you do, it is easy to slip into a feeling that life is treating you unfairly—and from there, to fall into a resigned depression that will only make things worse. After all, no matter how bad something is, remember that it will soon be over, as with all things in life, including your life itself.

Here, we see Stoicism overlap with Buddhism, an Eastern philosophy that emphasizes the impermanence of life and the transitory nature of existence. If you remember that desiring a certain outcome is a lose-lose proposition, you will know not to waste your short, precious life in search of worldly goods. The most important thing to pursue that will give you true happiness is virtue, because it sets you free from the chains of endless desire. Epictetus was actually a slave, and thanks to the teachings of Stoicism, he was able to live a fulfilling life. No wonder historian Paul Veyne described Stoicism like this: "Stoicism is not so much an ethic as it is a paradoxical recipe for happiness."

Take Away Lessons from This Book:

Chapter 2 and Chapter 3 introduced you to the two key exercises of stoicism: daily journaling and negative visualization. Journaling—morning and evening reflections—help you to achieve a clear vision and to learn important lessons from what you have done, whether good or bad, success or failure. On the subject of success and failure, try taking the advice of Microsoft founder and philanthropist Bill Gates "It's fine to celebrate success but it is more important to heed the lessons of failure." While journaling needs to be done every day to really have an impact, negative visualization, on the other hand, does not have to be a daily practice. It can be performed whenever you are about to embark on a new, intimidating event. Remember, the repeated exposure to negative imagery actually numbs you to it, and this makes it possible for you to bravely confront your worst fears—and to prepare for them in advance, so you'll never be surprised or caught off guard. It also reminds you that life is short, that everything is borrowed, and to appreciate what you have. Do not make a mountain out of a molehill!

Chapter 4 got you down into the trenches and told you about the value of decisive action. Once you make a decision, and set the wheels in motion, the stoics then give valuable, practical advice about increasing motivation by remembering the uncertainty of life (do not forget: you could be dead tomorrow, so stop procrastinating and get to work!). They teach us to have intense discipline, and that includes mastering your emotions. It also means a Stoic cane endure pain without complaint, and can push himself as hard as he can possibly go, and then pushes a little harder. At the same time, Stoic philosophy respects time for rest too. And it tells us about ideal ways to optimize your productivity by delegating, automating and letting go of the things that do not matter (because every person's time is limited!). Finally, when a project is finished, remember that a stoic leader takes ownership of any results, good or bad, and he perseveres through any challenges that he and his team will inevitably face.

Chapter 5 told you about the power of introspection and extrospection in influencing your life and work an entrepreneur. While it is important to know yourself profoundly, remember you do not exist in a vacuum. This means you also must objectively study those around you and strive to surround yourself with only the best people—that is, the people who bring out the best in you and help you live according to your virtue. Of course you must know your friends, but knowing your fellow businessmen and women (and how you will react to them) will provide you with an advantage when it comes to negotiating. In the end, however, the best result is one that goes along with nature and honors our interconnectedness. A compromise that respects both parties is always the best outcome.

Chapter 6 introduced to you the concept of *sympatheia* (interconnectedness) in order to give advice about how to improve various essential business relationships. It talks about how to handle your employees, especially if they are not performing. It also discusses the important role of developing good relationships with your business partners, which means knowing how to talk and listen to them from a Stoic perspective. Then, it gives you important advice about how to attract, maintain and troubleshoot problems with clients, especially in the early stages of growing your business. Then, it also takes a deeper look at negotiation and selling tactics for the stoic entrepreneur. Thanks to its emphasis on the fleeting nature of life, stoicism also has practical advice about personal wellness. By teaching people to focus on what truly matters and what they can actually control, stoicism teaches people how to conserve their precious energy, decrease anxiety, obtain balance and improve their time management skills. This chapter asked *you* to become a teacher, giving you a series of easy, practical and powerful exercises to give your team a week of stoicism at work.

We hope you enjoyed this introduction to Stoicism and entrepreneurship, and that in the process of reading, you have found inspiration and actionable advice that you can put to work for the benefit of yourself, of your business endeavors and of those around you. Remember, Stoicism is not an all or nothing proposition, even if the ancient Stoic seem like towering icons of perfection. It's not that you're either completely Stoic, or you're not Stoic at all. Stoicism is not about criticizing or evaluating how Stoic someone is, and it is not just for the mythical "sage." Stoics themselves recognized the value of the *prokopton*, the person who is "making progress." This sense of progress does not typically follow a straight line. Instead, as the Stoics themselves tell us repeatedly, is all about getting back up after you have been thrown down by life. If you take even the quickest read through the classic Stoic literature, you will see that failure is an accepted part of the process, so as you are reaching the end of this book, commit to returning regularly to its principles, so that you can make that most important of commitments, the commitment to improve yourself, no matter how long it takes. After all, when you start a new exercise routine in order to get into better shape, you would never start by trying to lift the same amount of weight or running the same distance as the people who have been training for years. You take stock of your current physical fitness, you assess your weaknesses and past experiences, and you start out with a lighter amount of weight or a shorter distance. And then you keep on going. Eventually you can start to increase the amount of weight, to run farther, and you take on new exercises, and eventually sign up for a marathon. Keep this same principle in mind as you continue your journey as a *prokopton,* and make sure to practice and develop your temperance, your self-control as you embrace this life-changing discipline.

Finally, we leave you with a few powerful reflections. One that is particularly resonant is Marcus Aurelius' thoughts on why you should get started today and live the stoic lifestyle described in this book. He writes: **"Remember how long you have been putting this off, how many extensions the gods gave you, and you didn't use them. At some point you have to recognize what the world it is that you belong to; what power rules it and from what source you spring; That there is a limit to the time assigned you, and if you do not use it to free yourself, it will be gone and will never return."** Epictetus also has a compelling exhortation to any of you who are still hesitating about getting started. He writes, "Now is the time to get serious about living your ideals. How long can you afford to put off who you really want to be? Your nobler self cannot wait any longer. Put your principles into practice – now. Stop the excuses and procrastination. This is your life! [...] Decide to be extraordinary and do what you need to do – now."

Now if that's not inspiration to stop reading and get to work, we do not know what is!

Further Reading

Today, stoicism is an incredibly popular topic, and no wonder, if you stop and consider all the successful world leaders who profess their allegiance to the stoic world view. Check out these resources to get more information about stoicism and learn how it can apply to your everyday life:

For general background, we recommend that you try the first introduction to stoic philosophy published in recent years:

Stoicism by John Sellars (2014)

Or: Stoicism: A Very Short Introduction by Brad Inwood (2018)

For more information on Marcus Aurelius, you should try:

The Inner Citadel (2001) and Philosophy as a Way of Life (1995) by Pierre Hadot

Marcus Aurelius by Matthew Arnold (essay)

For more information on Cato, you should try:

Rome's Last Citizen: The Life and Legacy of Cato, Mortal Enemy of Caesar by Rob Goodman and Jimmy Son (2014)

Cato the Younger by Plutarch and John Dryde (2013)

For practical applications of stoicism in today's modern world, you should check out:

The Daily Stoic: 366 Meditations on Wisdom, Perseverance, and the Art of Living

By Ryan Holiday, Stephen Hanselman (2016)

How to Be a Stoic: Using Ancient Philosophy to Live a Modern Life

By Massimo Pigliucci (2017)

The Practicing Stoic: A Philosophical User's Manual, by Ward Farnsworth (2018)

Stoicism and the Art of Happiness: Practical wisdom for everyday life: embrace perseverance, strength and happiness with stoic philosophy by Donald Robertson (2018)

Stoicism: A Stoic Approach to Modern Life by Tom Miles (2015)

A Guide to the Good Life: The Ancient Art of Stoic Joy, By William B. Irvine (2008)

For a memoir of true stoics who mastered themselves and beat the odds, you should try:

Can't Hurt Me by David Goggins (2018)

Or: Courage Under Fire: Testing Epictetus's Doctrines in a Laboratory of Human Behavior by James Stockdale (1993)

For original writings by Greek stoics, try the following:

Meditations by Marcus Aurelius

Letters from a Stoic by Seneca

On The Shortness of Life by Seneca

Discourses and Selected Writings by Epictetus

Fragments by Heraclitus

If you want a digital assistant to help you deepen your connection to stoicism—and provide a daily reminder to complete your practices, you should try the following top-rated apps:

Stoic Meditations, produced by the Stoa Nova in partnership with Adam Musial-Bright (currently available on the iTunes store, no Android version available). The meditations allow you to start your morning with a stoic thought and to perform Stoic self-improvement activities.

Stoic: Self Reflect Journaling is a free, top-rated app developed by Maciej Lobodinzski to help you learn to cope with stress and to start truly enjoying your life. It contains a morning and evening routine, reflective exercises, history, philosophy and wisdom. There is a premium subscription option.

Daily Stoic, developed by Brass Check, provides daily quotes from Marcus Aurelius, Seneca, Epictetus and others.

Stoic Library provides the most important classical stoic texts, including Marcus Aurelius, Seneca, Epictetus and others, in one convenient place.

Stoa is a meditation app for practitioners and doers. It has 2+ hours of guided meditations to help you embrace the stoic disciplines and apply them to your life.

Stoicism is now a popular topic for podcasts, so you can continue to learn about it while you are driving or exercising. You should check out:

The Tim Ferriss Show

Host: Tim Ferriss
Website: https://tim.blog/tag/stoicism/

Tim Ferris talks about a range of topics, including stoicism and how it applies to Ferriss' life and work.

The Practical Stoic Podcast

Hosted by: Simon Drew
Website: http://www.risetothegoodlife.com/practicalstoicpodcast/

Topic: The Practical Stoic Podcast features concrete advice from the ancient Stoic philosophers.

Stoic Mettle

Hosted by: Scott Hebert
Website: https://stoicmettle.com/

These podcasts are generally short and practical, with advice that is easy to put into action. He uses his personal life to teach

Stoic ideas and interviews contemporary Stoics to ask them to contribute further insights.

Stoic Meditations

Hosted by: Massimo Pigliucci

Website: https://anchor.fm/stoicmeditations

(For more from Pigliucci see the book How To Be A Stoic and the Stoic Meditations app above). A Professor of Philosophy at CUNY-City College, Massimo Pigliucci's Stoic Meditations are comprised of short readings from the ancient Stoics, with his scholarly commentary that makes them easy to understand in a modern context. Try adding it to your daily routine!

Good Fortune

Hosted by: Matt van Natta

Website: https://immoderatestoic.com/good-fortune/

Topic: Van Natta does readings of stoic texts and interprets them in the context of modern day life.

Stoic Philosophy Podcast

Hosted by: Justin Vacula

Website: http://justinvacula.com/

The Stoic Philosophy Podcast offers practical tidbits for daily living. It explores a broad set of topics that are relatable to everyday contemporary life.

The Sunday Stoic Podcast

Hosted by: Steve Karafiat
Website: https://sundaystoic.wixsite.com/home

Sunday Stoic is a podcast that focuses on readings of the ancient Stoics with modern applications of their most salient lessons.

REFERENCES

1. Stipancic, M., Renner, W., Schutz P., Dond, R. (2009). Effects of Neuro-Linguistic Psychotherapy on Psychological Difficulties and Perceived Quality of Life. *J. Counselling and Psychotherapy Research.* https://doi.org/10.1080/14733140903225240
2. Zaharia, C., Reiner, M., Schutz, P. (2015). Evidence-Based Neuro-Linguistic Psychotherapy: A Meta-Analysis. *J. Psychiatria Danubina.* Vol. 27, No. 4, pages 355–363.
3. Rubino, J. (n.d.). The Impact of Lacking Self-esteem on Business Professionals. Retrieved from https://bodymindinstitute.com/the-impact-of-lacking-self-esteem-on-business-professionals/ [28 June 2019].
4. Cherry, K. (2019). The 6 Types of Basic Emotions and Their Effect on Human Behavior. Retrieved from https://www.verywellmind.com/an-overview-of-the-types-of-emotions-4163976
5. Donaldson, M. (2019). Plutchik's Wheel of Emotions - 2017 Update • Six Seconds. Retrieved from https://www.6seconds.org/2017/04/27/plutchiks-model-of-emotions/
6. Goleman, Daniel. Emotional Intelligence: Why It Can Matter More Than Iq. New York: Bantam Books, 1995. Print.

7. Levine, M. (2019). Logic and Emotion. Retrieved from https://www.psychologytoday.com/us/blog/the-divided-mind/201207/logic-and-emotion
8. Salovey, P., Brackett, M., & Mayer, J. (2007). Emotional intelligence. Port Chester, N.Y.: Dude Pub.
9. Srivastava K. (2013). Emotional intelligence and organizational effectiveness. Industrial psychiatry journal, 22(2), 97–99. doi:10.4103/0972-6748.132912
10. Stosny, S. (2019). The Function of Emotions. Retrieved from https://www.psychologytoday.com/us/blog/anger-in-the-age-entitlement/201612/the-function-emotions

RESOURCES

1. https://www.planetnlp.com/nlp_techniques.html
2. https://en.m.wikipedia.org/wiki/Methods_of_neuro-linguistic_programming
3. https://en.m.wikipedia.org/wiki/Neuro-linguistic_programming
4. https://excellenceassured.com/2402/goal-setting-with-your-timeline-in-mind
5. https://www.planetnlp.com/submodalities_page2.html
6. https://www.planetnlp.com/nlp_submodalities.html
7. https://www.planetnlp.com/nlp_for_motivation.html
8. https://www.planetnlp.com/nlp_motivation_strategy.html
9. https://www.planetnlp.com/nlp_motivation.html
10. https://www.hypnosisdownloads.com/anxiety-treatment/anxiety-fear?3466!NT04
11. https://www.planetnlp.com/nlp_primer_content.html
12. https://www.planetnlp.com/nlp_primer_content_page2.html
13. https://www.planetnlp.com/nlp_primer_content_page3.html
14. https://www.planetnlp.com/nlp_submodality_worksheet.html
15. https://www.provensalestraining.com/how-to-get-motivated.html
16. https://www.transformdestiny.com/nlp-guide/nlp-motivation-strategies.asp
17. https://inlpcenter.org/change-your-thinking-nlp-motivation-strategy/amp/

18. https://www.nlpworld.co.uk/nlp-glossary/s/submodalities/
19. https://www.nlpworld.co.uk/nlp-glossary/r/representational-systems/
20. https://theplaidzebra.com
21. http://planetnlp.com/nlp_sales.html#objections
22. http://planetnlp.com/nlp_selling.html
23. http://planetnlp.com/nlp_sensory_acuity.html
24. http://planetnlp.com/nlp_language_patterns.html
25. http://planetnlp.com/nlp_sales.html
26. https://www.asiahrtraining.com/training/communication-skills-with-nlp/
27. https://inlpcenter.org/how-to-create-rapport-with-nlp/
28. https://inlpcenter.org/four-ways-to-harness-the-most-powerful-communication-phenomenon/
29. https://inlpcenter.org/communication-skills/?amp
30. http://www.altfeld.com/mastery/nlp-techniques.html
31. https://www.zinc.it/6-business-impacts-poor-communication/
32. https://smallbusiness.chron.com/effects-poor-communication-business-345.html
33. http://business.time.com/2012/06/05/effective-communication-for-entrepreneurs/
34. https://www.entrepreneur.com/amphtml/252555
35. https://www.tutorialspoint.com/entrepreneurship_skills/entrepreneurship_skills_effective_communication.htm
36. https://www.globalnlptraining.com/blog/how-to-know-how-someone-is-thinking/

37. https://www.psychmechanics.com/2015/03/what-are-nlp-eye-accessing-cues-and-how.html?m=1
38. https://www.nlpworld.co.uk/nlp-glossary/e/eye-accessing-cues/
39. https://www.coachingwithnlp.co/time-management-and-golf-balls/
40. https://www.abbyeagle.com/nlp-coaching-resources/nlp-time-management.php
41. https://www.nlp-techniques.org
42. https://www.nlp-techniques.org/what-is-nlp/visual-squash/
43. https://www.nlp-techniques.org/what-is-nlp/timeline/
44. https://www.nlp-techniques.org/what-is-nlp/sales/sales-attitude-useful-states-beliefs/
45. https://www.nlp-techniques.org/what-is-nlp/sales/
46. https://www.nlp-techniques.org/what-is-nlp/nlp-planning/nlp-plan-time-energy-focus/
47. https://hackernoon.com/10-tips-for-time-management-and-become-more-productive-as-entrepreneurs-a15192aaed6c
48. https://www.the-secret-of-mindpower-and-nlp.com/Overcoming-low-self-esteem.html
49. https://blog.iqmatrix.com/self-esteem-builder
50. https://www.nlpca.com/DCweb/selfesteemandthepowerofnl.html
51. http://planetnlp.com/nlp_eye_accessing.html
52. http://planetnlp.com/pacing_and_leading.html
53. http://planetnlp.com/nlp_rapport.html
54. http://planetnlp.com/nlp_exercise_tone.html

55. http://planetnlp.com/nlp_exercise_beliefcreator.html
56. http://planetnlp.com/nlp_exercise_beliefdisintegrator.html
57. http://planetnlp.com/nlp_reframing.html
58. https://finetofab.com/effects-of-a-low-self-esteem/
59. https://www.nlp-techniques.org/what-is-nlp/six-step-reframing/
60. http://nlpnotes.com/six-step-reframe/
61. https://nlp-mentor.com/six-step-reframe/
62. https://www.nlp-techniques.org/what-is-nlp/six-step-reframing/
63. https://blog.iqmatrix.com/self-esteem-enhancer
64. https://www.psychmechanics.com/2015/03/nlp-techniques-reframing.html?m=1

www.ingramcontent.com/pod-product-compliance
Lightning Source LLC
Chambersburg PA
CBHW071950110526
44592CB00012B/1050